ON·THE OTHER HAND

Passages from the letters of Sinclair Lewis and James M. Cain are used by permission of their respective estates. The lines from the Clifford Odets letter are reprinted with the permission of Walt Odets and Nora Odets.

Lyrics from "My Blue Heaven" © 1927 (renewed 1955) Donaldson Publishing Co. and George Whiting Publishing Co.

Design by Glen M. Edelstein

Library of Congress Cataloging-in-Publication Data

Wray, Fay.
    On the other hand : a life story / Fay Wray.
        p.   cm.
    ISBN 0-312-02265-4
    1. Wray, Fay, 1907—   .   2. Motion picture actors and actresses
    —United States—Biography.   I. Title.
    PN2287.W74A3 1988
    791.43′028′0924—dc 19   88-11567
    [B]

First Edition

10   9   8   7   6   5   4   3   2   1

ON·THE OTHER HAND

A Life Story

by
FAY·WRAY

St. Martin's Press
NEW YORK

For Susan, Robert, Victoria,
Nora, and Jacob

And for all the young-in-heart
who have liked
King Kong

16 I'm the Busiest Actress in Hollywood   131

17 Some Roles I Wanted But Didn't Get   143

18 Some People Behind the Camera   155

19 Oh, to Be in England!   165

20 Someone to Love   177

21 Summer Theater and Sinclair Lewis   182

22 Hollywood Again and Robert Riskin   199

23 Clifford Odets: Behind His Own Iron Curtain   204

24 The Reality of Robert Riskin   214

25 The Office of War Information   222

26 A Home on a Hill   232

27 A Broken Clock   239

28 A New Beginning   250

Filmography   257

Index   263

CONTENTS

Acknowledgments   ix

Prologue   xi

Introduction   xv

1 Northern Lights, Indian Dances   1

2 At the Age of Three, I Pledge Allegiance   11

3 Life Without Father   21

4 California: Red Streetcar to Hollywood   30

5 With My Mother Again   43

6 A Film Contract: The Beginning of Life in the
   Movies   52

7 A Big Step from the Little Westerns   61

8 *The Wedding March* with Erich von Stroheim   64

9 Romance and Marriage   80

10 A Troubled Honeymoon   93

11 Merian Cooper: Pre-Sound, Pre-King Kong   102

12 "My People Is Broke"   106

13 Dancing Is Better Than Crying   110

14 John's "Single Lady" Becomes My "Nikki" with Cary
    Grant   114

15 The Tallest, Darkest Leading Man   124

ACKNOWLEDGMENTS

I am thankful to my children, who urged me to write this; to Bob, who presented me with a personal computer and forgave me for not using it; to Vicki, for reviewing the work while in progress and giving me the benefit of her judgment; to Susan, whose enthusiasm helped to make my own spirit high; to my very good fortune for having the three of them.

PROLOGUE

Dear Kong:

This has to be an open letter because I've never had a precise address for you.

A few years ago, a Mr. Auerbach wrote in *The New York Times* that he had interviewed you at your island home. But I do not want to chance addressing you just at Skull Island; today, without a zip code—who knows?

Then I saw the cover of a Directors Guild magazine showing you in a large easy chair, wearing house slippers and watching scenes of yourself on television at the top of the Empire State Building. There were banana peels on the floor beside you and on a table nearby there was a framed photograph of me. I found that quite touching. It let me know I had been some influence in your life.

I wonder whether you know how strong a force you have been in mine?

For more than half a century, you have been the most dominant figure in my public life. To speak of me is to think of you. To speak *to* me is often a prelude to questions about you.

Sometimes, I am asked whether I get tired of hearing so much about you—of being asked so many questions. I say I don't get tired because I have good energy. I could go on to say that I also have respect for you. But that would be hard for people to understand, considering most would think you meant to do me harm.

I feel that you never did mean harm to me. My children knew that when they saw "our film" for the first time: "He didn't want to hurt you," they said, "he just liked you."

I admire you because you made only one film—and that became famous, whereas I made seventy-five or eighty and only the one I made with you became really famous. Another reason I respect you is that, although we never talked about it, I felt we had a tacit understanding that there were some beautiful moments in *King Kong;* that we both appreciated the location given us for the scene when you held me in your left hand and pulled at my skirt with your right hand, as though taking petals from a flower. That's the way I think of it because that's my disposition: to make a poetic metaphor. The background was inspired by the paintings of Gustave Doré, a wondrously quiet, mystical mountain right on the edge of outer space. You brought a petal of my skirt to your nose and sniffed at it.

At a recent film festival, this brought hoots from some young men in the audience: "Whoo, Whoo, Whew," they cried out. Later, outside the theater, they ran after me and apologized. They didn't have to do that. Their reaction showed they liked it—in their boyish way.

The other scene I find unforgettable is you in your last moments just before falling from the top of the Empire State Building. You had put me down very carefully as though wanting me to be safe. You felt your chest where you had been shot, knowing you were doomed. That scene puts a lump in my throat. When I told this to an interviewer for a French magazine, he cried, "At last, then, Kong has won!"

Your influence has affected the way people respond to me. It made Leonard Bernstein pick me up when we were first introduced in the lobby of a theater. It made Freddy de Cordova (who produces the "The Tonight Show") lift me up and whirl me around

INTRODUCTION

COINCIDENCE IN LIFE, OR SERENDIPITY . . . or the stronger
word, *destiny*, all deserve respect and in my case, appreciation: the events that led to the making of *King Kong*, the for-
tuitous timing of the completion of the Empire State Building, the
fact that the producer, Merian Cooper, was in New York soon
after and could visualize the ending of the film, all these combined.

What does it matter that many people think *King Kong* was my
only film? Again and again, I hear: "I saw your film." "Your
movie was on television the other night." *Kong* does not erase the
fact that I did many other films, but it is a fact that *Kong* is the
most widely known, the most enduring. And considering the im-
provement in tape and laser, it is likely to go on shaping and
enhancing the state of wonder in young people and even old.

My own sense of childhood wonder has always traveled with
me. And that has prompted me to look again at a span of time
that began in the Canadian Rockies and took me on a journey
sometimes wondrous, sometimes difficult . . . as all lived lives
are likely to have been.

in a restaurant. It made Tennessee Williams exclaim at our first meeting (as he held tightly onto my hand), "I am glad you got away from that big ape!"

Sometimes I fantasize that, with all that influence, you might be able to help bring about peace in the world. In my mind, I outline a script that has you buried under Fifth Avenue, where you fell after the airplanes shot you down. You have been sleeping there right into the 1980s! On an early morning, your furriness moves when discovered by subway repairmen. You push up, out, and across Manhattan (scaring people a lot) and wade into the Hudson River, bathing away your sleepiness. You sit for a while on the Jersey Palisades—then the top of the Empire State Building comes into your focus. You imagine you see Ann Darrow there—so, of course, you wade back across the Hudson, causing huge waves as you go and, once again, you climb to the top of that building where you last saw Ann. Only she isn't there now and all you can do is cling to the spire and to your memories.

You have accumulated so much affection over all the years that no one, absolutely no one wants to kill you. What the whole world wants is to save you. All military attitudes are suspended while your case is considered.

At the United Nations, you are foremost on the agenda; how to rescue you; where to give you safe haven. After offers from Russia, China, and even South Africa, there is a representative from Skull Island who gently proposes the obvious: Why not return you to your native island?

A great helicopter is obtained with a huge and comfortable net attached. The representative from Skull Island goes up and talks quietly to you so that you go willingly into the net.

Now every rooftop in New York is alive with citizens watching, waving, calling out fond farewells as the helicopter circles the city before heading south. Their affection goes with you.

I had thought of letting you drop onto a rocket as you reached Cape Canaveral but that gets a little fantastic and it's better to think of you in carpet slippers and at home, the way Mishkin pictured you on the cover of the Directors Guild magazine.

These reflections will let you know that I think of you and feel it only fair to tell you I am writing about a lot of times that have nothing to do with you—long before we met. Once we met, you had a pretty strong hold on me. On the other hand, there have been films, people, and places that also had a hold on me. I hope you don't look at television all the time and may read this.

Affectionately,

Jay

ON·THE
OTHER
HAND

A Life Story

CHAPTER I
NORTHERN LIGHTS, INDIAN DANCES

◆

I T HAD BEEN A BRIGHT, sunny day when we left the airport in
Great Falls, Montana. As we approached the Canadian border,
the sky was swept with somber hues. The landscape to right and
left was flat, seeming to go on to infinity—prairie land, wheat
land. The dusk had turned to dark.

We were three: the mayor of Cardston, his wife, and I. I had
received their invitation to return to Canada for a jubilee celebration—the seventy-fifth anniversary of the establishment of the
town of Cardston. The Prime Minister of Canada would be arriving from Ottawa, the Blood Band of the Blackfoot Indians would
be in dress regalia. There would be a rodeo; there would be a
banquet, parades, receptions, and I would get to see the red-
coated Northwest Mounted Police. All this was promised to me as
I rode beside the mayor, his wife reminding him—from her seat
in the back of the car—of planned details.

She knew the particular site where I had been born.

My own memories ran like an obligato to the conversation . . .
memories that had to precede three and a half years, for that was

my age when my family had left Canada for the warmer winters of Arizona.

First memory: carrying a bowl of water to my mother, who had fainted. I, the youngest of four, was eager to assist the three older ones and my father, who were attempting to revive a supine Mama. Never did she want to be called other than "Mama." And Papa was "Papa." Papa and Mama had gone to Canada just about the turn of the century. First, they had lived in a log cabin while Papa established a sawmill and built, with his own hands, a handsome two-story ranch house with a veranda along the entire front that looked onto a large meadow. He had made a playground with a teeter-totter and a swing for his children, fenced protectively against the mountain lions that sometimes neared the meadowland. Thoughts of going up and down on the teeter-totter while sitting in the lap of my eldest sister: the feel of her plaid cape as she had wrapped it around me . . . fine, strong, close-woven wool . . . the look of it, plaid, beige and greens . . . the warmth of her.

"The foothills of the Rockies"—that was the way my mother described our ranch-home, which was always referred to as "Wrayland." The entrance to the property was a covered gateway. At the base of one of the gateposts, a large stone, in which my father had chiseled the name "Wrayland," served to identify his homestead.

Mama loved to tell about life in the log cabin. At Christmastime, she lined the interior with very white sheets and my father brought in a Christmas tree from one of the thousands available in the nearby mountains. Papa worked at the mill. Mama kept an immaculate cabin, prepared her husband's lunch, placing the handle of the lunch pail in the mouth of their spaniel dog, saying, "Take this to Joe." The dog would fly away through the meadow. Sometimes she would ask the dog to carry just a note to Joe. In the early years, it might have been simply to say, "I love you." Later, all of that would change.

There is a chill in my soul now when I realize how much it changed. There was something glorious in hearing about the sweet beginnings of their love, to know they had been happy living in so primitive a way. I heard, too, about the natural beauties of that land: the Rockies rising high and sheltering above them, the exquisite look of wild spring flowers—forget-me-nots and wild strawberries. Me, she called "Forget-me-not." There was a blue-eyed girl before me whom she had named Willow. Papa's eyes were blue, large, expressive. He had a fine straight nose, curly black hair. This was how my mother saw him in the beginning. All the enchantment of the springtime—birch trees in leaf, wildflowers in bloom—and a strong and handsome home, her own abilities as a former schoolteacher in instructing her own, brought her fulfillment.

She told me that I said "Mama" at the age of five months, but only when she placed me in a darkened room and went away. I visualize her showing this response to friends who waited in a cluster just outside a closed door. Later, she taught me recitations. I still remember poems I was asked to recite to her friends. I remember the poems, not the occasions.

Springtimes became wintertimes. Wintertimes became bitter times. Snow in five-foot-high drifts made Mama a prisoner. What had seemed a romantic wonderland because it was five miles removed from the nearest post office (Mountain View) and twenty-five miles from Cardston (the nearest town) became a remote and difficult existence. The last of our winters in Canada, my brother, the eldest child, got pneumonia from a circumstance in which I shared. We were on a sled, I on his big-brotherly lap. He would have been nine or ten. An older boy was pulling us over the icy surface of a lake. We came to a wide crack in the ice. Our friend attempted to yank the sled across the crack. The sled went down into the icy water. I do not remember being frightened or even cold, I just remember seeing my brother's two brown shoes sticking up out of the water. I am told he righted himself and held me up until our friend could get us out. That experience was bad for us and for my mother. The temperature dropped that winter to fifty-five below. Not long after that, she suffered a miscarriage. And then she had a nervous breakdown—which took her away from us and into a hospital for several months. Her children were parceled out into the homes of doctor friends in Cardston. The two eldest stayed with a veterinarian, Dr. Christie; Willow, just older than I, with a Dr. and Mrs. Lynn. I stayed with a Dr. and Mrs. Stackpoole. These were probably all the doctors there were in so small a town, but they were ready to care for the Wray children. I guess my papa stayed at the ranch getting it ready to be sold. We never went back there again. Once, he came to get us in a buggy and took us through birch trees over a creek to visit a Dr. and Mrs. Weeks. There I saw a beautiful machine called a milk separator and, even more beautiful, a great green table for billiards. Again, a doctor was a friend. My mama once said she had a dream while in the hospital that no matter how difficult life had become or might continue to be, there would always be a "Dr. Stacy" to stay and see that her family was well. Now, as I write this and am married to a doctor, her dream seems to have foretold the future.

Memories are so selective that one's life is a record of those choices. Among the gifts my mother had was the ability to sew. She was often at her machine, her foot on the pedal, her delicate hands guiding the cloth under the whirring needle. She enjoyed tea, and most particularly in a cup of very thin china. She had taken her tea to the machine and sipped it between stitchings. When she had finished, I asked permission to carry the cup to the kitchen—a privilege usually given to Willow.

As I started to walk with the cup and saucer, I saw my sister's big blue reproachful eyes. Would I be able to get all the way past that look and into the kitchen? I dropped the cup; I dropped the saucer. All went smash. "Willow did it," I cried.

I have no memory of the punishment that followed. The spanking, the scolding went on and on, Mama holding me, she said, with her left hand, spanking with the right, I running in a circle around her trying to escape. "Willow did it. Willow did it." Considering how I still remember, as if in a close-up, my sister's eyes, it's not surprising that I never gave in.

It is appropriate to use the term *close-up* for the vision a child has of the world. Little ones do not see a lot beyond a very few yards.

From the time I went to stay with the Stackpooles, my world became larger. It included the look of an entire room where I could lie on a big black mohair sofa and poke my fingers into its deeply-buttoned recesses while I listened to Dr. Stackpoole play the piano. I loved Dr. Harry Stackpoole. It began then, I think, that I would love someone, especially a male someone, for a particular talent. My three-year-oldness thought him a great big-mustachioed wonder and I was happiest while I was sitting on his lap watching his fingers dance along the black-and-white keyboard.

The mayor brought his car to a stop beside a small, dimly lighted structure. His wife was saying we were now at the border. A sentry came out, acknowledged us, and sent us on—into Canada. The mayor said friends in Cardston were waiting to give us a nightcap, even though it was exceptional in a Mormon town where Mormons didn't drink even coffee or tea. Surely they were trying to make a lady from Hollywood welcome in the way they thought most suitable. But I thought none of the welcoming friends was disappointed when I said I was already much too stimulated to have a drink. Goodnights having been said, we set out for the Prince of Wales Hotel, which lies about ten miles to the west of Cardston, on the shore of the Waterton Lakes. We drove in darkness and I knew it would be morning before I could see all the beauty of the land. Then suddenly, great shafts of light were sweeping up over the horizon. The brightened sky outlined the form of an antlered deer that grazed near the edge of the lake. We all got out of the car. My friends said they had not seen such a display of northern lights for twenty years. It was a real dazzler. I took it very personally: a symbolic welcoming! There was absolute silence in every direction but there was also a sense of music, a tremendous rhapsody of midnight blue-white blues.

In the morning, when I looked out on the lake and the pines and the clean blue white-clouded sky and the strength of the Rocky Mountains embracing all of it, I thought I understood why my mother had been glad to bear her brood of "little Canucks" in this land.

My parents had met in Salt Lake City. My mother had been born there in 1871, one of fourteen children. I know more of my grandfather than I do of my grandmother because he had the kindness to write his autobiography. He was orphaned at the age of eleven, in Missouri, apprenticed to a saddle maker until he was seventeen, when he volunteered to fight in the war with Mexico. There he learned to read and write Spanish and became fond of the Mexican people.

After the war, enroute to California with a large trading company, the hammer of his pistol caught on the edge of his holster, causing the gun to go off: "The ball ranged downward, entering the groin and thigh, passing through some fourteen inches of flesh." The company expected that the youth would die and must, therefore, be abandoned. But the company guide thought that if the youth was to be left behind, he should at least be abandoned to the possible care of nearby Indians. He went to fetch them. My grandfather wrote: "I can never forget their looks of kindness. They offered to take me and try to cure me." The company, thus challenged, made a frame to carry the wounded boy on the back of a mule for the remaining fifteen day's journey into Salt Lake Valley. "I felt almost disappointed not to go with the Indians for my heart was melted toward them and I felt as though I could always be their friend and trust them." In Salt Lake City, Mormons nurtured him to recovery and inspired him to join the church and forego continuing on to California.

In 1852, he married Miss Emily Colton, whom he would never cease loving. She appreciated his view of the Indians and supported his willingness to befriend them and his efforts to obtain fair treatment for them. She loved her husband, Daniel Webster Jones, too much to tolerate the recommendation of the church that he take a second wife. The devoted pair produced fourteen children. My mother was their tenth.

She was fourteen when her mother died at the age of forty during a storm. My mother's responsibilities as "mother" to the younger ones and housekeeper for her father increased her antagonism to the church. She had seen her mother's anguish at the thought of a polygamous household. Of all the children, she was the one who rebelled.

She had an impudent kind of beauty—a retroussé nose, gray-green eyes, very fair skin, and an abundance of curly Titian-red hair. She liked to recall for her children the beauty of her youthful figure. She attended the University of Utah (then Deseret University) and earned credentials to become a schoolteacher. She assisted her father in arranging the manuscript of his book *Forty Years Among the Indians* (1890).

At the age of seventeen, my mother had the misfortune, out of innocence and ignorance, to marry a man who was physically unable to "consummate a marriage." "Spunk" was one of her favorite words, but it must have been love, as well, that caused her to run off to Canada with my father after enduring six years of that hapless first marriage.

My parents-to-be published their intention to run away together even as they were in flight—a legality in lieu of divorce, my mother would tell us. The date of their actual marriage is uncertain. In the *Geneology of Daniel Webster Jones*, it is May 23, 1900. In her own handwriting, in the family Bible, my mother puts it down as June 10, 1900. A certificate of marriage signed by F. Sandeman De Mattos, Ph.D., rector of St. Mary's Church, joined in holy matrimony:

Vina Marguerite Jones [her maiden name]
and
Joseph Herber Wray
The date, December 16, 1910. The place,
Brandon, Manitoba, Canada.

By that time she had four children and at least one miscarriage. Brandon was where she had gone to be hospitalized. A whole avalanche of questions followed my recent discovery of the marriage certificate. Perhaps the first possible opportunity for a non-Mormon marriage was in Brandon. I would have been more interested in her own views of all these circumstances than in the precision of dates.

But, whatever they were, I am *here*. I am reminded of a story about a husband who arrived home late one night to a worried and reproachful wife who scolded him for his lateness on and on and on. When, finally, he said, "But I am *here!*" she became quiet and embraced him.

While my mother was in the hospital, my father took me with him on a train trip to Ottowa. What I remember about him is that he was all fur. He was a long raccoon coat more than he was a person and up at the top of the coat, there was a tobacco pipe. His fur coat had big bullets for buttons. I was a fur person, too. I had a cape of white fur and a muff to match. My hands could be tucked in from either side of the muff and kept warm. If he liked being a fur person as much as I did, he felt good.

My mother did not become an absolutely real person to me until she returned from Brandon. I did not know how much I had missed the sight, the feel, the smell of her. But when I saw her, I ran to her and held her around the knees and put my face into the folds of her white-dotted blue challis skirt. She was waiting for me outside a row-type rooming house in Cardston. I had to run up a little hill to reach her. She was beautiful! She was beautiful again the next day when she came to get me at the Stackpooles'. She was wearing an auburn chiffon scarf over her hair. She knelt down outside the white picket fence. I studied her loveliness through the fence and she told me she had come to take me with her.

Inside the house, Mrs. Stackpoole said it was impossible for her to get my things together; she simply could not do it. I said with "spunk," which pleased my mother, that I would pack my own things. I knew I had to go with this wonderful mother person. There was enough difficulty in getting my clothes together that we went away with only what I could be dressed in. Even though it took a while for me to find the missing mate of a pair of shoes, Mrs. Stackpoole and her adopted daughter, Marjorie, who was a little older than I, gave no assistance. They had been very good to me but they were not *mine*. A few days later, in the street, Marjorie told me she was going to keep my clothes for herself. My mother told me I answered, "My Papa can buy me plenty more!" "Spunk," again.

At the Prince of Wales Hotel, I slept lightly, my head searching the past and anticipating what the next day would bring. Would it be possible to identify anything out of my little-girl memories?

The sweep of land between the hotel and the town was so grand that the lady who came to call for me the next morning, quite used to the look of it all, must have thought my "oohs, aahs, how beautiful!" were extravagant. The wooden figure of a Northwest Mounted Policeman, perhaps twenty feet high, stood guard at the entrance to the town. The main street was not long and as I looked eagerly up the side streets, I imagined I saw (and maybe really did see) the Stackpoole house with the picket fence around it.

The first of the ceremonies was a meeting at a town hall. As I entered, I was greeted with, "My mother delivered you!" "My cousin was the midwife when you were born!" This was repeated so many times and with such affectionate tones that I felt multiplied.

In the days that followed, there would be a parade, a rodeo, a ceremony to make me an honorary member of the Blood Band of the Blackfoot Indian Confederacy, under the name of Kisk-sta-ki-aki (Beaver Woman). Fifteen Indian chiefs, in white buckskin and feathered headdresses, initiated me into their Indian world. Their names were as colorful as their costumes. Consider that of the head chief: Jim-Shot-on-Both-Sides. As soon as I accepted my Indianhood, I told them about my grandfather and the heritage I had from him of caring about them. Then there was dancing in an ever-widening circle as we were joined by the squaws and younger people. Many of the squaws and young ones looked as though they were enduring inherited illness—and not all the chiefs looked hale and handsome. There is something painful in realizing that the strength and energy of these people seems to have diminished. My romantic head imagines all of them as Hiawathas. My romantic heart wants that to be true.

The days were clear, the air clean, not a fleck of smog anywhere; white clouds dramatized the deep blue background of the sky.

At a banquet to honor Prime Minister and Mrs. Diefenbacker, I spoke of the pleasure it was to breathe this air, to see this land, and said I would like to carry a handful of Canadian soil home with me. A more significant souvenir had already been arranged.

Rains came, gray clouds hovered low over the Waterton Lakes—but regardless of weather, a caravan of four or five cars undertook the trip to the place once known as "Wrayland." The rain-soaked, rich black soil set the tires to spinning, causing the rear of our cars to fishtail. My hostess-driver was a lady who resembled Loretta Young, slender and delicate. She whirled the steering wheel far to the right, then far to the left to counter the fishtailing and brought us safely into a clearing at the foot of the mountains where cowboys had gone ahead earlier in the morning, taking with them the "Wrayland" stone. They had placed it in the center of the meadow where the ranch house once had been. The grass was short, no more than six inches high. The land had been remote when my parents first came upon it; it was still remote today. Not far from the "Wrayland" stone, I saw a square of discarded metal: the iron oven door of a kitchen range—the only sign that there ever had been any inhabitants.

The presence of the people who had made this journey warmed the moment. The gray mist seemed as a curtain over the memories that only my parents would have been able to recall. I saw the word *malleable* on the iron oven door. "Capable of being reformed or transformed. Not fixed in any given direction." My parents' lives had been transformed and redirected. Loyalty to the memory of my parents had kept the "Wrayland" stone safe. I wished their redirection had been protected and guarded equally well.

CHAPTER 2
AT THE AGE OF THREE, I PLEDGE ALLEGIANCE

♦

A CCORDING TO IMMIGRATION RECORDS, IT was in June 1911 that my family crossed the border into the United States. There were:

Joseph Vivien Wray	11 years
Vaida Viola Wray	9 years
Willow Winona Wray	5 years
Vina Fay Wray	3 years

That "Fay" is almost as a punctuation mark to the longer, fancier names my mother favored. She had been disappointed not to have had a boy, so my father took the opportunity to name me after both his wife and a former lady friend.

We went by train through great mountains, something called the Royal Gorge. A young man sat with us and teased me by taking my silver cup and apparently hanging it on a hook outside the train window. Out, to my despair—in again, to my delight.

Over and over. It was exciting and I would tell about it afterward, feeling a lot of love for that wonderful young man and his magic.

We boarded a ship at Seattle, where, for phonetic reason, I expected to "see cattle." Not too unreasonable for a child born on a ranch.

The port of Los Angeles was then at Redondo. Before landing, Mama told me I should say the piece that she had taught me: "I pledge allegiance to the flag of the United States . . ." She was passionately patriotic and happy to be back in her native land. She must have had a sense of drama to make that moment memorable for me. It served her in two ways: It saluted her return to America and it pleased her that her youngest learned easily and remembered well. If I had an inherent feeling for drama, it was, throughout my young years, enlivened by her enthusiasm when I appeared in school plays and by her admiration for some of the actors and actresses she had seen while growing up in Salt Lake City: E. H. Sothern, Julia Marlowe, Minnie Maddern Fiske, Eleanora Duse, and Maude Adams—who had been born in Salt Lake City.

Her memories of having heard the magnificent voices of Nellie Melba and Jenny Lind may have had an equal influence on my sisters. But their musical talent, their ability to sing, came from our father. He was born in Hull, England, but I would later think that the tone of his voice was touched with the wondrous timbres of the Welsh or the Irish.

Mama had two brothers living in the territory of Arizona. That was to be our destination. Los Angeles *was* red geraniums, everywhere geraniums; and then we were on a train again and hot, hot, hot. Only the look of Mama's white-and-lavender voile blouse was cool, and I rested my head there. The train paused in Colton. Colton was my grandmother's maiden name. But Colton was hot, too, and then there was Arizona—120 in the shade.

We stayed at my Uncle Dan's. Among other things, he grew strawberries. He took me through the rows of berries. I saw yellow-skinned pickers at work. I refused the offer of a berry, telling him the color of the workers' skins did not look clean. He took me to the end of the rows where there were large wooden tubs. He said the workers bathed there every day. "Very clean," he said.

This was my mother's oldest brother. He was later Speaker of the House in Arizona.

During our stay, my sister Willow and I found a bottle of Castoria, liked the taste, and drank it all. There was consternation in the house as to why we had to be up all through the night.

My first memorable meal was of fresh bread, milk still warm from the cow, and the tartness of just-picked gooseberries—all eaten while sitting on the porch steps after sundown.

Another Uncle, Edward, had large fig trees at his place. It was fun watching them plucked off into tin cans that were nailed to poles long enough to reach high into the trees. Some tree-ripened figs plopped down and split open as they hit the ground. The taste of figs was very unpleasant.

My father soon had a place for his family: twenty acres planted in alfalfa, lots of chickens, some cows, a guinea hen whose eggs were said to be reserved for me. There were umbrella trees lining the driveway, a covered well in the back, and an irrigation canal at the far end of the property where we occasionally went to cool our bodies. There were ants and tarantulas to be worried about. Also, there was a little boy who wanted to play doctor by listening to my sister's and my bare chests.

I had a minor accident when I fell onto a paint bucket, cutting the skin alongside my mouth; and I soon learned my first long word: erysipelas. I also learned that a bad-smelling, black tarry medicine could be a good thing if it healed you.

A little brother was born—very little, about five pounds. The first time I was really aware of him was when he disappeared. The baby had been put to nap on my mother's bed. Where could he have gone? Who could have taken him? There was wild concern; everyone was running in and out of the house looking in every direction. Finally, a baby-sound came from the back of the bed where little Richard had squirmed himself off of it and onto an egg crate. He was resting unharmed and happy.

I do not remember any sibling rivalry, but I do remember the affection expressed for me by a childless couple who lived not a great distance away. "We wish you were our little girl," they said. With the selfishness of four years, I packed my suitcase and told my mother I would be going to live with them. She went outside with me to the long road that led to my "future home." She pointed out that in order to get there, I would have to pass several ferocious dogs. These dogs, she said, always came out and rushed at anyone passing by. I had seen those dogs. They were *very* large. I decided to go on living at home.

To overcome the persistent heat, my father devised a rectangular fan that was suspended from the ceiling over the dining table. With pulleys and ropes and a foot pedal in front of his place, he was able to make the fringed fan sweep the length of the table and give us some comfort during the family meal.

Where he was the night of the cyclone, I do not know. Our house was trembling; dishes were falling from the shelves. Large trees around the house were uprooted. All of us were clinging to my mother's skirts; she was trying to calm us and to hold tiny Richard close. It was her thought that the house might be picked up and carried away and that she should try to get us to a more substantial structure across the road—an electric plant made of cement. Four children at her side, one in her arms, she attempted to open the front door. The wind slammed it back and held it shut tight, and then she knew the impossibility of her plan. She put the baby back on the bed, observing that she had been holding him upside down. While the wind had uprooted trees, it had left wooden "congress" chairs on the veranda undisturbed, except that a straw had been driven straight through the arm of one of the chairs. In the calm morning light, that fact became a focus of interest.

It was not the storm that drove us from Arizona. Although my father had resourcefulness and an inventive mind that had made his Canadian ranch and his sawmill prosper, alfalfa that grew poorly and chickens that grew sick combined to spell disaster. Two years after arriving in Mesa, Arizona, we found ourselves arriving in Salt Lake City. And we found that we were poor.

For the first time in our lives, we were "city children," even though we were well on the outskirts of Salt Lake City; the street-car line ended soon after passing in front of our house. Our house was not really ours but was owned by people named Woodbury who lived in a much larger home on the opposite corner. Around their home, there was a fence heavily laden with sweet-pea vines. There was a vegetable garden.

Early in the morning Mrs. Woodbury tended to the vines and vegetables. She sprayed her blooms and plants with a fine-nozzled hose. She appeared so neat, so orderly, so in charge of her corner of the world that I imagined the sunrise itself might have been her responsibility, that she might have knocked on the door of the sun to wake him up.

In contrast to the large two-story look of their house, ours was a small single-story: two large rooms in tandem. Behind them a kind of pantry room and a small screened porch. The "front room" served as parlor and bedroom, sliding doors separating it from the second "kitchen and dining room." These sliding doors were not often open. My father got a job as night watchman at a mill in one of the canyons near the city. He had to sleep through the day; we had to be quiet. We stayed outside as much as possible.

Being on a corner, we had a sense of greater expanse than the house itself afforded. I say "we" but I am really speaking only for my own five-year-old self. There were sights besides Mrs. Wood-bury. Every afternoon, a woman in an untidy housedress waited on the corner where the streetcar would stop. While she waited, she dug at the pimples on her face with the corner of her apron. As the streetcar arrived, she smoothed out her apron, waiting like an obedient puppy. The streetcar clanged to a stop, her husband came down the steps, she put her arm through his and they walked home together. My mother said that was because she was afraid of her husband.

Many afternoons, a man who looked like Mr. Jiggs in the funny papers walked past our house. He wore a white vest under a dark coat, white spats, a red carnation in his lapel, and carried a cane. He walked very slowly, a little unsteadily; he had a large red nose. My mother said that was because he drank whiskey.

My brother Vivien created a particular excitement when he got a job selling soft drinks, rolling a push-cart into our yard at the end of one day with enough bottled drinks to go around. He gave us each a bottle of "pop" for absolutely nothing! He probably earned a little bit more than just the right to give away the drinks.

My mother, too, began to earn some money, sewing a green satin gown for a neighbor who was rich enough to give a children's Easter party, a cotton carrot-hugging rabbit at each and every place.

There were jobs for all next door at the Woodburys' when it was time to shuck the corn. Pulling off the husks, loving the feel of the yellow silk strands that clung to the ears, smelling their sweetness and watching the pile of husks grow higher and higher until darkness came, was a proud and earthy pleasure. Sore hands did not matter much.

A tall man, a cousin, came to see us sometimes. He took me to a movie theater called the Kinema. A beam of light and pictures of people who were part of the light were shining out over all the people in the theater and making them feel happy. He called the place that was up front where the pictures were, a screen. He asked me whether I would like to be up there. I thought it would be nice to be on a screen like that if it would make people happy. My answer to him was "yes."

A Mr. Rosenbaum came to see us, too. He had money to help my papa with an invention: a can opener especially for condensed milk. The clever idea was that the opener could punch two holes in the can and then cover them up to keep the milk sanitary. The opener was shaped like an arch, with round rubber pieces at each end for the sealers. I went to the factory where the parts were being made. Mr. Rosenbaum was very nice to me. He gave me this letter from a typewriter.

> To whom it may concern:
> This is to certify that I think Fay Wray is the prettiest little girl in
> Salt Lake City and when she grows up I want her to be my
> secretary.

On the day he gave me the letter, he also gave me a nickel. I said, "No, thank you," believing it was not polite to accept. My father said that since it was from Mr. Rosenbaum it was all right. We three were on the sidewalk in the uptown of the city. They were both in a good mood. They helped me up to get a drink from a street fountain. Then they asked me which of two names I would choose for them to go and have a drink too. I made a choice. They laughed in a happy way. We were standing right in front of my choice, they said. But little girls had to stay outside. They went through swinging doors. I stood on the sidewalk holding the letter and the nickle. They were not gone long. I was proud to have the letter and kept it for many years. It was like a promise of wonderful times to be.

The factory didn't stay open for long. What was left, after, was a can opener that we used for ourselves, never once using it without respect for the cleverness of my papa.

The Whittier School was within walking distance. In a school Christmas play, I was given the role of Mrs. Santa Claus. Mrs. Santa Claus just sat and made lots of stitches. Still, it was an honor and a nice name.

In the spring of 1914 there were new and very loud sounds in our street. On all four corners, newsboys in knickers were shouting, "Extra! Extra! War is declared!" That sounded as though it was going to change everything in the world. The only thing it changed for us right away was that my father went to work in a copper-mill town about twenty miles outside of Salt Lake City. The town had a very pretty name: Lark.

At the end of June that year, Willow and I were sent to sleep over at the Woodburys'. We came home the following morning to find a new baby brother—Victor. Mama was wearing a soft, flowing robe, a look we were not used to seeing. She seemed weak and tired. She said she had given her wedding ring to pay the doctor who had come to deliver the baby.

When my new baby brother was two months old and Mama felt strong enough, we followed my papa to Lark. We went in a large horse-drawn buggy that was called a stage. As we approached a place that the driver said was Lark, I wondered how long we would have to live in a little town that seemed to be all dust and no trees. Overcoming that unhappy feeling was the thought that I was just about to have my seventh birthday. That was exciting. And it was exciting to think about seeing my papa again.

Lark was a town of perhaps four hundred people, many being transients, working at the mill or at a coal mine nearby. There was a Mormon church, a Methodist church, one general store, one livery stable, one four-room schoolhouse (grades one through eight), one tiny post office, a drugstore, and a long building at the lower end of town that was divided lengthwise—one side a pool hall (the inside of which we never saw), the other side a long room where we went as often as possible, a hall of enchantment. There we saw Mary Pickford, her brother Jack Pickford, Marguerite Clark, Douglas Fairbanks, Wallace Reid, Sessue Hayakawa, Marie Doro, Dustin and William Farnum, and Jack Holt. In the back of the hall a player piano underscored the moods we saw on the screen. We came close to weeping for the troubles and predicaments of our heroes and heroines and we laughed at Chaplin and Harold Lloyd and Snub Pollard and a comedian named Musty Suffer who, I suspect, was Wallace Beery.

My mother was always working hard and didn't have time to talk about things very much, only to give rules. Rules were pretty much the same as they had been in Salt Lake City. The hardest one to follow was: "Don't play with any of the children in this town." We had been in Lark only a few days when a little boy named Scott came to ask her whether he and his friends could give me a birthday party. His friends—about six of them—were lined up behind him. I stood close in back of my mother hoping to hear her say "yes." She didn't say just "no." She said, "Absolutely not."

Other rules were; "Hold your heads high. Don't forget that John Marshall, Chief Justice of the Supreme Court of the United States of America, may have been one of your ancestors; that John Paul Jones, when his name was just John Paul, lived with your grandfather's family in Virginia at one time and liked them so well, he took their name for his own."

Heritage she considered important. Even most of her contemporary relatives were better off then we were; but the basis of the pride she wanted us to have in ourselves had nothing to do with having or not having money or relatives of affluence. She honestly believed that she and, therefore, we, her children, were better than most. The conditions in Lark certainly brought all those considerations to the surface. We gave her no argument. For myself, I believed in and actually enjoyed the aura she created. But that didn't help the disappointment I felt when she consistently said her "Absolutely not."

She didn't know much about my father's background, so in the equation of equality, she simply counted him out. If she had loved him once, that love was fading and easy to tell, even if there was no way to have any understanding of the tensions that were building up between them. There was often argument, especially when the grocery bill was to be paid and the hundred dollars he brought home was "just not going to be enough."

Mama's nephew, Wesley Jones, who had moved to Lark even before we did, went on a train trip and came back to tell us he was going to be married. What luck for him and for us! Helen, his wife, made a difference in all our lives. She gave Willow and Vaida piano lessons; she cooked, she made chocolate layer cake. She laughed a lot. She was a happy woman. Helen was a life-giving person and not someone just surviving. She had been born in California and the thought that enveloped the fact was that she had been born in and absorbed the famous sunshine. *California!*

On the first Thanksgiving she was in Lark, we went to her house for dinner. Her sunny personality might have held off a heavy snowfall, might have been enough to keep me from getting a feverish illness. But I felt very sick. My mother carried me home, struggling through the heavy snow. By the time we got home, she was hemorrhaging. I felt that I had been the cause of "another miscarriage."

Mama was resourceful at her machine. She seemed to be happiest there, as though grateful to turn her back on the washing, the ironing, the breadmaking, the supervision of seven baths in tin tubs on Saturday nights (eight including her own). Rainwater had to be caught and saved for shampooing—or snow melted. Our curly heads had to be kept beautiful. There was no end to the endlessness of work. Once I saw her lying in a hammock on the porch reading a book and I felt almost weak with joy at the sight.

She surprised me and I guess all of us when she decided to leave her chores and go into Salt Lake to the wedding reception of her friend Annie Woodbury. The happy part is, she took me with her! At the reception people were talking about the sculptor Aavard Fairbanks being there. I saw him. He was good-looking, which is what I expected because he was an artist. In a way, there was something of an artist about my papa. When you add up the way he could sing, the way he could entertain and tell stories if company came in—even without company, he could be entertaining, sitting in the rocker and singing "Ole Black Joe," letting his baritone voice go very deep at the last "Ole Black Joe." He could play the harmonica and he could do wood carving. He made a long chain out of a solid piece of wood and finished it off with a rectangular "cage" with a ball inside it, which could roll around and around. How clever he was! He made a scythe for me when I was given the part of Father Time in a school play. He made the scythe fast because I had to learn the part very quickly when the teacher realized the boy who was doing it couldn't remember his lines. He made me an hourglass, too. My family thought that for a nine-year-old girl, I was a very good Father Time.

Once, during the night, there was a great fire at the livery stable. And another night when there was even a greater fire that burned the mill where my father worked. This was the closest the war came to us, for my mother said she was sure it had been set afire by Germans who knew that copper was an important and useful metal in fighting the war. That fire made a difference in our lives. Papa had to go to find a job in the nearby town of Bingham. When he found one, we went to visit him once but we were not to see him except maybe once or twice after that. There wasn't any special talk about my parents separating. Papa was gone. He was gone and Mama seemed glad. There was a vague awfulness about that. She was too glad. "Street Angel, Home Devil," she said of him.

CHAPTER 3

LIFE WITHOUT FATHER

◆

A FTER A FEW MONTHS, ONE of the young men who had come home wounded from the war helped Mama load up a truck with all the little bits of furniture we had. Mama sat up front beside him and we children sat in the back on top of whatever we could. The young man drove us to Salt Lake City. We went to a street named Hampton Avenue and to a house with the number 236. Two thirty-six So. Hampton Ave. That had a fine sound. This was the first precise address of our lives. Mama was resourceful in getting that house for us. Maybe one of her rich relatives had helped. The rent was twenty-five dollars a month. There were five rooms, a vine-sheltered outhouse, the excitement of a telephone on the wall, a lamp with beaded fringe that hung over a round golden-oak dining table, and a rose-colored silk shade on a ceiling lamp in one of the two bedrooms, making that room seem cozy and warm even though it never was. The house was brick, far stronger and more secure than we'd had in Lark.

And there was shade. The street was lined with poplars. There

◆ 21 ◆

was green all around the bungalow. The small front yard was covered with grass and bordered with a low hedge. The backyard had a wild glory about it. Yellow golden glow tangled with tall green weeds. We worked at clearing out the weeds in the early morning, letting our bodies brush against the dew-covered growth. We battled through until we came to a tree at the side of the house where we found a swing suspended.

It was Vaida who pushed the swing and ran full-strength under it so that I got a thrilling start. At the very top, there was a "snap" that kept the swing from going up-up-up and over into a complete circle—a perilously perfect moment.

The atmosphere in the house was happier than I had known for a long while. There was not the tension that had existed between my mother and father because now there was only my mother. One thing made me unhappy: to see my little brothers, Richard, age six, and Victor, age four, sleeping on the floor on a mattress in the rear bedroom.

About one block away, there was a grocery store. I had seen the grocer's son, Fred Henriod, working there. Fred was my own age, eleven, bright-faced and friendly to me. If he could be working at our age, I could be working, too. I would speak to his father; his father would give me a job; I would give the money I earned to my mother; my mother would buy a bed for my brothers so they wouldn't have to sleep on the floor. It never occurred to me to consult my mother. It was simply a matter of doing what had to be done. I thought it would have to be done very early in the morning.

I was at the store as soon as Mr. Henriod got it open, so that only he and I were there. I presented my case with urgency and said nothing about my brothers, only that I wanted to work, just like Fred worked. Then he did a terrible thing. He questioned me about *why* I should want a job, what was the *reason*. With a reddened face, I told him I thought my family needed my help, and then he did something worse. He said, "Why don't you appeal to the Ladies' Aid Society?" I left the store, my face hot and unhappy. I felt much worse than disappointed. I felt that Mr.

Henriod should have known that I wasn't asking for such a thing as charity.

My friend Fred grew up to become the Chief Justice of the Supreme Court of Utah. I found that out when he wrote to me just a few years ago. I was glad to hear from him and to have a picture that he had taken of me on Hampton Avenue. I was astounded that he had kept it all those years. We wrote back and forth a few times, remembering that we had admired each other when we were little.

Vaida did get a job. My mother's cousin had a husband with a friend who had a printing business. He gave Vaida an office job. His name was Roy Porte. Vaida would dress very neatly and go to work by streetcar, which was only a block away. That same streetcar would bring people to visit us, especially young men who were attracted to Vaida. "There's safety in numbers," my mother would say.

Mama rented an upright piano. Vaida and Willow sang duets together: "I Love You Truly" and "The Rose of No-Man's Land." Mama made over a white linen suit of her cousin's for Vaida, who walked in a parade as a tribute to the Red Cross nurses.

After Mama rented the piano, she also rented a horse for me to practice on—up and down, up and down on Hampton Avenue. In a newspaper, the Salt Lake *Telegram*, it was advertised that there was to be a contest to see who would have the lead in a motion picture about the early days in Utah. The leading lady would have to ride. The contestants would have to get new subscribers for the paper. That's what the contest was really all about. Mama made me a cotton plaid suit and I went from door to door, feeling like I was on a crusade. I won the contest simply because I got the most subscriptions.

The immediate reward for that was a screen test. The test was made on the grounds of the county court house, right in the heart of the city. I sat on a bench there, holding a bunch of red roses. The director told me to lift the roses to my face and then look up to heaven as though the fragrance was just wonderful. I did what he said and soon the "test" was shown on the screen in an uptown theater. It went so fast, it was hard to tell much about it. After that, I was told I was really going to be the leading lady. I was now twelve years old.

We went to Fort Douglas, where the soldiers dressed in nineteenth-century uniforms, and I was put into a period dress and then onto the horse. I was in the center of the group of soldiers, as though I were their leader, and we all rode together toward the camera when we were told to and then stopped when we were told to. The movie also stopped right there. No further scene was made. The paper had its new subscribers, the "director" left Salt Lake City, perhaps to make arrangements with a newspaper in another city. But the circulation manager was very pleased with me and proud enough that he gave me a job at the paper stuffing envelopes every day after school. At the paper, I met an older girl who was doing the same thing. She had been promised a character role in the movie. She never got a chance to do that, of course, but the whole idea of it stimulated her and her family to go to California, where I would find her later and she would become my good friend. Her name was Katherine Wright.

It was around Halloween when I got paid for stuffing the envelopes. I went to a party at school and left my money in my pocket in the coatroom. It disappeared during the Halloween fun. Nine dollars was a lot to lose.

Willow's talents were more productive creatively. Even if she didn't get paid for it, she was chosen to sing in Handel's *Messiah*. A man named Squire Coop was the director of the Mormon Tabernacle Choir and he thought her fourteen-year-old contralto was good enough to sing in that great oratorio.

Vaida and I shared a bed in the room with the rose-colored lampshade. As the winter came, the room was so cold that we had to wear sweaters at night. She had a good red and green Canadian cardigan. She would pull my back close up to her, forming a lap for me. She was a warming person. She had a coloratura voice and was as beautiful as anyone I've ever seen.

My brother Vivien went off to work at a place called Silver City, so he wasn't home when the great influenza epidemic of

1918 came upon us that winter. Every person in our house was ill. My mother was too ill to help any of us. Mr. Porte sent a registered nurse to look after us. Cots were pulled toward the warmer area of the house and a kind of ward was created so the nurse could watch over us all. Vaida was put in the "front" room; I was put in the dining room. When I heard Vaida coughing, it seemed to make my own chest hurt even more and I coughed back at her. "Mama," she called out, "Fay is copying me." And I was, I know, and now that's horrible to think about. The nurse put a plaster of lard and turpentine on my chest and by the following morning, just like a miracle, all the tormenting tightness had gone and I seemed to be well again.

But during the night, Vaida had been taken to the hospital. I had been sleeping and didn't know. In a few days, my mother went there to see her. When she came back, she said that Vaida would not come home again. She said that her lungs had filled with water.

There was a terrible dark mystery all over everywhere, a dark force that must have moved through the whole Salt Lake Valley looking for her, finding her, saying to her, "I'm going to take you with me. You're mine." But that dark, mysterious force had no shape and no face, so you couldn't go and find it and say, "*No. She's mine!*"

We moved, when we were better, to a smaller house. The address was 814 Sherman Avenue. The rent was twelve dollars a month. The house had two rooms, one in back of the other, the two being joined together by a smaller space that was scarcely a room at all. From the outside, the house looked narrow and small and very, very sad. My first thought about it was that Vaida would have found it miserable and not a suitable place for her young men to come calling.

I have a letter from that time in which my mother writes a relative of her concern about me. The tone is close to desperate, with a list of multiple symptoms, a prognosis of maybe ten more days to live if my "tonsils were not removed." Our cousin, Dr. Warren Colton, found a specialist who did the operation right in his office. Afterward, he ordered strawberry malted milks to be delivered to our house every single day. He came to the house and saw me drinking the malted milk and watched me getting better.

My mother had more than just me to be concerned about. A letter that I have only recently discovered came to her from Vivien in Silver City.

My Dear Mother:

It is with more appreciation than anything that I have yet received, that I received your letter. I think I have found something in you that I never before realized. As I have always said, nothing is without its purpose. What you have had to go through has made you understand things that you never would have otherwise. I know that if I had told you about myself a few years ago, you would have nearly been frantic. A more common sense letter I do not believe could have been written. It pleased me more than any other thing, as I have found you almost perfect in all but that one respect. You have extremely fine views but you have always seemed to hold to them so rigidly, that you condemned all that did not conform to them. The greatest and broadest viewpoint concedes and allows for everything, no matter what it is, for life is as much unpleasant things as pleasant. You see what you have gained and what has been the purpose of your life. You know, troubles cease when you have become big enough and broad enough to overcome them and refuse to be affected by them. In definite words, you transcend them and their existence is like the the possibility of poverty to a genius . . . something that no less exists but is insignificant to him and his powers.

The letter continues, but it is this quoted passage that suggests my mother may have learned then what I am able to understand only now, and that I feel sure would have been difficult for her to accept: that Vivien had discovered he was homosexual. But I see that only in retrospect and with the awareness that life and living brings. He had a keen and sensitive intellect. He was a good student; he wrote a lot—essays on Matter and Energy—and he wrote poetry. I thought he knew all things.

*   *   *

Vivien sent money as he could, and Willow got a job at a photographic studio owned by a lady named Ida Wilcox. Willow's work was to tint the black-and-white photos with life-giving pink cheeks and eye and hair colors. This was before color photography and the tinting was a popular enhancement. Now we were able to move to a larger two-story house. It was a fine and roomy place for the twenty-five dollars rent and was near a school where I went for the summer months to make up for the winter of illness.

One evening, Willow brought a friend home whom she had met at the studio. When he came in, he seemed to take charge of the room, to vitalize it with talk and energy. He was very lean, slim-faced, and with insistent blue eyes and blond hair cut to suggest a recent service in the army. What he talked about were things artistic: his own experience as a student at the Art Students League in New York; his travels to Greece under the patronage of the brother of Sumner Gerard, who had been United States Ambassador to Germany; about his family having come from Schleswieg-Holstein; about having taught art at the East Side High School in Salt Lake City. And one evening he talked about the theater and playwrights. He brought a large white cardboard on which he had written in electric-blue ink a quotation about what it was that a playwright had to do: "with the pitiless precision of the skillful surgeon, he probes the souls of men. . . ." There was probably more before those words and after them, but the cadence of that sentence carried a high excitement for me. My mother served watermelon and a cake she had made with cocoa and buttermilk.

He invited Willow to go to the theater and invited me to go with them. We went to the Orpheum. There were people on the stage telling jokes that were not easy to understand; there were acrobats and jugglers who sent colorful Indian clubs flying at each other, always catching them. The theater itself was beautiful. I felt warm and yet uncertain about the jokes and looked to see whether Willow's friend William Mortensen laughed at them. Mostly, he did.

Soon, my mother told me that William Mortensen was going to

Los Angeles and that she had decided to let me go with him. What I heard her tell our friends was this: She did not want me to go through another cold winter. Her cousin Rose was planning to go to California before long and then I could stay with her. In the meantime, I could stay with friends of William's. She told her friends that he and my sister Willow were engaged and so she felt it perfectly proper that I should travel with him.

California! California! I went upstairs and sat in the window looking at the night sky. There was a large crescent moon with a star near the lower tip of the crescent. I saw them as glowing symbols of everything in the future.

For the next few days, or maybe a week, while plans and preparations for my going away were taking place, I was very nearly in a trance; it was all so amazing. At the same time that I was dreaming, some very practical things were being accomplished.

My mother took me to a department store and bought me a brown wool dress with a belt made of beads; brown single-strap button shoes; and a blue velvet tam. Her cousin Rose went to the train and gave me a challis combing jacket that she said I must wear over my dress to protect it from the train soot. The train seats were heavy red velvet. The air that came in the window was hot; my dress was, too, and the challis jacket made it seem even warmer.

William turned toward me and began telling me what he said he had been thinking since he first saw me. He painted a word picture that made me feel beautiful and special and unique. The surprise of this was absolutely enormous.

"My sister. It's my sister you like."

"It's you."

He didn't reach out to touch me. He just went on talking about the quality he had seen.

Oh Willow, I thought. This is a "triangle." I felt old, as old as a fourteen-year-old could feel. I felt happy that he admired me; I felt guilty that he did. The train rushed on and my face felt hot. I stared at the pattern in the combing jacket. To hear that he had not cared for my sister, as my mother had said, made me feel awful, even though I liked hearing what he had to say about me. I was feeling an appreciation of myself beyond what I had ever felt; at the same time, it was terribly uncomfortable to feel so old. The combing jacket had a pattern of little pink roses. I looked at them and at the blue satin binding that went around the edge of the jacket. He went on talking.

His friends in California were Christian Scientists. Their name was Gordon. They knew King Vidor and Florence Vidor because they were Christian Scientists, too. This faith, he said, demonstrated the great power of the mind. The Vidors had proved this power when they had been able to make a train wait for them after realizing they might be late for its scheduled departure.

CHAPTER 4

~~~~~~~~~~~

CALIFORNIA:
RED STREETCAR
TO HOLLYWOOD

◆

WHEN WE GOT TO LOS ANGELES, we went on a red streetcar to a place he said was the Garden Court Apartments. At the entrance, he spoke into a mouthpiece and said, "This is Michelangelo." He made himself feel very happy by saying that, and the Gordons—who were listening to him—it seemed, were happy, too. It was as though he and they couldn't wait to see each other. When we got to their apartment, there was a lot of gladness in the greetings. The Gordons were handsome. He was dark-eyed; she, white-skinned and blond. She had been an actress in the theater in New York. Her stage name was Alma Francis.

It was getting toward the end of the day and it was decided to take us to an apartment the Gordons had bought on Highland Avenue at the corner of Yucca. They had bought it to rent, but it hadn't been rented yet. It was freshly furnished, with everything looking as though it had just come from the store. They opened the bed for me and the sheets made sounds of crispness. I was very soon drifting off to sleep. Then I heard a sound on the far side of the room and saw that William was lying on the floor against the wall. He was fully dressed.

When I woke up in the morning, he was gone. There was no one at all in the apartment. I thought about a time when my mother's sister Myra had come to visit us in Salt Lake City. Aunt Myra was always beautifully dressed and touched her cheeks with rouge. She had been wearing a black velvet hat with pink ostrich plumes. My mother thought Myra was inclined to overdress. Myra was talking about her sons and said that one of them had been sleeping with a girl and that the girl was expecting a baby. Mama said she shouldn't talk of such things "in front of my children" and she asked Aunt Myra to leave!

I had slept in the same room with William.

It seemed a very long time before the Gordons and William came back; then we went to eat at a Chinese restaurant. Nothing tasted good. The soy sauce made me feel ill.

Later, they took me to meet Robert Gordon's mother, a Mrs. Comer, and she said I could stay with her. She was very plump and very kind and also a Christian Scientist. She was not at home very much, but she said I could have anything I liked from the refrigerator. There was very good mustardy mayonnaise.

The next afternoon, William came and sat beside me on a window seat. He ran his hand over my dress, feeling the shape of my breasts. I sat absolutely still, not moving at all, even to look at him. He got up and left the house, leaving me worried and wondering why, when I stood up, there was moisture on my skirt.

The next time he arrived, he had a splendid Harley-Davidson motorcycle painted a shiny dark green with a thin stripe of gold going all around it. It had a sidecar, painted in the same way, with a door to it and a little step-up and inside the car there was a lap robe.

He was dressed in riding pants and boots, a slim jacket with a russet-colored herringbone pattern, and a visored cap to match, where his goggles rested. He had goggles for me, too. He said he was going to take me to friends of his family who lived in Van

Nuys. It seemed a long ride over bumpy dirt roads, but the side car was cozy and comfortable.

His friends, whose name was Staley, welcomed us to their house, with the good smell of corn growing in their backyard. I was not only in a new world but in a succession of new situations.

A few days later, he took me to the home of Ferdinand Pinney Earle, a big two-story house on Highland Avenue that was almost directly across from the Hollywood Bowl. Mr. Earle was producing a film based on *The Rubáiyát of Omar Khayyám,* and William had the job of painting the interiors of Persian palaces on canvas boards that were about two feet by three feet. He said they were to be photographed and then rephotographed with people in the foreground, so that it would seem as though the people were really inside the palaces. Mr. Earle gave me a job being one of those people.

With five other girls in Oriental clothes, I stood on a raised beam-sized board. All we had to do was stand quietly. Mr. Earle came and made comments about our bare feet. There were large banks of lights called Cooper-Hewitts, which made our skin look ghostly green and our lips a purplish-black. They also made our eyes sore. There was a shimmering quality in the lighting, an effect of eerie otherworldliness, as though a studio was not like any other place on earth.

The palatial paintings were the first I had seen of William's work; I saw marble halls, great arches, and pillars look so real that you felt you could walk into them—even if they *were* only two feet by three.

I was given a room on the second floor at the Earles', the largest and most personal space I had ever known. There was a phonograph and I could play it and dance and look out onto pepper trees on one side of the house and onto a curved pebble driveway on the Highland Avenue side. I whirled and twirled to whatever music it was and one day whirled close to a window and saw two men in a tree, watching me. They were tree trimmers who had stopped their work for my dancing. That was a startling surprise! I stopped my dancing for the day, but only for the day, and next time looked to be sure there were no tree people outside! When

Mr. Earle went off to work in his big open car, Mrs. Earle would stand on the running board all the way to the street and then walk back sadly, seeming sorry to see him go. She was slim, gray-eyed Norwegian and a beautiful pianist. People came to hear her play Liszt. There were musical afternoons and evenings and there was talk about Lawrence Tibbett and the excitement they felt that he was going to create with the Metropolitan Opera Company. There was lots of wicker furniture in the room where the piano was and there were certain impressive other things, such as silver bread-and-butter plates that were used at every meal, including breakfast.

Mrs. Earle told me one afternoon that she and I were to join Mr. Earle and a friend at a place called Musso Frank and then go to see the film *The Cabinet of Doctor Caligari*. We had a little snack just before we left, so she expressed surprise when I said I would have the same meal that the two gentlemen ordered. She ate nothing! Although I was embarrassed, I felt committed to the steak that was brought and I ate it all, which was probably a good way to fortify myself for the unforgettably scary experience of seeing *Caligari*.

When walking from the Earle's house down Highland Avenue to Hollywood Boulevard, there was the fragrance of orange blossoms. The air itself was soft and gently warm as if satisfied because it was in California. On Hollywood Boulevard pepper trees shaded the street. The long slender branches of the trees were filled with gray-green leaves that partly covered tiny red berries clustered near the tips of the branches, smelling very pungent like real pepper. On the corner of Hollywood and Highland, the Hollywood Hotel had a long veranda that was edged with bright red geraniums. The look and feel of everything was caressingly beautiful. After the disturbing feelings I had had on the train, I returned to being young again and loving the look and the smells and the soft warm air, and the thought that there were other studios besides Mr. Earle's where there might be magic even greater than I had seen in his.

For instance, it was said that Lillian Gish had a large mouth but the makeup she used made it seem as small as a dime. Also, I was told that for the same reason, you wouldn't know Rudolph Valentino on the street if you looked right at him; it was his makeup that made him so handsome. So you couldn't tell whether you were seeing a movie star. One day, when I was told it was Betty Blythe who was carrying a parasol and strolling along under the pepper trees on Hollywood Boulevard, I believed it! She moved as though she were floating.

Mortensen took me to the Mack Sennett studios. We just walked about inside the studio. We saw a blond man in pale blue comic-looking overalls: Larry Semon, the comedian and director. He played Scarecrow in the first *Wizard of Oz*. We saw a beautiful brunette girl walking with two men on each side of her. She looked straight at me and smiled a beautiful, friendly smile. My mixed feelings were that she was perhaps a careless kind of person but that she was probably so happy being a movie star that she loved absolutely everybody, including strangers. Her name was Olive Borden, and she was a leading lady of silent films, as well as of the early talkies.

Mr. Earle was big, with small blue eyes and narrow red lips that he kept constantly moist by running his tongue over them. His head and arms were heavy with black hair. Mortensen told me he was known as "Affinity" Earle because once when he was in a trial about another man's wife, he had explained his feeling for her by saying that she was his "Affinity."

One night there was a tapping on my door; the knob was turning and the big arm of Ferdinand Pinney Earle was opening the door. I ran and pushed at the door with all my might. Mr. Earle went away. The next night, I pulled a chest of drawers in front of the door. I heard a tapping again and knew the door was opening only a very little—and couldn't open any further because of the drawers.

At breakfast the following morning, Mr. Earle told his wife about me putting furniture in front of the door. He laughed a big wet-lipped laugh. Charlotte Earle didn't laugh, but it was hard to tell what she thought because she said nothing. I looked at my silver bread-and-butter plate all through the breakfast.

Perhaps Charlotte Earle told Mortensen. Later, he telephoned me and said to be up very early, to go quietly down to the kitchen, make sandwiches, and meet him in front of the house. There was lots of bread in the kitchen but not much to put in sandwiches. I found some huge jars of apricot jam.

Like a little thief, I worked fast and got the jam sandwiches made; then I met him and we rode for a long way into the country. He said we were in Topanga Canyon when we stopped. We sat under a tree and put out the sandwiches.

We sat for a while without eating. He was very serious, saying what seemed to be important thoughts: that the most powerful urge in the world was the urge between men and women. It seemed that what he said had nothing to do with him and me— only that I should be aware. I felt unhappy and very old again— and wished there wouldn't be any such things to worry about. I was sorry he was making me feel old again, but I thought he cared about me. There might be terrible future trouble, but it wouldn't be between him and me. And from that moment, I felt comfortable with him and had a sense of belonging.

It was that day, or soon after, that we went to a large hotel in downtown Los Angeles. Here he found stationery at a desk in the lobby. I sat beside him while he wrote a letter to an actor named Warren Kerrigan, asking him and his wife to take me into their home. Then he rented a room for me where he was staying in the 1700 block of North Alexandria Avenue. He was sharing a room with a young man named Paul Detleffson. The cost of my room was a dollar a night.

Paul was always saying funny things. He was a short person and the flat cap he wore made him look even shorter, but he told very big and very funny jokes and his eyes twinkled all the time. He called Mortensen "Bill." I began to do that, too.

Mr. and Mrs. Quinby owned a clean, neat house. Mr. Quinby sat on the front porch a lot, reading letters he had written to the *Times*. Mrs. Quinby did all the housework and sometimes asked me to help her when she changed the bed linens. They were very sad about their daughter who had gone away when her engagement to be married had been broken. To emphasize her sadness, Mrs. Quinby showed Bill all the lovely unworn clothes that had been her daughter's trousseau.

I saw these clothes first when Bill took me to the Wetzel Photographic Studio on Hollywood Boulevard. It was a Sunday. He had borrowed the studio, borrowed the dresses, and for several hours, he photographed me. I changed dresses and my hair each time, all my feelings flowing along with his enthusiasm. I felt grown-up and admired and lovely in the laces and taffetas. And later, when he showed me the prints, I knew it was possible for me to look at least seventeen or maybe more. There was a person in those pictures I hadn't seen before, even if I had suspected she could be there. And he had stimulated all of that.

There was a lunch place near the Quinbys' house where you could get a fresh-fruit salad piled high with whipped cream for thirty cents. Bill and Paul and I went there often. Bill liked to talk about the time he went to the Art Students League in New York and about Robert Henri being a fine American artist. He also talked about Titian and Tintoretto and about the time he went to study in Greece (the beauty of the ancient statues) and he told this limerick:

> There was a young sculptor named Phidias
> Whose sculptures were perfectly hideous.
> He carved Aphrodite without any nightie
> And shocked the ultrafastidious.

So sophisticated, I thought. He had a leather-bound copy of *Plutarch's Lives* and got me to read some of it to him and Paul. Days passed and there was no response from Warren Kerrigan.

I told Bill about Katherine Wright, who had moved to California earlier. We found her living with her family on South St. Andrews, near Thirty-fourth Street. Their house was not yet completed; the inner walls still showed tar paper between the raw-wood uprights. Outside, there was hard dry ground, as yet un-turned for any planting. We asked whether I could stay with them. Almost at once, I became the fifth member of that family. There wasn't enough space, but their welcome was large and im-mediate. They, too, were Christian Scientists, a coincidence that enlivened the meeting between them and Bill.

Mr. Wright looked like Will Rogers and was a carpenter who went out to work, thereby neglecting the carpentry needs of his own home. Mrs. Wright, whose gentle brown eyes appeared to be ready either to laugh or cry—her feelings so sweetly on the sur-face—cooked over a coal-oil stove. Everything was temporary in a material way; everything was permanent and enduring in the spirit they brought to their daily living.

Katherine no longer imagined herself an actress, and she worked as a milliner in downtown Los Angeles. Her sister, Hazel, shared a bed with her. The outside edge of that bed became mine. Hazel was not entirely happy to yield that space and showed her resentment by throwing a bucket of water over me one day as I was drying my hair in the sun. She was justified because Katherine treated me as a favorite little sister, making dresses for me and sometimes taking me with her on the red car—as the streetcar was called—all the way to Venice, where we walked along the beach and bought ice cream sandwiches.

I registered for school at the Thirtieth Street Junior High School, within easy walking distance. It was understood, because the Wrights did not have a telephone, that William Mortensen would get me on the weekends. His motorcycle would come bounding over the bumps in the front yard at a given time. He expected punctuality.

Sometimes he arranged for me to stay at the Quinbys' and sometimes with ladies he thought might be helpful to me; for ex-ample, the sister of Carol Dempster. Carol had starred in D. W. Griffith films, or the sister of the cameraman Robert De Grasse. He also arranged for me to spend a few Saturday mornings in a ballet class at the studio of Theodore Kosloff, who had acted and danced in Cecil B. De Mille films. I did the best I could to imitate the dancers, dressed in a pink silk tunic and shorts that Katherine had made for me.

I spent a weekend at the home of a writers' agent name Edna Schley. She was short and round and had an air of great efficiency. She had been married to a naval officer and had traveled a lot, especially to the Orient. Her snow-white hair was worn in a Dutch cut so that the bangs would cover a scar where she had had brain surgery to remove a blood clot. She said that during the operation, she had gotten out of her body and watched the surgeons while they worked.

She woke me up one night when she came home from a dinner party. There was only moonlight in the room, coming through louvered shutters. She sat on the edge of my bed, saying over and over, "You're a lovely girl. A very lovely girl." There was a strong chemical smell about her and the moonlight made her face look very red. I was glad when she went away. That was the first time I had been so close to anyone who had been drinking. It seemed as though she didn't really know what she was saying. Later, she was to become an important person in my life.

For my fifteenth birthday in September my mother sent some yardage of "changeable" taffeta, the colors blending from bronze to turquoise. By Thanksgiving, Katherine had made it into a dress, and I went with Bill to have dinner at the Pig 'n Whistle on Hollywood Boulevard. The dinner cost eighty-five cents per person. We sat at a small table, opposite each other. He had presents for me. First, glass beads of a bluish tone that went very well with the dress I was wearing. Then two books, bound in black leather, both by Mary Baker Eddy: *Science and Health* and *Key to the Scriptures*. His large blue eyes watched for my reaction. Something of material beauty—the glass beads—and something of spiritual value—the books. That made a wholeness of caring. I felt wonderfully fortunate to have him care about me. I wouldn't have known how to say that. I expect I just looked at the beads and then at him and said, "How beautiful," and put them on and looked at the books and then at him. I probably said, "Thank you," and found a place for the books at the side of the table, so there would be room for the food. I knew that he wanted everything good for me.

Katherine was glad I had that book and encouraged me to memorize the "Statement of Being," which was easy to do, but I thought the last part contradicted the first and I have never yet been able to reconcile that difficulty.

My pleasure in going to the Thirtieth Street Junior High School was enhanced by realizing that Bill Mortensen was adding to my learning almost as a tutor might. I liked ancient history all the more because he had been to Greece. I liked preparing speeches from Shakespeare for the oral English class. I wrote a poem for the *Annual*—"Mountains," which was fairly good and was later published in *Theatre* magazine when I was in a film with Emil Jannings called *The Street of Sin*. Probably it was published *because* I was in a film with Emil Jannings.

All my grades, even in algebra, were good. I gave my report cards to Bill for his signature. Mr. Tritt, the principal, asked why it was that they were signed by this person who added the word *guardian* after his name. Mr. Tritt seemed worried about how unusual this was, but after I explained it to him, he didn't seem worried anymore.

There was a night at the Quinby house when the room I usually had was not available, and Bill said the three of us, he and Paul and I, could keep all our clothes on—even our shoes—and sleep on top of the bedclothes in their room. That's what we did. I was on the outside of the bed, staring at the ceiling and feeling that I was moving faraway from what my mother would want me to do. I was also feeling tired, and I slept.

Bill was working at the Wetzel Photographic Studio, doing tinting on the black-and-white photos. He took me with him to deliver some of these to a customer, Richard Jones, who was head of the Mack Sennett studio. Mr. Jones was not at home, but I remembered his name when he became head of the Hal Roach studio, and I went there to ask him for a job.

* * *

By the time summer vacation came, Bill had found space in a large house on Wilshire Boulevard, somewhere between Vermont and Western. It had once been a fine home and was now a rooming house run by a lady named Mrs. Brett. Bill lived over the garage in a space large enough to make into a studio. He was constantly at work, creating papier-mâché masks in the style of Benda, making costume jewelry, dyeing batik silks, and setting up a darkroom for his photography.

Mrs. Brett gave me a small room upstairs in the main house. She sometimes made breakfast for me—large slices of ham and browned potatoes. I was astonished that she took this kind of generous breakfasting for granted. She was widowed, I think, because there was no Mr. Brett around the place. But there was a son, Quentin—big and strong, a noble sadness in his features, as though he had been sculpted from some melancholy stone. His sadness may have come from having been in the war and returning home blind in one eye. He had brought a souvenir bayonet home with him. He and Bill and I played mumblety-peg with it, pinning squares of paper into the big front lawn.

Going up the stairs to the studio, the smells of glue and clay were heavy and oppressive. The masks were first modeled in clay and then glued paper was molded over them. To reverse that process, Bill wanted to make a life mask of me. It meant first covering my face with a heavy coat of Vaseline—from my hairline to under my chin—and placing straws in my nostrils so I could breathe while he poured plaster of paris over my entire face; it also meant holding very still until the plaster set, which seemed like a very long time to me. All the while, he kept talking and assuring me that there was nothing to be concerned about, even when the liquid plaster seemed to have heat like smoke vaporizing from it. But then, when it touched my face, it wasn't hot at all. When finally he pulled the plaster away, there was the shape of my face inside the cast.

Whatever work he was doing was of the utmost interest and urgency to him. He worked at a fever pitch. He began in that same way to make the garage room into a photographic studio. He took some draped figure photographs of me, teaching me what was the line of action and the line of inaction. I posed a lot, feeling the sense of grace for which he was looking. "Never," he said, "let anyone photograph you so as to show any 'local color.'" Local color I understood to be pubic hair and undraped breasts. He made some lovely photographs. I developed an awareness and sense of my own body, much as a dancer might.

He also took some casual pictures of me and Quentin alongside the shiny Harley-Davidson. I was beginning to feel freedom and a stylishness of behavior that reflected some of the actresses of the day—even the femme fatale Theda Bara—and I looked into the camera, trying to show that I could imitate her sultry look.

I was happy to send some photos to my mother. I didn't take the trouble to explain that I was posing, "putting on" the Theda Bara style.

It would be a month or so before the shock of this would bring her to California. In the meantime, Bill found a studio in the center of Hollywood: a large room at the back of a big old house on Hollywood Boulevard. Once again, he shared a room inside the big house with Paul, and on the occasions when I stayed over, I had a bunk bed in the studio.

One afternoon, he brought me a pale-green-taffeta evening dress and told me I was to wear it to work the next morning as an extra at the Century comedy studios. Early in the morning, he came into his studio and helped me put on makeup; then he drove me to the Century studio, which was at the corner of Sunset and Gower. Well! Now I was in the movies.

The star of the Century comedy was a girl, a very pretty blonde. I watched her more than I watched anything else on the set, wondering what it was and why it was that she was the star of the movie we were doing. I've forgotten her name.

Many years later, I would learn that she married into the family of the writer-producer Dore Schary. His family was in the bakery business. That pretty lady, then a whole lot plumper, was running the bakery shop in our neighborhood supermarket.

Very soon, Bill told me that the same studio wanted me to do a bit part. I was to perform a clown dance in a theater scene. Bill got me a dark-green, white-trimmed clown suit. I don't know who decided my face should stay free of clown makeup, but when they were ready for me to go up on the stage and dance, I improvised what I thought was a screamingly funny little dance—part clownish, part Charleston, and I felt just marvelous showing off that way.

At school, too, I was developing a sense of my power to be oh, so entertaining! At recess the girls sat in a circle letting me make up funny stories and we had a very good time.

CHAPTER 5

~~~~~~~~~~~~~~~

WITH MY MOTHER AGAIN

◆

T HE FALL TERM HAD NOT been going very long when I looked out the front window at the Wrights' and saw my mother walking toward the house. She marched rather than walked because there was an invisible army on either side of her. She looked much smaller than when I had seen her last. She was wearing serious black. Her step was very measured, very sober, and none of this manner changed to joy when she entered the house and saw me. There were courteous exchanges with the Wrights but no great warmth or thank-you's for the enormous kindness they had shown me.

I was to gather my belongings and go with her. I did that obediently. She was my mother, a little general of a dark invading army. But my mother—mother—I felt stunned into silence. Whatever thoughts were spinning in her head were not to be let out until she was absolutely ready. In the meantime, we got to the place where she had located herself along with my two little brothers: a boarding house on Hollywood Boulevard east of Vine

Street that was run by an English woman whose narrow nose was narrowed further by pince-nez.

Most of the occupants rocked on the veranda, especially one who was recovering from tuberculosis. He was thin, as Leslie Howard would later look. Mrs. Pince-Nez served everybody at a long table. A chunky blond girl never sat down to eat but stopped at the table to tell about the wonderful parties she would be going to with her big producer friend, someone named Lazarus. There was always pudding and my little brothers liked that. I felt as though a large stone had come hurtling down off a high building and thumped me into numbness.

Then my mother took me to Lafayette Park. She was ready to talk. She told me that she had gone to a spiritualist after she saw my "Theda" look, and that the woman had spoken to her in the voice of my sister Vaida. She said that my mother should get to California as soon as possible to save me from the most awful dangers, and that she, Vaida, would keep Bill away from me until my mother could arrive.

We were sitting on a bench in a quiet area of the park—which is now known as MacArthur Park. Now, it is often very rowdy but then, it was peaceful. I wondered to myself how my lovely sister could have said any such things. I felt an avalanche of unhappiness.

"Now. What was the worst thing that happened?" my mother wanted to know.

I thought. Then I told her about a time when Bill and I drove up the coast carrying his Graflex camera and lots of pale-blue-chiffon yardage. We walked from the highway, after parking the Harley-Davidson, and when we got onto a beach below the palisade and found an enormous rock, he told me to go behind it and drape myself with the chiffon while he set up his camera. The tide was low. The sand was firm where the surf touched it and it was easy to run fast, even when the foamy water was lapping at my feet. That was what he wanted. And he wanted the ends of the chiffon to fly in back of me and my loosened hair to fly back in the same way. I ran away from where he waited with his camera on a tripod, and listened for him to say, "Now," so that I was coordinated with the incoming surf. And so I ran, to and fro, to and fro. And then I saw a highway patrolman coming down the narrow path on the palisade that we ourselves had used. I waited while he approached Bill. "People up there on the highway say that you are down here taking nude photographs." "You can see for yourself that isn't so," Bill said to him. He looked at me, nodded. "Even so," he said, "I think you ought to pack up and move along."

There was a lot of disgrace about hearing that: "pack up and move along." My face burned. The sting of that moment remained. It was hard to tell my mother about it but I thought I had to.

After a moment of absorbing this confession, she went on. "Did he have his way with you?"

"What do you mean? What does that mean . . . have his way?"

"It means," she said, "that I have been afraid you would have a baby."

Oh! There were those two times when I had slept all night in the same room with Bill. Is that what Vaida wanted her to know? Maybe I had had a baby like my Aunt Myra had talked about and maybe I had lost it like my mother had lost babies more than once when she had bled a lot and said she had had a miscarriage. Maybe I had had a miscarriage one time when I had bled a lot during one of my periods. I said those thoughts out loud to my mother and she seemed satisfied. We went back to the rooming house.

I should have been glad to see my little brothers. But, I was missing the great lighted-up look of Bill's enthusiastic blue eyes. I was silenced by my mother's renewed silence. I sat in a rocker near the man who was recovering from tuberculosis and listened to him tell how wonderful it had been at Lake Saranac, New York, where there was a place to help people with his illness.

Bill Mortensen's studio was not many blocks away. After my mother found a four-room permanent house in a "court" on Van Ness Avenue, she and I went to call on Bill Mortensen.

He obliged her by bringing out a stack of Graflex negatives: "every negative you have ever taken of her." He placed them in a stack as she indicated—beside the chair in which she sat. I stood near the door; he, on the far side of the room. I saw in his expression astonishment and nonresistance to what my mother did then. She smashed each negative. Each plate of glass splintered down onto the one just smashed, until she had done them *all*. She seemed to be naming them as she struck one on top of another: Sin! Sin! Ugly! Sinful! She didn't speak but her energy was eloquent. Bill was only a few yards away from me but every good, exciting, creative moment that the past year with him had meant to me was distanced, going farther and farther away with every splintering sound. Was this true? Was this really happening— this great erasure? This amputation? It wasn't *good,* her fury was saying. It was evil, evil, *evil!* I looked at him. Both of us were letting this awful moment condemn us. But there was no question of *not* letting it happen. The only question was whether it was true; was she right; was a mother the one who would *know* even without *knowing?* Mothers were supposed to be very close to God.

She said we should go.

"You are not to set a foot out of this house," she said when we got to the house on Van Ness Avenue. It was painful to be isolated, not to be seeing Bill. For more than a year, he had had charge of my life. He was my mentor, my friend.

The tragedy of my mother's actions was that she was assuming we had a physical relationship. Out of complete ignorance I had contributed to that assumption. It would be a long time before I would know what a physical relationship was. William Mortensen had never tried to embrace me. Perhaps if he had, as my mother imagined, I would have been compelled to walk out of the house and go to him. It was numbing to think that in her eyes, all the time I had been in California, I had been a very wicked person.

Katherine Wright telephoned one day, speaking quickly, urgently. She and Bill had a plan: to take me out of the country and bring me back under another name! But she didn't call again.

My sister Willow arrived from Salt Lake City, bringing her chiropractor husband, Reed, with her. She was expecting a child. My mother was quite happy about this marriage. My sister would be happy, too, for a few years. Her husband was a gentle, tentative person, ducking his head to cover laughter as though to apologize. "Forgive me but that is pretty funny." He had a brother in the same profession who lived in Redlands.

The first time I was allowed out of the house was to go with Willow and Reed to see him. Willow sat in the back of their Ford to allow her large abdomen more comfort. For a few moments, Reed let me operate the gas accelerator, which, at that time, was situated inside the circumference of the steering wheel.

Willow told my mother, later that day, that she hated those few moments. As soon as she told my mother, my mother told *me*. I was in the bathtub. She flew into the room, slamming the door behind her, and began hitting me about the head and shoulders, saying, "Huzzy, huzzy! Willow has told me about you, you huzzy, sitting close to Reed in the car." I tried to protect my head but I couldn't protect myself from the overwhelming sense of injustice.

Her anger was like a seal, a validation of the guilt she had already made my identification. Anyone who has ever had feelings of guilt imposed by a parent will know that it doesn't go away quickly. It didn't seem to matter that it was she who had sent me off on the train with William Mortensen; that it was entirely her choice, her decision. I think as time went by and she became fearful that she might have made a mistake in that decision, she had to find someone or multiple ones to blame, and the object of her concern was the most obvious. It would have helped enormously to have been able to understand her psychology then. As it was, there would be no escape from the feeling of wrongful responsibility she placed upon me—not for a long, long time.

The wrong was to be complicated again and again because of that lack of understanding and insight. All I had then was the instinctive knowledge that I could survive any wrongful accusation. I had that understanding about myself. What I did not have was an understanding about *her*. And the love I felt for her blurred any possibility of seeing her clearly. If I could have, perhaps I would have loved her more.

*   *   *

After about a month, rescue came in the person of a lady from the Board of Education. An ample-bodied Minerva arrived at the house to question my absence from school.

The excitement of returning to school was tremendous. At the corner of Highland and Sunset, Hollywood High School was fronted with broad, sweeping lawns; the buildings bordered with poinsettias. *Poinsettia* was the name of the yearbook and the emblem placed on certificates given for excellent grades. I was proud to receive one of these signed by the feisty, much-respected principal, Mr. Snyder.

Mr. Arthur Kachel taught drama. He had a liberated personality. He would sometimes do readings for us, especially "Disraeli." When he directed play rehearsals in the evenings, he took his very attractive lady friend along with him.

In Booth Tarkington's *Seventeen,* I had only a small part; the leading lady was Mary McCallister. Harry Warner's son Lewis was on the stage crew. Lewis was very good-looking. He and his friend Joe Sauer (later, as an actor, Joe Sawyer) invited some of us to the Warner home on Rossmore Avenue.

There, we walked on thick Oriental rugs and stood around watching the boys play billiards. Lewis's sister Betty tells me that on the ceiling there were paintings of the Warner children as angels, but even if I had looked up, I wouldn't have known. It is very interesting to imagine what they were like. Lewis died not long after. He had gone on a visit to Cuba. While there, he had been troubled by an impacted wisdom tooth. He went back home, but by that time the infection had spread through his body. There was no such thing as penicillin then to save him. We were all sad and shocked, most of all his close friend Joe. For years after, I noticed that Joe was almost a constant as a character actor in Warner Brothers films. That just seemed nice to me.

Another big house we got to see was the Hamburger home. Two Hamburger sisters went to Hollywood High. Their family owned a large department store downtown, now The May Company. We were invited into the kitchen only. It was big and almost too immaculate.

To raise funds for a pipe organ for the school auditorium, we presented *The Pied Piper of Hamelin* at the Hollywood Bowl. Only now do I note the coincidence of "pipe organ" and "piper." Here, again, I had a small part—rather, I was one of the crowd. I was "auditioned" for a speaking role but, however I tried, my voice didn't carry from the stage all the way to the top of the Bowl. I probably tried too hard, squeezing my larynx down with the effort. It would be a long time before I would understand that enunciation might have been more effective than loudness. To compensate, I worked hard at selling tickets for the event. For the first time ever, my picture was in a Los Angeles daily paper.

Mr. Kachel liked me and promised me that I could do *Friend Hannah*, a play about a Quaker girl, the following year. In the meantime, he included me in an invitation to about six students (four boys, two girls) to apply for extra parts in *The Pilgrimage Play*, in which he was to play Pontius Pilate. Through his consideration, we all got jobs and trudged about the hills, as background for the awesome happenings in Jerusalem and Gethsemane. The play had been presented for many summers in a natural setting quite near the Hollywood Bowl. Sometimes later, while listening to a concert at the Bowl, I could hear a vocal crescendo rising from the hills opposite and recognize the approximate progress of the play.

My mother's cousin—my "Aunt" Rose—who was supposed to have come to California soon after my arrival, finally did arrive. Her brother came, too. He was rich enough to buy a small apartment house on Cassil Place, where Rose lived. Walking to school was convenient from there and she gave me good things for breakfast and let me have some of my girlfriends over after school for cake. I didn't stay permanently, just occasionally, and was as happy as my family to be able to decrease the crowding in the tiny house on Van Ness.

I won the interest of a few girls to act in an adaptation I chose to make from a section of *Ivanhoe*. I won their initial interest, not their sustained interest, which shouldn't have puzzled me as much as it did. One of the girls, Bonnie Cashin, cared about another art form. She became a leading fashion designer.

There was a day when William Mortensen's past efforts on my behalf were freshly realized. My mother and I were walking along Sunset Boulevard. As we neared the corner of Gower, two men came out of the Century studio where I had worked. They waited for us, as if to be sure they recognized me. One of them asked whether I would like to be a leading lady in a comedy that was to begin shooting in a few days. They were the Stern Brothers, cousins to the Laemmle family. One is credited with having said about the foolishness of selectivity for location sites: "A tree is a tree, a rock is a rock; shoot it in Griffith Park."

Now, I thought, I was going to become a comedienne! They had probably seen my clown dance and wanted me for my comic style. I could be funny like Mary Pickford or even Mabel Normand!

The Stern brothers went along and my mother and I stayed right on the spot, fairly transfixed by the moment. We were *both* happy and she said at once that I'd have to have a new dress and I knew she was right and we went off to find one. Nice but inexpensive.

A few days later, in a new cotton dress and long, well-combed curls, I was ready to begin my comic career. Looking up at the tall, fat leading man, I made a marvelously funny face . . . or so I thought. The director called out, "*No, no*. Don't try to be funny. Just look pretty. Keep looking pretty!" That was a letdown. It seemed odd to be in a comedy without having the opportunity to be funny. "Just look pretty!"

At the Fox studio on Western Avenue, I was given a screen test for a leading-lady role with Robert Gordon, that same Robert Gordon who knew William Mortensen as Michelangelo. More than one girl was being tested for this. The producer said I got the part because he could see I had a "fighting spirit." Robert Gordon's wife was on the set a lot, bringing large amounts of orange juice processed on the spot with a juicer she was promoting. The set wasn't really a set but an outdoor "rock and tree location." Again, I was the look-pretty leading lady.

The Gordons and I didn't talk about William Mortensen. I had a clear sense of severance and didn't even wonder whether he might have been in any way responsible for my getting the part with Gordon.

Steps leading to my next leading-lady role are elusive. I reach back to the thought that it was my mother who learned about Bud Barsky. He was "established" on Beechwood Drive just back of the Columbia studios. He was to make a feature film, *The Coast Patrol*. It would have scenes on the ocean and in a lighthouse, so it would be a lot more than a "rock and a tree" production.

Bud Barsky was round-faced and enthusiastic. He chewed on a cigar but that didn't keep his smile from showing. He was so pleased to have me in his picture that he wanted to change my name to June Darling! That may have been caring a lot about me and my future from his point of view, but from mine, I would be losing what I understood myself to be. Certainly *not* June Darling!

My mother accompanied me most of the time on this picture; there was also a tutor, so it must have been during school term. We paid sixteen dollars for a pretty silk-print dress. I had a grandfather in the picture, so I had more to do than just look pretty. I think I had to worry about him. Everyone in the company, especially Mr. Barsky, had to worry about me after I had spent a whole day doing scenes in a dinghy on the ocean. The makeup either did not protect me from the sun and/or intensified the burning that made my face swell to twice its size. What an expensive few days followed for Mr. Barsky until the swelling reduced and I could worry about my grandfather with a recognizable face. Perhaps Barsky would have wanted me to do more films, but it's possible that too much of his funds were lost in those days of waiting.

CHAPTER 6
A FILM CONTRACT:
THE BEGINNING
OF LIFE
IN THE MOVIES

◆

THE REALITY OF WORKING WAS a growing fact. I thought I had stepped strongly enough into the world of movies not to go back to school, much as I loved it. I read about a new production head at the Hal Roach studio: Richard Jones. I recognized the name of the man to whom Bill had attempted to deliver some tinted photos. Perhaps, subconsciously, both names made me feel comfortable having been within my mother's family. I went to the Hal Roach studio, asked to see Mr. Jones, and was admitted to his office. He twinkled; his eyes, his mustache, all of him, it seemed, was cautiously merry. I don't think I sat down, but I said what I had to say fast: that I wanted to work and would like to work at the Hal Roach studio. "Well." He twinkled. "I think we can give you a six months' contract." When I've told this story, it has seemed incredible even to me that it could have happened so fast, so simply. He was my instant, immediate sponsor, a kindly twinkle that gave me a six months' contract at sixty dollars a week. He didn't hand me a contract right that minute, of course. But he said I could go to work. He was, to me, implicitly my friend and I had a warm respect for him, except once when he said "Goddamn" in front of me. He must have lost his twinkle for a moment when I objected. I saw him perhaps not more than three times after I was given my contract, although I went to the studio every day. Being under contract meant that you had to be available for any possible bit part or even extra work or to be a leading lady in case *that* opportunity arose. You waited in your dressing room. I shared mine with a girl named Marjorie Winter who taught me a little about improving my makeup. If there wasn't work in a film, there were publicity pictures to be made. Arthur Hagermann and "Mike" Boylan ran the publicity department. At various times, I was costumed as Kiki, as a farm girl, as an athlete waiting for the starting gun in appropriate shorts and sweater. Young reporters from the newspapers stopped by occasionally. Their friendly kindness got some of these pictures printed.

Two of the stars in the studio were Charlie Chase and Stan Laurel. I got to do a lead with Charlie Chase that was directed by Leo McCarey. He was to become a great director, particularly of comedy-drama with Irene Dunne and Cary Grant. And I had an ingenue lead with Stan Laurel. Stan Laurel had not yet teamed with Oliver Hardy, although he, too, was in the studio. The particular magic that magnetized these two into a team lit up the sky for Hal Roach and for audiences everywhere. The Roach studio was in Culver City, a distance from where I lived. My mother borrowed $600 from Mr. Roy Porte in Salt Lake City to buy a model T Ford. My brother Vivien, who by now had arrived in California, taught me to drive.

Very often, I would go up Vine Street, turn left on Selma Avenue, and pick up Janet Gaynor, who also worked at Hal Roach. Janet was good company. She had a head full of curly, red hair, very correct petite features, and carnelian-brown eyes that danced to a wry little smile. There was an elfin wisdom about her, as though she might know certain charming secrets. She never said "because" but always "on account of." I found that fun to imitate and later it would be copied from me for the character Nikki in

John Monk Saunders's *Single Lady*. Saunders was the screen-writer whom I would later marry.

At Christmastime, Mr. Roach gave all the girls under contract beautiful beaded bags. It was really nice to be "in the movies" at the Hal Roach studio. The salary I got made it possible to rent a better house, this time on Fairfax Avenue near Fountain. Hedda Hopper lived up the street and also Mary Philbin. Mary had been in *Phantom of the Opera* with Lon Chaney and also in *Merry-Go-Round*, directed by Erich von Stroheim.

One of the young men who came to call on me was Paul Kohner. My mother was pleased: Paul was Jewish. She had once read *Daniel Deronda* by George Eliot and through that had come to admire the Jewish character. Also, Paul was a musician, a pianist.

He took me to meet his friends, the Petchnikoffs. There was Lili, who played the violin. Her iron-gray hair rose full and round over her Russian features, gray eyes heavily ringed with dark circles; all of her looked distinguished. There was Sergei, her young son, and Nadja, her still younger daughter. Her mother and her aunt wore long black taffeta and played double solitaire with tiny playing cards.

There was always company; there were sometimes conductors who would be performing at the Hollywood Bowl, just directly across from the Petchnikoff home. I met Eugene Goosens. I met Bruno Walter. I heard Lili play. There was an artistic energy in this household. If you just looked and listened, you absorbed a lot of good feeling.

Paul played the piano sometimes. He occasionally took me to dinner, always with people from the Universal studio. He was not related to the Laemmles but was like one of the family, having come from "the old country." I don't know when he became casting director at Universal, but when my six months at Hal Roach were over, I went to Universal. Janet did, too. We moved upward and onward together. Now we had contracts that implied great futures, renewable by the year with salaries increasing gradually over a period of seven such years, so that if you looked at the amount set down for the final year, you could feel all that great potential.

Universal's bread-and-butter pictures were Westerns, two-reel, four-reel, and five. Two-reelers were twenty to twenty-five minutes long and usually shown before a feature film. Janet began in two-reelers with Pee Wee Holmes. I began with Eddie Cobb, also in two-reelers. Janet and I shared a dressing room. If there was such a thing as a makeup department, we knew nothing of it. We put on our own greasepaint, making our faces very light, our mouths very dark. This was the recommended contrast suitable for the film of the time. It also helped our faces to register in the long shots.

In the Westerns, there were very few close-ups. We had to be in the studio early because the pictures were almost always shot outside and work began as soon as the sun was up. The sun was a great friend to moviemaking, but to leading ladies who had to look up adoringly at tall cowboys, it could be literal pain. Reflectors (large boards covered with tinfoil and angled to turn the sun's light onto a scene) could make it a struggle just to keep your eyes open.

My progress at Universal was from two-reel Westerns all the way to a five-reeler with their biggest star, Hoot Gibson. Eddie Cobb, Art Acord, and Jack Hoxie were the stars of the shorter-length films. Eddie Cobb was the most gentle of men, a shy and apologetic wonderment in all that he said: "Oh, my. I'll be darned. Oh, my!"

Art Acord sometimes had to be awakened by the assistant director on the way to location. It seemed that he wouldn't stir out of bed until pulled from it. We would all wait in the car until he came out, looking grim, saying nothing, smelling of alcohol. It was said he was part Indian but he had blue eyes, except the part that was streaked red from the alcohol. He was a handsome, sad-appearing fellow. He wore his cowboy clothes with style. But because of his sadness and silence and the alcohol, it wasn't comfortable to do scenes with him.

Mostly, there were day locations, perhaps an hour's drive out into the San Fernando Valley. Sometimes we worked on the back lot, where a cable car swung on a cable over a great gulley. Fights between heroes and villains took place in that little car; girls were rescued from it. It was probably dangerous but I had an abiding faith in the crew and in the cowboys who were responsible for all the action scenes. In *The Wild Horse Stampede*, I didn't hesitate to lie low on the ground covering a child with my body while stampeding horses came roaring toward us. I was certain the cowboys would deflect the horses to the right and left of us "just in time."

I rode a supposedly runaway horse and lay across the saddle, my head hanging down on one side of the horse, one foot tied to the stirrup on the far side. A crew member behind the camera shook his head, asking me silently not to do it.

Rarely, we shot on a set inside the studio. It was then that I learned that for fight scenes, glass windows were really made of sheets of candy; that furniture flung about or used to bash a cowboy over the head couldn't hurt him very much because they were made of yucca. Yucca plants grow in the Hollywood Hills and are called "God's candlesticks" because they have tall, slender clusterings of white bloom. The wood part is porous and almost hollow, yet strong enough to be shaped into chairs or whatever is needed to "furnish" a fight scene.

Janet had a friend, Herbert Moulton, a writer who worked on *The Los Angeles Times*. Sometimes we double-dated with Herbert's friend, Whitney Williams, who was also a journalist. I think it must have been they who got Janet and me the special privilege of being "pages" in Renaissance costumes at The Writers' Club, which demanded only that we stand at each side of the proscenium arch "looking pretty."

It was these young writers who nominated Janet and me to be WAMPAS Baby Stars of 1926. WAMPAS stood for Western Association of Motion Picture Advertisers. The organization of press personnel was designed to select a dozen potential starlets and to present them at a formal evening. The list that particular year was strong: Mary Astor, Joan Crawford, Dolores Costello, Marceline

Day, Dolores Del Rio, Janet Gaynor, and Fay Wray among others.

Universal was pleased to have its young players nominated. The wardrobe department made a gown for me of rose-colored taffeta trimmed with rhinestones, and they chose one of their most successful directors to be my escort. It was an awesome moment when William Seiter arrived at my house in a limousine. He was dressed in white tie and tails and wore a high silk hat and a white silk muffler about his throat. I was nearly speechless and remained that way during the drive to the Ambassador Hotel ballroom, keeping myself far away from him and what I thought was his super-sophistication. About ten years later when I was in a film he directed, *The Richest Girl in the World*, we laughed about how scared I seemed to be. Not seemed—was.

None of the WAMPAS girls was required to perform, just to be individually presented and then collectively photographed. But Dolores Del Rio, exquisitely beautiful in a grand Spanish shawl, did do some moments of solo dancing.

Not long after this, Janet left Universal, and for the most wonderful reason. She went to do a film with the director F. W. Murnau—*Sunrise!*—and after that she did *Seventh Heaven*, under the direction of Frank Borzage.

She was enchanting in both and won the first Academy Award as Best Actress for 1927–1928. All over the town, there were life-size statues of Janet in her *Seventh Heaven* costume. They were, it's true, put up by the Adohr Milk Company, but they were done in such good taste that the commercial emphasis was minimized and they seemed to be a total tribute to Janet. Janet's figure was on top of a large plinth that had Adohr Milk Company written discreetly across the face of it. But Janet was *on top*. She had made a tremendous leap straight from the little Westerns. I hoped that I might make a leap from the little Westerns, too.

Until such time, which I felt sure would come, there was a warm pleasure in working at Universal, mostly because of the family feeling that grew out of being with the kith and kin of "Uncle" Carl Laemmle. It was said that he brought the entire

town of his native Laupheim over from Germany. There was Ernst
Laemmle, a nephew, who directed me in a two-reeler; there was
William Wyler, also a relative, with whom I worked in a four-
reeler, *Lazy Lightning*.

This was a dramatic little story that had me watching over a
little boy who was dying. Willy wanted tears from me as I sat at
the bedside by candlelight. From the far side of the bed beside
the camera, Willy talked quietly and intensely to me. I'm not sure
that the tears were as abundant as Willy wanted, but the experience took on a quality that would make me remember him—and
make me understand why he later became one of the "greats."
His parents were often in the studio; his mother, Melanie,
brought me many charming little antiques from her collection: an
ivory minature, a crystal perfume bottle. Ernst Laemmle's parents, too, were often present. Ernst taught me German phrases to
greet them and to congratulate his mother on her birthday.

Lone Pine was the location for two Jack Hoxie films directed by
Al Rogell (not a Laemmle relative). I was to have done them both,
one immediately following the other. The scenic background of
the mountains was fine, the night sky brilliant with stars, the
mornings cold and sparkling and rich with outdoor aromas of
breakfast prepared for the entire company.

The final scenes on the first film had been completed and I was
resting in my small hotel room in the evening when I heard voices
through the wall from the room adjoining. Al Rogell was saying
he wanted me sent back to the studio; he wanted a blonde, a
particular blonde for the next film. As one or two other voices
protested, he insisted loudly that it had to be that particular
blonde; it had to be—not *me*. It was decided, then. The exchange
would take place the next day.

I went out to the hall and knocked on their door. "I just want
you to know I heard every word you have said. The walls in this
hotel are very thin." The only thing that helped at that moment
was my own feelings. I felt very good about letting them know that
I knew.

The company manager rode back with me the next day. He was

a considerate person and said I shouldn't take this as a rejection; rather, that he knew Al Rogell to be crazy about the particular blonde. That's what it was all about, he said. It's true; they were married soon after. Paul Kohner was as kind as the company manager, dismissing my concerns with, "These things happen. . . ." He was soon to be even more considerate.

If there was an aura of quality about Universal, it was a leftover from the films of Erich von Stroheim. He had written, directed, and acted in *Blind Husbands* and *Foolish Wives,* and written and directed *Merry-Go-Round.* All of these were strong successes. The word *genius* was suitably applied to him. To think of von Stroheim was to think of the single most exciting talent of the time. Although he had left Universal a few years earlier, it was there that I walked directly into the possibility of doing a film with him.

I was on my way to the commissary when I saw Edna Schley. She came toward me, as though we had an appointment. Actually, I had not seen her for a long time. Knowing her to be an agent for writers, I assumed she was in the studio in relation to her work. When she told me that Erich von Stroheim was looking for a leading lady and she thought I would be wonderful in the role, a warm rain of pleasure poured over me. She said she would make an appointment for the following day to take me to meet von Stroheim if I would be free to do that. Oh, yes! Free, free! There wasn't a thought in my head about being under contract to Universal. The only thought was to meet von Stroheim, to be in a film with him, to be in this particular film, *The Wedding March.*

I made myself look as grown-up as possible, piling my hair high on my head, wearing my best blue-chiffon dress and my high-heeled patent-leather slippers.

We drove along Sunset Boulevard east to Broadway, then turned north until we came to the Selig studio. We were admitted to the office of Mr. Emil Offeman, vice-president of Celebrity Pictures. He was a smallish man with slanting blue-gray eyes. These eyes looked me over after Mrs. Schley explained why we were there. A French accent came from his small pursed lips, saying, "Non, absolutely non. There is no use for you to see von

Stroheim. You are too tall. He is a short man. You are a brunette. He is dark. He wants a blonde. You would not do. Absolutely non!" While he was saying these things, my thoughts were flying along: Too tall! Maybe if I let my hair hang down . . . if I wear flat shoes. "May I come back tomorrow? I will look different tomorrow!" My head, my heart, my whole self knew that I was going to be in *The Wedding March*. He *must* say yes; he *must* say yes!

After a moment, he said, "Yes. Very well, yes. Come back tomorrow."

CHAPTER 7

A BIG STEP
FROM THE LITTLE
WESTERNS

◆

THE FOLLOWING DAY, WEARING LOW heels, and with my hair hanging down, I went back to Mr. Emil Offeman's office with Edna. He greeted us, made no comment about my changed appearance, opened the door at the rear of his office, and showed us a pathway that would lead to the office of Erich von Stroheim.

It was a warm day. Two steps up to a screen door and we were inside a long, low bungalow. There he was. He was sitting in a high-backed chair behind a desk whose length ran with the length of the room. He rose from his chair, which seemed to be red and gold, and came around the desk to greet us, looking not at all imperial or arrogant but warm-weather casual. He asked me to sit against a wall opposite his desk in a high-backed armchair similar to his own. He asked Mrs. Schley to sit somewhere toward the end of the desk. I was conscious only of him, of his very dark eyes, of his skin showing a warm amber color against the white of his linen shirt, of his compactness, his energy. He began to pace back and forth along the length of the desk, centering a look on me each time he passed. And then as he paced, he told the story of *The Wedding March*. I held on to the arms of my chair and heard about Nicki and Mitzi and Franz Josef and the beauty of Vienna, about Cecelia and Schani, about the romance of Nicki and Mitzi and the joy and pain that romance would bring to them both. He was going to play Nicki. He stood in front of me. "Do you think," he asked, "that you could play Mitzi?"

"I know I could." I stood to meet his eyes. He held out his hand. "Good-bye, Mitzi."

Perhaps he had said that to every possible Mitzi he had interviewed, but because this very sure and certain person called me Mitzi in a way that christened me, it meant, "Yes, absolutely yes, you will be my Mitzi." I looked at his hand. I wanted to take it, but my eyes were filling and I covered my face with both hands. The lovely tensions of the past few moments were released and I went on crying inside my covering palms. I heard him saying, "Oh! Oh! I can work with her!" I uncovered my face and saw him move toward Mrs. Schley and back again to me. "Yes, yes. I can work with her!" Then the two of them left the office, saying something about "going to see Mr. Offeman."

I sat alone, wiping my face and knowing that nothing would alter what had just happened.

My next appointment at the studio was again with Emil Offeman. He was crisp, businesslike, with not a shade of emotion as he told me that von Stroheim did want me to play Mitzi but that I must understand it would be impossible to sign me for the role unless I could free myself from Universal. His pale, taut face became paler as he set forth the reasons: If Universal knew that Celebrity wanted me for *The Wedding March*, they would certainly not let me out of my contract; they would want, instead, to loan me at some impossibly high price. This, Celebrity Pictures could not do, both for financial reasons and also because they would not give me a role that would enhance my career for the benefit of Universal. Borrowing me would be out of the question. So the question—the very delicate question—was, how could I get a release from Universal without that company having even the slightest suspicion of *why*. "It is up to you to find the answer, to devise some ruse. Perhaps even to tell them some lie . . ."

Not some lie, I thought, as I drove home. Truth. Truth would find someone at Universal understanding. My meeting with von Stroheim had been so strong that the extension of that feeling must have the force of truth when I went to Universal to tell someone exactly what had happened. That understanding someone, I thought, would be Paul Kohner.

Sometimes, we plan, anticipate, and imagine situations in advance. Oftentimes, the realities are very different from what we have imagined. In the case of von Stroheim and, again, Paul Kohner, my anticipations were fulfilled. Paul *was* understanding and ready to be helpful. His admiration for von Stroheim, and a certain very real appreciation of me were unified. He saw the situation as correct and made an appointment to take me with him to Carl Laemmle's office. This was probably not the same day, but the following. Even so, we were given time at the very end of the office day, as though "Uncle Carl" was conceding a few extra moments of time to Paul, whom he considered to be part of his family. Paul did not tell me in advance what he expected from the meeting. I had vaguely mixed feelings as we sat side by side across the desk from Mr. Laemmle, and I heard Paul saying that the studio had no particular plans for me and because I was not very happy with what I had done during my time there, he wanted to recommend the cancellation of my contract.

It seemed an easy decision for Mr. Laemmle. He smiled and nodded his agreement. His rimless glasses caught a flash of light from his desk lamp, adding some sparkle to his agreeability. It was the only time I ever saw Carl Laemmle, Sr.

Later, when I was under contract to Paramount, a writer, Benjamin Glazier, paid me a compliment about my work in a film with Emil Jannings. I said I was grateful. "Never say you're grateful. Never be grateful to anyone in this business." He had never had the good fortune to know an altruistic experience such as I had known with Paul Kohner.

CHAPTER 8

THE WEDDING MARCH WITH ERICH VON STROHEIM

◆

Edna Schley, then, became my first agent. Her contract called for 25 percent of the $500 a week I would be getting from Celebrity Pictures—a large increase over the $75 I'd been receiving from Universal. The thought of so much money was exciting, but I did not want that to come between me and the far greater excitement it would be to work with von Stroheim.

Patrick Powers, the president of Celebrity Pictures, invited me, Mrs. Schley, and my mother to his home in Flintridge—a mansion with massive furniture, a pipe organ, Oriental rugs, and extensive gardens. I had never seen so large a home. If there had ever been a wife or a lady in his life, there was none present. Later, I would hear that he had many lady friends.

He was tall, with a kind of Paddy Irish face, bushy black eyebrows, and an easy, kindly manner. He was fatherly toward me and would be my fatherly friend for many years. During those years I would learn that he had owned a company known as Castle Films, where Walt Disney had done his earliest work. (I would learn from Walt Disney himself that he had found Pat Powers too tough a businessman.) Pat Powers also owned the Western Costume Company, a building on Seventh Avenue in New York, and the studio where *The Wedding March* would be filmed in 1926 and 1927. I believe he thought his business acumen would guide him to know how to cope with von Stroheim's extravagances, but it was probably their mutual Catholicism that brought them together.

Von Stroheim's house, in sharp contrast to Mr. Powers's, was a small frame bungalow on Oxford Street near Beverly Boulevard. At first it was surprising that so great a man would be living in such a modest little home. But his vivid personal quality and the warm manner of his handsome wife, Valerie, soon erased such thoughts.

I tried on clothes there one evening. They had been brought from Mr. Powers's Western Costume Company. Every detail was important to von Stroheim. There was no mirror but I could see my reflection in his expressive face. When he was certain, it was certain he was right. All flowed along with a precision as though he were dressing the Mitzi character from memory and loving the remembering. She must have been in his life because he knew so much about her. But what was wonderful was that he didn't pour me into the mold of that memory or make an arbitrary shape for me to fill. He watched me, observing my mannerisms, and would say, "Keep that. Do that." For instance, shyness made me sometimes bite my lower lip. "Do that!" It was as if I was not learning about Mitzi any more than Mitzi about me. He was making a blend, coloring the character with his own rememberings and what he was seeing in me. He had loved that Mitzi and so there was that feeling of his love surrounding the character and that was the best garment of all.

The last things chosen were the nightgown, slippers, overskirt, and paisley shawl for the seduction scene. He wanted my coral-and-silver earrings to be a half-inch shorter, so he removed the lowest segment himself and found the correct balance. He asked Valerie for some brandy and she brought little glasses filled with a dark liquor. I took the glass she offered, sipped it, and felt a sharp thump in the center of my forehead. This first drink of spirits made me wonder why anyone should want it.

In the studio, there was to be testing to decide whether or not I should wear makeup. Von Stroheim's naturally dark skin required none. A luminous lighting made me look almost blond. A kind of gossamer shimmering tone was an enhancement so great, I saw myself transformed by the photography. Gone, gone the contrasty black-and-white face of the girl in the little Westerns. Magic had happened! So, then, I would not have to use makeup, even though there was a makeup-hairdresser person; I would do these things for myself. Mitzi would not have had that kind of help!

The first scenes would be in the wine garden, all of them night shots, and it was planned that by the time they were ready for me, I would have learned how to simulate playing the harp. A lady harpist came to my dressing room every evening and showed me how to pluck the strings for an old Viennese piece called "Paradise." It was a long lot of nights before I was called to the set. After a while, the lady harpist went away and the harp was left with me. Then the harp, too, was taken and I knew that if the harp was needed on the set, I should soon be needed, also. It was the thirtieth night when I went to see the beautiful wine garden. There were apple blossoms everywhere, the heavily laden branches making a roof over all the brightly dressed tables. Von Stroheim was there at one of the tables, in a long white officer's overcoat, brass-buttoned and trimmed with accents of red and black. The shiny visor of his cap was reflecting gleams from the "moonlight" that filtered through the "apple trees." There was a small stage to one side where my harp waited.

Before I went up onto the stage, I was introduced to Harry Carr, who had written the script with von Stroheim and was the much-respected drama critic of *The Los Angeles Times*. He stood behind the camera and watched as the scene went on. I was playing as part of a quartet, but playing only for the watchful Prince Nicki while musicians in the background made real music. When the scene was done, Harry Carr's nose twiggled (twitched and wiggled). I would learn that was a sign that he liked what he saw.

A scene at the table with von Stroheim wasn't completed until the dawn was beginning to rob the setting of its moonlight. By that time, he was weary and had forgotten some of his lines. I was able to "cue" him by changing the lines without stopping the scene. He was happily excited about that. He called me a "pro." It was a good beginning. I felt a rapport with him that I would never lose. It was as though there were just the two of us, no cameras anywhere, so easy it was to believe in him and with him.

In the early morning, I drove home with my right hand on the wheel of the car, my left hand holding a heavy forehead. But I was richly happy and wanted to sleep "fast" so as to be back in the studio again. I would always want to be back in the studio. Being there was life, now.

I was never given a script of *The Wedding March*. I knew the story only from von Stroheim's telling it.

Prince Nicholaus (Nicki) is the son of aristocratic but self-indulgent parents whose fortunes are diminished. Nicki is self-indulgent also. As First Lieutenant in the Mounted Guards of Emperor Franz Josef, he is a compelling figure. His parents think he should use his magnetism to attract a bride with enough money to support him lavishly. They have in mind the daughter of a wealthy merchant. Unfortunately, she is lame and painfully insecure and timid. This role (Cecilia) was played by Zasu Pitts. (Zasu had worked with von Stroheim before in a film some consider his masterpiece—*Greed*.) Nicki cynically accepts his parents' proposition. But that is before he meets Mitzi.

Nicki and Mitzi meet at the celebration of Corpus Christi. The celebration brings much of the population to Vienna to the square in front of Saint Stephen's Cathedral. Everyone wants to see the pomp and circumstance, the Emperor Franz Josef in his carriage, and a procession that includes the elegant officers of the Emperor's Guard on horseback.

One of those officers (Nicki) brings his horse to a standing position alongside a group that includes Mitzi. She is there with her parents and Schani, an oafish fellow she finds crude and repulsive. He is a butcher who has his shop near the wine garden that is run by her parents. It is the hope of Mitzi's mother that Schani and Mitzi will marry. A vendor of violets comes by. Schani buys Mitzi a bunch of violets. Nicki, on horseback, has been observing the behavior of the little group with some amusement. Their various attitudes are clear to him. Very subtly, he gets Mitzi's attention. She looks up and sees . . . someone wonderful. She is compelled to steal another look—and another. She hides her face in the violets, but then she has to look again. He signals to her to put some of the violets into the top of his well-polished boot. She manages to do that without anyone seeing. She is being rash but she has to be because the moment is so compelling. There is a rifle salute to the Emperor, the horses rear up, and a hoof comes down on Mitzi's ankle. She faints and is taken away on a stretcher.

There were two von Stroheims to be seen during the filming of the Corpus Christi sequence. There was the character Nicki, who looked at Mitzi not just with his eyes but with his mind, not just seeing her but mentally absorbing her, showing her his understanding of her predicament. Their flirtation was so winning, so certain, that she would never be free of him nor would she want to be.

The other von Stroheim was loud, commanding. He directed the crowd through a megaphone, yelling at them, telling them to be restless, surly, tired of the heat, of the long wait to see the Emperor, angry at having to look at the rears of the horses. "You are sick of seeing horses rosettes!" he shouted.

As director, he wore the same hot-weather clothes he wore the first day I had met him. His sleeveless shirt was shaped like a BVD but made of fine linen. He wore a gold crucifix around his neck, and on one wrist a gold watch. On the other wrist, he wore a gold chain bracelet. His nails were perfectly manicured. Many of the people on the set referred to him as Mr. Von. It was, I thought, as though Mr. Von was short for Mr. Vonderful.

The story unfolded more as an experience than as a piece of writing. There was never much dialogue, but when there was, he showed me the script so I could learn the written words.

Following Corpus Christi, Nicki goes to find Mitzi in the hospital, taking her a huge box of chocolates. Soon, he goes to visit her in the wine garden where she lives.

She is willing to be loved by him, knowing it may be tragic for her.

She goes to confession.

Nicki's father and Cecilia's father make a contract for the marriage of their children. This scene takes place in a brothel, revealing the licentious character of both parents.

Mitzi's mother is insistent that she should marry Schani.

Mitzi has to fight off the advances of Schani. Schani vows to kill Nicki and goes to Saint Stephen's, where the wedding of Nicki and Cecilia is taking place. Mitzi goes too, and holds on to Schani's arm so that he cannot remove his gun from his pocket. As Nicki and Cecilia drive away in their elegant carriage, Schani lifts a weeping Mitzi onto his shoulder to force her to look at Nicki for the last time.

In the carriage, Cecilia, who is carrying a bouquet of apple blossoms, wonders about the girl who is crying. Nicki replies, "I never saw her before in my life."

With that line, one-third of the story had been told. Because of the studio's heavy editing, when the film was released, that was the final scene.*

The second third of the story tells about the arrival of Nicki and Cecilia at his family's estate in the Tyrolean Alps, where the bride and groom are to spend their honeymoon. Nicki gives Cecilia champagne. When she speaks of the beauty of her apple blossom bouquet, he thinks of Mitzi and leaves Cecilia alone on their wedding night.

In Vienna, Mitzi has agreed to marry Schani if he promises not to pursue Nicki. The ceremony begins but Mitzi cannot say the final words. She faints.

An enraged Schani begins the climb up the mountain to kill Nicki.

A desparate Mitzi follows, hoping to warn Nicki.

The Wedding March is available on cassette.

Schani arrives at the mountain lodge and accidentally shoots Cecilia instead of Nicki. Schani escapes.

Mitzi arrives at the lodge in time to share a death-bed vigil for Cecilia. In the morning, Mitzi bids farewell to Nicki and returns to Vienna.

Nicki rejoins his parents in Vienna. They are happy. Now they have not only Cecilia's dowry, but her inheritance as well. Nicki is shocked at their callousness.

After a little time, he goes to the wine garden to look for Mitzi. The wine garden is deserted; there are For Sale signs on it. He goes out to the orchard. All the apple blossoms are gone. Cobwebs cover the abandoned carriage where he had made love to Mitzi.

The rest of the story was in the script but never was put on film. Condensed to its simplest elements, it told about Mitzi entering a convent, about the beginning of the First World War, about Nicki finding Mitzi when his regiment stopped for a rest nearby, about the marriage of the two there in the convent, and Nicki's immediate departure with his regiment.

How simple it seems to tell the story line of that film. How impossible to relate the mood, the enormous capacity von Stroheim had for every minute detail of the setting, the costuming, the emphasis of symbolism, the richness of understanding about human behavior, the evident knowledge of old Vienna. *His* Vienna. There was never any sense of having to compete with time. Time was his, he owned it. He used it as it should be used by an artist: He ignored it.

There was always a trio of musicians on the set with a portable piano, a cello, and a violin. They played Viennese waltzes and marches that transported the time and place to the Austria of 1914.

The setting of the wine garden included the apple orchard. Fifty-thousand handmade wax blossoms, it was said, were attached to the trees. And there were paper petals, as well, that fell over Nicki and me during love scenes that took place in an abandoned carriage in the orchard. "You mustn't say the things to me that you say to your fine ladies . . . because I might believe them." This was the peasant wisdom of Mitzi, her way of asking him never to pretend to her. There was very little to disturb the reality of the setting. Sometimes lions roared at the Selig zoo next door, but Wanda, their caretaker-trainer, could be relied upon to quiet them. And the Viennese music would always prevail.

Visitors sometimes came to the set: Lawrence Tibbett and his wife Grace; Paul Whiteman and his wife. There was often a priest, a close friend of von Stroheim.

When it came time for the seduction scene in the orchard, I was glad that I had seen the film, *The Sea Beast*, with John Barrymore and Dolores Costello. In a full-figure shot of those two embracing, she had let her arm suddenly fall, a gesture of complete surrender. I knew that was right for the moment when Nicki embraced Mitzi just before he picked her up to take her to the carriage; but I didn't tell von Stroheim I had "borrowed."

He directed me very little in scenes between the two of us. There was a natural and easy flow. In scenes other than the ones he was in, he found reason two or three times to be very angry with me. When Mitzi was on crutches because of her broken ankle and was to beat Schani over the head with one of the crutches, he simply couldn't understand how difficult it was while hopping about on one foot to come down hard on the head of a man who was much taller than I. And he couldn't understand, he said, that I continued to look beautiful even with mud all over my face after falling in a big puddle—as though that angered him.

A confessional scene went on almost an entire day. At the end of the confession, he wanted me to blow my nose. In his mind, it should have been done vigorously. When he called out, "Now blow your nose," and I simply pressed my folded handkerchief to my nose, he was angry, saying that a whole series of preceding lap dissolves would be ruined.

But when he looked at the scene in the rushes, he decided not to do it over. I became entranced with all of this; the good and the intuitively right and the misery of the wrong moments. I use the word *intuitively* because I had had no training, no preparation to perform in any other way.

There was a period for almost a month when I was not allowed in the studio. No! Not because he was angry at me. Because he was shooting scenes in a brothel. It was Mr. Offeman who told me it had been decided that it wouldn't be appropriate for me to be in the studio at all, much less on the set. They would let me know when my scenes would be resumed.

Ernst Laemmle came to take me to dinner and said there was much concerned talk at Universal that von Stroheim had done a seduction scene with me. I thought what we had done was a love scene and had no idea why there should be any concern. Perhaps it was simply that Ernst could see that I was fascinated with von Stroheim. I was. Even when he was angry, I saw him as being passionately involved in what he wanted to achieve.

By the time I returned to the studio, my frustration at not having been there had grown. I had loved all of it; I had been feeling deprived, like a lovesick, youngster might feel. I wanted to tell, to talk about this to von Stroheim.

We were walking through a corridor in the wine garden that led from one setting to another—only we two. He looked at me. "What's troubling you?" I wanted to tell him what I had been feeling about missing work, missing him, but what I said instead of all that was something I felt but not at all in the way he was going to understand. "What's troubling you?" I said, "I love you!" In a flash, he had me pinned against the corridor wall, his body pressing against mine. He looked and looked into my eyes. I don't think I said a word. I know I didn't push him away even though I wanted to, knowing that I should. Perhaps he heard someone coming. He let me go. I heard nothing, only my own heartbeat saying, What has happened? What have I done? Each day thereafter, he would say he had thought of me the night before.

Soon, Mrs. Schley was saying to me that she thought it would be good for me to have an experience with von Stroheim. What did she mean by that? Soon, Mr. Powers was telling me that he wouldn't believe anything about me unless I told him myself. Mickey, the script girl, was saying, was whispering, "If you don't make him leave his wife, I will help you." Help me what? At the dark end of one day, she asked me to go with her to "Mr. Von's" office. We went in. "Wait here," she said. She went out. Mr. von Stroheim came in. Again, he pressed himself against me, bending me backward over the desk. "Someone is coming," I said. "I hear someone coming." What I meant was *I wanted* to hear someone coming. But he believed me and left me and went out the rear of the office, leaving me free to go out the way I had come in, where there was no one at all.

Where before all had been happiness, or if misery, miserable happiness, now there was a wondering what? Why? A something I had clearly started but didn't want to face; it all seemed so urgent, so physical, so unrelated to the lyrical joy I wanted it to be. Soon, von Stroheim had "instructions" for me. I was to go to the Western Costume Company downtown on Hill Street to be fitted for a nun's costume that I would wear in the second half of the film. He spoke to me quietly. I was to go at a certain hour of the morning. He himself would arrive soon after. His wife's brother, George Gemomprez, was his chauffeur, so von Stroheim couldn't be seen going directly there. He would apparently be going to the large department store across the street. He would go in the *hause*door, he said . . . in the *hause*door . . . go through the store and around to the Western Costume Company.

Having said all that in a very low tone, he left me to think about what he had said. *Hause*door. Mrs. von Stroheim's brother. The only way I knew how to handle these things was one way: not to go.

On the night of the day that didn't happen, we were to make scenes in the wine garden, where Nicki comes and stands below Mitzi's window and throws a stone up to awaken her. She comes to the window in her long flannel nightie. Her underclothes are hanging to dry on a line just outside her window. She leans out the window. He looks up at her. He is supposed to smile at her with anticipation, with joy. Von Stroheim couldn't smile that night. The camera looked down on him from my point of view. I smiled. I tried to make funny faces, one that he had laughed at before: my bee-stung lips like those of a star he had recently directed, Mae Murray. Art Jell, the violinist, made funny faces and played funny music. Von Stroheim the director could *not* force von Stroheim the actor to smile. He only stared and stared up at me, grim and solemn. I knew, of course, but had no caring for that grimness. I wanted only that the scene should be realized, that Nicki should smile. But von Stroheim wouldn't let him do that. We stopped work for that night.

Innocence can be a force for evil. A small amount of research much, much later would lead me to find that Henry James had written about that. I did not know that what I had done could lead to misery for him. I just knew he had asked me to do something that I suspected was wrong.

If Harry Carr knew of this, I cannot tell. Most everyone close to von Stroheim may have known. The effects of that unhappy day and night were not sustained. The awful feelings went away. Maybe he talked to the priest. I think about that only now. Soon, there was good feeling between us again. But the interesting thing is, that he never questioned me about why I didn't go.

By Christmastime, it was wonderful to hear a knock at my dressing room door and see him standing there in his uniform carrying a very large box that seemed to be encrusted with rubies . . . at least very large red stones. Inside, he said, there were chocolates. I loved the look of him, the precise bow he made, and I took the chocolates, feeling they were the loveliest of all gifts. He also presented me with an alabaster powder box with a pink figure of a dancing lady on top of it. And he invited me to go to the von Stroheim house on Christmas Eve.

There, Valerie had real lighted candles on the Christmas tree. I was feeling uncertain about everything and decided it would be best if I didn't thank Valerie for the gifts von Stroheim had already taken to my dressing room. Afterward, he told me he wondered why I hadn't.

Harry Carr had asked me if I would be home Christmas morning and I said I would be. However, when he arrived, I wasn't there, having thoughtlessly, heartlessly forgotten what I had told him. He had brought violets. It had been a long journey for him . . . all the way from the Los Feliz area where he lived. But he had a special good feeling for me that included forgiveness. The

violets were associated with the film . . . with the first meeting of
Mitzi and Nicki when they had met in front of Saint Stephen's
Cathedral for the celebration of Corpus Christi.

There had been a large group of extras on that set. Visitors
came, too, to see the beautiful reproduction of St. Stephen's.
Jesse Lasky came, wearing a hard straw hat and his pince-nez.
His company was going to release the film, had partially financed
it, and, unhappily for von Stroheim, before very long would be
taking the film away from him. Of me, Jesse Lasky said, "She has
an exceptional quality; she's a lady." Or so I was told. I think it
was Harry Carr who told me.

There was absolutely no idea of this film being publicized or
me being exploited. I look back in appreciation and wonder that
this should have been so. Harry Carr did write an article about
me for a motion-picture magazine. I treasure it beyond any ever
done about me. He was a sensitive man. As a writer, he had
patiently collaborated with von Stroheim, who was more mercurial
than he. He told me he had pretended to be typing the scenario
when von Stroheim had a fallow period. The stimulus was effective and von Stroheim reignited.

Harry Carr admired Lillian Gish more than any other actress.
He took me to meet her. She lived at the beach. We arrived in
the evening. She was sitting before large windows that looked
onto the moonlit ocean. She was brushing her long blond hair.
She continued to do that while we talked—while *they* talked—
and I watched with wonder how lovely it was to see her in this
informal way. I told her about this a year or so ago and she said
that she had never in her entire life gone into a beauty shop.
Perhaps she should be given a special award just for that!

Harry encouraged me to buy box seats at the Hollywood Bowl
and to become a charter subscriber to the soon-to-be-published
Time magazine. Sitting on the side of the set, Harry and I sometimes talked about things philosophical—about Schopenhauer
and viewpoints, about the choices to be made of looking at the
wooden strips that made a lattice or at the vistas made by the
spaces in between. About Pola Negri, who had made a powerful,

vital film, *Passion*, in Germany, where she looked like a fiercely wild, exciting, ungroomed gypsy. It was this film that had brought her to America and now that she was here, she had been "groomed and polished" and her palette of colors scraped away by the company she had joined: Paramount Famous Lasky Corporation. That same thing would, before long, be happening to me!

Grace Tibbett became my friend, taking me to have tea with Mrs. Richard Day, the wife of Captain Richard Day, who did the sets for *The Wedding March*. Plain thin bread and butter, the bread buttered just before slicing, tasted unforgettably good.

Richard Day's sets were so realistic that the cameraman, Hal Mohr, and his fiancée, a young actress named Evelyn Venable, chose to be married in St. Stephen's. She was brilliant and later became a professor of both Latin and Greek at UCLA. I was not invited to the wedding but that was during the time I was not supposed to be in the studio. Could that have added to my feeling of being left out? I was also left out when the company went on a weekend to Laguna or La Jolla. Zasu Pitts went. It was undoubtedly Harry Carr (who *did* go) who said it wouldn't have been appropriate for me because there had been drinking.

And there was an evening when I chose to be left out while we were on location at Mount Whitney. That's a place in California where it surely does snow, but on that location it was only very cold. Mount Whitney is about three hundred miles northeast of Los Angeles, in the High Sierras. On the way there, my mother sprained her ankle. A caravan of cars wound up the mountain. We stopped for lunch and as she left the bright sunshine and walked into the dark interior of the restaurant, she missed a step and was almost immediately in great pain. Von Stroheim took charge. He ordered a pan of hot water to be brought and he knelt in front of her, encouraging her to try to endure the heat. Where was the man who had been advertised as "The Man You Love to Hate"? On his knees there before her in the little mountain restaurant, he was totally kind and gently caring.

The increasing steepness of the remainder of the journey was somehow helpful as an anesthetic. My mother was fearful enough of the tortuous turns to be distracted from her suffering. As soon

as I had got her into bed in the lodging assigned to us, von
Stroheim came into the room with a tumbler more than half full of
whiskey. He "directed" her to drink it, she who never had had a
drink. His insistence overcame her resistance; she swallowed it
down and was very soon sleepy. He said the company would be
meeting together later and I should join them. I sat with her for a
while and watched her and listened as she began to sing. The
whiskey was making my mother deliriously happy! And then she
fell sound asleep and I went to look for the company.

It was easy to find. Voices and laughter came through the night
air at the back of the lodge. I went into a room that was packed
tight with people, everyone drinking in a bluish haze of cigarette
smoke. I saw Mrs. von Stroheim sitting on the lap of the second
assistant director. I pushed my way back to the door and as I
went out, I heard von Stroheim say, "What is the matter with
her?!" Well, then, I guess it was all right with him for his wife to
be sitting on another man's lap, but it didn't seem right to me.
The smoke and the crowding was well left behind, I thought, as I
went and climbed onto a boulder and looked at the stars. Although I was eighteen years old, I had never before been in a
drinking party atmosphere. I wanted fiercely to be left out. Out
alone in the dark, I wanted to be very, very lonely!

After only a few days of shooting exteriors at Mt. Whitney, we
were back in the studio—this time using space at Paramount—
where great sets of snow-laden mountains had been built. It was
in this background that Mitzi was to climb to the lodge to tell
Nicki that his life was endangered. The mountains in the studio
were more realistic than the real mountains could have been—
and "snow" drifted down over us as was needed from overhead
wire trays full of finely cut white feathers. The sifted feathers
danced around us in the gusts of air just as snowflakes float and
swirl. Mitzi's own life was endangered more than once during the
climb and she stopped at each shrine to weep and to pray for
Nicki. Von Stroheim wanted lots of weeping even in the rehearsals. That was something new—to want tears even in rehearsal. And if "the fount ran dry," he would put drops of
glycerine in the corners of my eyes. He showed me that he had

only to concentrate on the memory of his father and his eyes would fill so quickly, so easily.

After all night at the bedside of the dying Cecilia, Mitzi is ready to return to Vienna. Nicki comes outside with her to say farewell.

It is startling for me to realize now that the farewell between Nicki and Mitzi was also the farewell between me and von Stroheim. He who had the most uncanny sense of fate and destiny, and had made fate a theme of *The Wedding March*, could not have been aware of the personal significance of that scene. Now, as I write this, I see the fateful meaning for both of us. I would not see him again for fourteen years.

Nothing had been said during our time at Paramount that Mr. Powers had any intention of stopping production. We were to continue filming at the Selig studio. There was a period of a few days when I heard nothing from the company. I went to the Selig studio one morning to find some members of the crew sitting together, very still, as though they had been playing the game of Statue and had come to the moment when the name of the game is called and all the players have to freeze in place and to remain that way until the music begins again. The music would not begin again. It was official. Production had been stopped.

If the news was difficult for the crew to accept, how much greater it must have been for "Mr. Von."

I spent some hours in a vacuum of bewilderment. Then Mr. Powers invited me to his home in Flintridge and told me over dinner that he had given control of the film to Paramount, that my contract, as well, had been taken over by them. He said he would continue to be interested in how things went for me. I knew he would be—but Mr. Powers was a businessman, and the kind of creative force I had met in von Stroheim I would never see again.

There is a beautiful book titled *The Wedding March of Erich von Stroheim* by Herman G. Weinberg for The American Film Institute. Mr. Weinberg writes a very scholarly and appreciative foreword and there are more than two hundred and fifty stills that illustrate the film. Because still photographers are not given credit with the presentation of a film, Mr. Weinberg did not know who had taken the photos. I wish someone had asked me. William Fraker was responsible for some magnificent photographs.

From that same book I learned about the editing of the film. Von Stroheim brought 200,000 feet of film to a rough cut of 50,000 feet—then to approximately 44,000 feet, which he wanted released in two showings of three hours each. Paramount was adamant about wanting one film only. The impasse led Paramount to request that Josef von Sternberg take over the editing. Finally, two films did result (as von Stroheim had wanted) although greatly shortened. Part One: 10,852 feet released on 14 reels accompanied by 14 discs of the synchronized musical score. Part Two was reduced to 9,000 feet (2,000 of which was reprise film from Part One) and entitled *The Honeymoon*. It was released in Europe.

The only known print of *The Honeymoon* was burned in a fire at the Cinémathèque Française in Paris five days after von Stroheim's death in 1957. Henri Langlois, curator of Cinémathèque, said (according to Mr. Weinberg) that the film died voluntarily out of humiliation, out of affront at its dismemberment and not wishing to outlive its creator.

CHAPTER 9
ROMANCE AND MARRIAGE

◆

M R. POWERS'S IDEA OF WHAT was a good role was the length of it—how much footage; that was the measure of a good part, he said. He wanted me to be aware of that and, too, that *sound* was being introduced to film. *The Jazz Singer* had been released and he thought that by the time von Stroheim had finished editing *The Wedding March,* the sound of bells from the steeple of St. Stephen's would have to be introduced.

It seemed to me that seeing a silent film was a total experience and that sound would be an intrusion. He was patient with my viewpoint but assured me that future films would include sound. It was not immediate.

I was to do three silent films at Paramount. The first, *Legion of the Condemned,* had been written by John Monk Saunders, a young man who had also written *Wings,* the story of war in the air. Mr. Powers was eager to have me meet this young man, who, he said, was very personable and had been a Rhodes scholar. He wanted to invite us both to join him at a gala that was to be held at the Biltmore Hotel the following month.

Before Mr. Powers had the opportunity to introduce us, I met John Monk Saunders at the studio. I was leaving through the front entrance. He was just arriving and called my name as our paths crossed. I turned to see a very handsome man. It was a warm summer afternoon. He was dressed in white flannels, a dark-blue blazer, and wore a white Panama hat. I thought he was astonishingly good-looking. Astonishing because the name Monk suggested someone less wonderfully well-groomed.

Legion of the Condemned, a story about flyers in the Foreign Legion, was directed by a veteran flyer, William Wellman. He had the enthusiasm of an entire rooting section and the physical energy to support it. He was tough and unsubtle but absolutely wild with the pleasure of making films, especially if the studio management kept out of his way. He could praise his actors. His almost belligerent appreciation was stimulating.

Gary Cooper was the leading man. A small part in the earlier *Wings* had brought him a flurry of fan mail, and the studio was delighted to make immediate co-stars of Gary and me. There was one bit of difficulty with that. Gary Cooper and I both had the inherent instinct and style to understate. We each needed a more aggressive personality for counterbalance. I didn't really understand that then. I just thought Gary was mostly sleepy and unalive! He *did* have the capacity to fall asleep in between scenes. And he almost never talked. The shape of his face was wonderful; he had long smoky lashes and a grin that caused his entire forehead to roll back, as if opening up all feelings in spite of his reticence and shyness.

Shame on me—that I didn't know then Gary was going to be one of the greatest movie stars of all time, that he would be devastatingly attractive to many glamorous women, that he would become a symbol of the heroic American. During the unhappy time of the Watergate hearings, years after Gary had died, *Time* magazine put him on a cover. The caption read: Where are you now, Gary Cooper, when we need you?

When, in the spring of 1988, the President of the United States went to the Soviet Union for a summit conference, he carried with him a presentation print of a film that Gary had starred in:

Friendly Persuasion. The significance was in the subject of the film: nonviolence. My heart beat faster to think a motion picture was considered a possible instrument toward international understanding.

John Monk Saunders, as author of *Legion of the Condemned*, was sometimes on the set. He sat beside me one day when we were filming at a small airfield in the San Fernando Valley. It was hot and his white shirt sleeves were rolled to the elbow. There was dust everywhere; only *he* seemed immaculately clean. During our conversation, as he touched my arm, a current of sensory feeling went through me. I knew, instinctively, it meant that there would probably be no turning away from him if his thoughts should turn toward me.

All I remember about the gala evening, where we were invited by Patrick Powers, is the ride home in the limousine. I wore a white velvet dress trimmed with seed pearls and a corsage of gardenias that John had sent me. They became quite crushed on the way home, John embracing me and telling me that he loved me. I told my mother at once. She was happy.

One of my mother's cousins soon came to the house and was also told. She said never to forget that all men were selfish. I knew she was bitter because her husband had run away with his secretary. I felt sorry for her. My mother seemed to become younger because John called her by her first name. She never questioned how much time I spent with John. That time began to be longer and longer. One evening only turned out to be brief. When he called for me, he stood at the door saying, "I'm lit. Do you still want to go out with me?" I didn't ask what that meant but said, "Of course," and he drove up to the Hollywood Hills and I found myself battling him just as I had once battled a boy when I was at Hollywood High School. So I found out that "lit" meant he had been drinking and "lit" made him a different person.

John lived in a small house on Cheremoya above Beechwood Drive. After one long evening with him there, he drank champagne—his way of celebrating. The next day, we met for lunch at a little Oriental restaurant opposite Grauman's Chinese. We had bowls of rice with cream and nutmeg. Sitting across from him in the red-lacquered wooden booth, feeling that my body was no longer my own, that the sensory changes were so great I would never go back to being just me but was now a part of him, I was half-glad and partly dismayed and, with a sense of gentle bewilderment, trying to cope with all the newfound feelings. John and I were now one fact. That oneness was there in the red-lacquered booth, but the oneness was very physical. The more significant and important oneness was to be a search of many years. I was nineteen and John was twenty-nine.

My mother would have to know my discovery about myself, and when I told her, I felt sure she would be exultant and say that all the concerns we had shared in Lafayette Park were (happily) wildly absurd. I thought she would embrace me and say wonderful, grateful words. Instead, she became very quiet but she didn't question me and never challenged the hours I spent away from home.

Legion of the Condemned was well received and thrust the studio executives into a fever of excitement about Gary Cooper and me as a team: "Paramount's glorious young lovers." Half a day was set aside in the portrait studio, where Gene Ritchie photographed us embracing, looking deeply into each other's eyes, both of us realizing that no excitement or electricity was sweeping us away. We were performing, it was tacitly understood; so when we emerged from the portrait gallery and I found my mother pacing about and murmuring, "dreadful . . . dreadful to be spending such a long, long time taking romantic pictures of a young girl who is engaged," I recognized her to be wrong. She was wrong, wrong on three counts: This was a professional session and not to be considered personal; it was essential to the exploitation of the film; and—*engaged*? I was not engaged—nor did I expect John to ask me to marry him.

The awareness of possibly being totally enveloped and absorbed by him placed a shadowy figure between me and what I hoped would be the fullness of working and growing as an actress. That shadowy figure was touched with a feather-light melancholia.

John's love did not glow with joy but with a sweet regret that there was no escape from the overwhelming power of love. It was a theme that he was to repeat over and over.

In spite of that, he did ask me to marry him. We were in a Russian restaurant on Sunset Boulevard.

> Just turn to the right,
> A little white light
> Will lead you to my Blue Heaven.
> Just Molly and me
> And baby makes three.
> We're happy in our Blue Heaven.

If it wasn't actually being played, it was playing in my head. By now he had told me about his attachment to Bessie (Mrs. Jesse Lasky).

"And Bessie makes three . . ."

In spite of that, as soon as he asked me, I said yes. Even now, I feel the sweet regret that she was in his life . . . and others, too—and that the numbers would increase.

Having asked me, he said he felt more secure. No, he didn't spoil the immediate moment with that but would later say it—that he hoped marriage would be a protection to him against the attention and desires of women, women, women. He was one of the most handsome men in Hollywood and, with the additional assets of athletic prowess and a superior education, infinitely attractive. An actress who had been sharing his life announced their engagement as soon as she was aware of me. As soon as she did, he rejected her.

The first showing of *Wings* was to be at the Biltmore Theatre, preceded by a dinner to which John invited me. Just prior to that, I invited him to a preview of *The Wedding March* at a theater in Long Beach. I loved the film and felt very good about myself in it, and I think John did too, so it was with a strong apology that he told me on the way home that Bessie Lasky had said she had expected him to escort her to the showing of *Wings*. He said that he hoped I would understand, because he felt he should not disappoint her. Would I mind? Yes, I said, I really would.

So at the dinner party for about twenty people, I sat between John and Sam Goldwyn, and looked across the table to see Bessie Lasky for the first time. She looked at me in what seemed a purposefully detached manner. The detachment, I soon felt, was not because of me but was part of her personality, giving her an air of apparent serenity. I could admire that. She had willful red hair that stood away from both sides of a delicate, if not pretty, face. She was older than John by about ten years. He was older than I by ten. So I saw her as a lady who was destined to lose the attention of a young man who had already told me that her neck showed signs of aging! That had given him concern! That she was married and had three children had not given him concern—or at least not enough to keep him from being a frequent houseguest wherever the Laskys established a ménage. First, in New York, where they had met through mutual friends in the publishing world. Later, at the Ambassador Hotel, where the Laskys had a large bungalow, and then at a Santa Monica house that she may well have bought to please John, who, being a champion swimmer, loved living on the ocean. She had a sort of Bridge of Sighs built between his room and hers. It was little by little that he volunteered details that I didn't even want to know. He liked telling. He told a lot about a lot of ladies.

He had had one marriage. He had felt scarred by events that led to a divorce: She, he said, had been unfaithful to him. She was Avis Hughes, the stepdaughter of Rupert Hughes, who was the uncle of Howard Hughes. Rupert was a successful novelist and for a while after their marriage, John and Avis lived in his home. John's stories about that time were vivid: Avis's mother was a beautiful lady who had brought two children, Avis and a son, Rush, into her marriage with Rupert—as well as a predisposition for alcohol that could not be satisfied with what Prohibition had to offer. She drank anyway—anything—sometimes wandering from her bedroom at night to rob the medicine chests of even toilet lotion.

If Rupert was gifted as a writer, he also had a talent for di-

atribe. As head of the household, he lectured, verbally condemned, reproached, reproved, denounced, accused, and, within
all of that, expressed subheadings of listed dire results from the
misbehaviors of all within earshot.

For John, these were not good memories. He hoped, he said, to
be healed from remembered scars of that marriage. He hoped to
be healed by me. "I love you more than all the houses and all the
people. I will love you until you are a little lavender old lady."

John's birthplace was Minnesota; by the age of nine, he was
living in the state of Washington. He was one of eight children
whose father became federal attorney in the city of Seattle, and
whose kindly mother believed that going to church each Sunday
morning was essential to the Christian nourishing of her brood.
John performed in a way that brought pride to both his parents.

His education at the University of Washington was interrupted
by the First World War. In response to the sounds of a recruit-
ing band, he joined the Air Service, became a pursuit pilot
(second lieutenant), and felt enormously cheated when the war
came to an end. He had been made an instructor in aerial acrobatics, and was at a flying field in Florida at the time of the
Armistice. He said that on that night, he went out to the field,
leaned against the wing of his plane, and wept. It was that longing, that wish to have been a triumpant ace in the skies over
France, that led him to write *Wings, Legion of the Condemned,
The Dawn Patrol, The Eagle and the Hawk, Ace of Aces, West
Point of the Air*, and *Devil Dogs of the Air*. Of course, he might
not have continued that string of aviation films were it not for the
fact that Hollywood wants successes repeated—and *Wings* had
been a tremendous success, winning the first Academy Award for
Best Picture.

Returning for two years at the university after the war brought
him his degree, a Rhodes scholarship, and a total change in his
appetite for life. In his heart, he had always resented the march
to church each Sunday, the eight children literally walking in
double file behind their parents. The demands of that church-
liness came into sharp conflict with the world he found at Oxford.

He was more often in pubs than in pews; English ladies welcomed him into their salons at teatime or at any time, and at least one wealthy wedded lady wanted to desert her husband and run away with him to Africa. After all of this, he could not "go home again."

In New York, he found a place on the editorial staff of the New York *Tribune*, then an associate editorship on the *American Magazine*. He sold his first short story to *Cosmopolitan* magazine. He found Avis, then lost her. His short story, listed as one of the best of 1923, was bought by Famous Players–Lasky and made into a film, *Too Many Kisses*. He found Jesse Lasky and Bessie Lasky. Jesse saw him as a brilliant and personable young man, and was intrigued with his idea of doing a film of war in the air. Believing that only John could write the story, he invited him to go to California with him—and with Bessie.

If only it would snow in California, chronology might be simpler. Was it Christmastime or springtime when I made the next film at Paramount? *The Street of Sin* starred Emil Jannings and was directed by Mauritz Stiller, who had brought Garbo to this country and who was miserable during the filming because Garbo had fallen out of love with him and in love with John Gilbert. He didn't talk about it but there was "talk." He had the natural look of sadness. One eye was blue, one eye was gray, his face large-boned and mournful. He left the film before completion.

Emil played a "bruiser," a real roughneck. The setting was Soho in London. Olga Baclanova played a lady of the night. This was a natural milieu for the Salvation Army, and that army was me and a little fellow who was really the property man on the production. At the time, there was no Screen Actors Guild and casting was oftentimes done on the spur of the moment. For instance, the Madame in *The Wedding March* was a plump lady from Valerie von Stroheim's hair salon.

The *Street of Sin* was silent, so Mr. Stiller could talk throughout the scenes. "Don't go before you don't start, FayWray," he said, as though the two names were one. The same was true with Emil Jannings: "Have zee ans in ze pans, FayWray?" This he had been coached to say, tilting his head away from me to see my reaction. And Mauritz Stiller again: "More open, more open, FayWray. Make the face more open."

Emil didn't seem to want to learn English. He didn't want to know the language or to eat the studio food. His white-jacketed valet brought his lunch from home each day. He liked to watch the dailies and when he saw a death scene that had been given to me, he arranged for the story to be changed to a death scene for him. The film, itself, died, I think, not because of those changes but because the nature of all things at Paramount was in limbo. Between the silents and the oncoming sound films, all was tenuous and uncertain.

Jannings, himself, was a giant of an actor. *The Blue Angel*, *The Last Laugh*, *The Patriot*—he was magnificent in many more than these. But the energy to learn the language was more than he wanted to expend. He was energized, it seemed, to return to Germany.

Josef von Sternberg had just returned from Germany. He brought back with him a passion for an actress. He asked me to his office to talk about *The Street of Sin*, which had been his story, and to talk to me about *The Wedding March*, which had been turned over to him for editing. Then he talked about Marlene Dietrich. He had become enchanted. He was more than confiding, he was affirming.

Before the release of her first Paramount film, twenty-four sheet-size billboards announced: SHE WILL SET A STANDARD BY WHICH THE GREAT SHALL BE JUDGED. The *great* was clearly Greta Garbo.

Von Sternberg's strong enthusiasm for Marlene emphasized the regret I felt that von Stroheim would not be making films at Paramount. Mrs. Schley realized, too, that I was now in the "hopper," that no particular person would be concerned with special roles for me. She faded away, except as to her share of my salary, which my mother began to realize was an unreasonably large portion. She asked me to go to Mrs. Schley and discuss a revision. "No," Mrs. Schley said. "If I don't get it, your family will."

I told Mr. Powers and he told me the name of an attorney. After I saw the attorney and the decision was made to sue for an adjustment, Mr. Powers said he hadn't meant for me to sue. "Always let the other party do that." But, we had already gone forward. For a year then, my salary was impounded.

The trial lasted for five days and is memorable for the testimony of Mr. Emil Offeman, who told his version of my first meeting with von Stroheim: ". . . and the girl she cry and evereeboddy was deeelighted!" There was laughter in the courtroom. After a few days of "taking the case under advisement," the judge determined in my behalf; the contract with Mrs. Schley was canceled. For several years after that, I had no representation.

Except for John. He introduced me to Roy Pomeroy, who was head of the newly established sound department, in the hope that Roy would let me test my voice under his personal supervision. John suggested I learn something from *Alice in Wonderland:* "You are old, Father William . . ." I sounded tinny, I thought, but at least could be heard quite clearly and distinctly. It was a time of transition and very worrisome to all who had begun in silents. The news that John Gilbert's voice was too high-pitched to be believable was disarming. He was a top star who, because of sound, had toppled. I passed the test, and the studio went forward with plans to star Gary Cooper and me in *The First Kiss,* to be made in Maryland.

William Mortensen, too, had come into the orbit of Patrick Powers. At Powers's Western Costume Company on Hill Street, he established a studio, where he had the use of costumes, wigs, and paraphernalia that would dramatize his subjects. He asked me to go for a sitting. With no objection from my mother, I arrived at the studio to find that he had already selected costumes and wigs of the eighteenth and nineteenth centuries. It was as though the first exciting sitting that we had had together was continuing. We were both totally involved in the moods that were developing with the change of each costume and there wasn't a word about the traumatic time when we had last seen each other. His enthusiasm, as before, was great. He had developed a process that made his prints appear to be paintings rather than photographs, and he sent me some enlargements.

By now we had a house of our own that my mother had purchased for three thousand dollars at 1332 Sierra Bonita Avenue. It wasn't quite so nice as the recently rented one, but it was *ours*. She had a small room added as a dressing room for me. Mr. Powers told us where and how to buy some furniture—wholesale. So we bought some fairly suitable things, and from the neighborhood piano store, a baby grand! I wanted that with all my heart and was soon playing "Wien" and "Fur Elise" and other pieces, not very well but very happily. Willow had her own home now and so I was in charge of the music department. Vivien, as usual, had the poorest room. He was put at the back of the house in a small space that he probably found satisfactory enough because he had a place in which to paint. Friends who came to see him were mostly young male artists. One young Spanish painter did an imaginary portrait of me on a panel of maroon velvet. Another brought a portfolio of caricatures. There was an Italian poet, too—Virgil.

There was money for my mother to have a checkup at the Presbyterian Hospital on Vermont Avenue. She was to be there for a few days. I was at the piano, playing away at "Wien, Wien," when my brother Vivien came and sat on the piano bench beside me. He leaned close to me, breathing heavily onto my face, searching for my mouth. *Oh, oh!* Something horribly wrong was happening! I got up and ran. How soon could I get to my mother—to tell her? At the hospital, where she was walking about in her room, I had no feeling that perhaps I shouldn't have disturbed her. She had to *know*! She listened. She didn't seem shocked. She didn't seem surprised, neither did she reproach me for going to her. Apparently it was time for her to go home anyway. That must have been it. Because I knew I couldn't be in the house again without her there.

My mother talked with the family doctor who thougth that Vivien should have some supervision in a small hospital. She talked with John and they came to the mutual judgment that, as soon as the doctor would permit, Vivien should go for a long vacation with her loyal friends in Canada.

Before he left for Canada, my mother and I were already on our way to Maryland. The cast and crew of *The First Kiss* filled one railroad car. In Kansas City, while we were waiting for the car to be switched to another railroad line, Gary Cooper and his pal Lane Chandler went into the city, missed our departure time, and had to hire an airplane to catch us at a later stop. It seemed wonderfully careless and exciting of them.

St. Michaels is a fishing village on Chesapeake Bay. It was not the happiest location, for at least three of us were reluctant to leave our loves in Hollywood. Gary was in love with Evelyn Brent, Leslie Fenton with Ann Dvorak, and I with John Saunders. Gary always seemed to have "dibs" on the one telephone booth where the company stayed, so a kind-hearted assistant director arranged to drive Leslie and me to a nearby town where, in the quiet of a private home, we could talk to our loved ones. I don't know about the others or the ache they felt, but I was sad and weepy after hearing John's great misery at missing me. And I was worried about my brother.

Word came: Vivien had taken the train as far as Lodi, California; he had fallen accidentally (or purposefully) between the railroad cars! Willow went to "take care of everything." Numbness. About two days later, I was doing a scene with Gary and when I looked up at him, *he* seemed to be my brother. It was the first moment of sensitive perception that my brother was actually gone. Professional people are supposed to be able to handle these moments. But I wasn't yet such a professional. We stopped work for the day.

John said he would soon be arriving in St. Michaels. When he came, he asked my mother if we could be married. Of course, she said, "Of course." John went to the little Methodist church, arranged for the minister, and bought a wedding band; and the director, Rowland V. Lee, and his wife and Gary and my mother witnessed our wedding. I was now twenty years old. John was thirty.

The film at that point was near completion. It was almost embarrassing to leave my mother and the company and go to stay at a little hotel with John. And now *I* would never go home again.

CHAPTER 10

A TROUBLED HONEYMOON

◆

W HEN THE COMPANY RETURNED TO Hollywood, John took
me to Foxcroft in Middleburg, Virginia, where Avis had
gone to school. He wanted me to meet Miss Charlotte, the head-
mistress who rode to hounds on a sidesaddle. She swept into the
reception room in her riding habit, white-haired, vibrant, saying
we should stay to a wedding reception that was to be held at the
school the same evening. Afterward, we joined former friends of
John and Avis at a private home. I was surprised to see John sit
on the floor before an attractive older woman, rest his crossed
arms on her lap, and say, "You have the most beautiful teeth I
have ever seen!" I thought he was meaning her breasts, which
were very large. I knew he was a little bit drunk.

In Washington at the Mayflower Hotel, we, rather *he*, ate cher-
rystone clams and had portraits made by the hotel photographer—together and singly. John looked splendid with and
without his Panama hat; I looked a little pale. We visited a lady
who had been a friend of his and Avis's, the widow of a career

army man. She lived in Georgetown among antiques and Oriental rugs.

In New York, we went to see Avis *herself*, up three flights of stairs on Washington Square. Now she was Mrs. Jack Golden. Her husband sat at the piano, as if interrupted at practicing. He was an accompanist to Marian Harris, a popular blues singer who had been married to Rush Hughes, Avis's brother. Marian was in love with Cesar Romero, who was then a ballroom dancer at a nightclub, and John and I went to see the handsome Cuban dance.

We went for a weekend to the country home of Adolph Zukor, where the ladies wore chalk-white evening dresses to show off their tans and their emeralds. We went to Cartier to buy an engagement ring for me: a lovely emerald-cut diamond.

I waited in our room at the Plaza Hotel while John kept an appointment with Bessie Lasky at the Lasky apartment on Fifth Avenue. Her son Jesse Jr. has written in his book, *Whatever Happened to Hollywood?*: "When John Saunders married Fay Wray, it almost broke Bessie's heart. She considered him her own admirer."

If it was a painful meeting for John, he didn't say so. But pain for him was just ahead. A telegram came from my mother asking him to "ignore current issue of a certain motion picture magazine. Picture of Fay is a composite." He went out at once and came back holding the article up for me to. "See, see, *see* this story about your going to California with a photographer! See what it can do to you! Paramount will cancel your contract!" (There is really no use to try to remember the exact words.) He went on and on: Disaster lay ahead for me!

There was a picture of me sitting in the sidecar alongside William Mortensen on the Harley-Davidson at the top of the page; and at the bottom, a picture of me, barefooted, my torso draped in silk taffeta. It was *not* a composite. It was a picture Mortensen had taken when he'd had his studio over the garage on Wilshire Boulevard. John threw the magazine on the floor, as if throwing me away with it—as if to say, I thought you were so *perfect*!

With every wave of words, I felt shock after shock. It was as though life itself was over. I was in a whirlpool of desperation. All the guilt that my mother had made me feel was compounded a thousand times. Certainly in my ignorance, I had caused her to see me that way, but now . . . "You are pure," John had said it so often, and now he thought I was not. I didn't pick the magazine up. I didn't care. I didn't read it then or at any time after. All my feelings were for the horrible chasm that had opened between John and me. If he thought this was so devastating, perhaps it was. He the well-educated, he the sophisticated, he the first, the only person I had loved. He, who was seeming to feel more scarred by this than by any past wounds that he had described to me. The worst part seemed to have been traveling with Mortensen from Salt Lake City to Los Angeles; the second worst, the bare legs, the bare shoulders that, to his willing mind, could suggest more revealing photos. No assurance by me could relieve that anxiety.

After a five-day train trip we arrived back in Los Angeles; a crisis meeting was held at the studio with my mother and John and Barney Hutchinson of the Paramount Publicity Department. I waited in my dressing room; I saw the three meeting and standing together in apparent consultation. What would their judgment be? Some way to correct all the wrong that had been done to me and by me? What wrong? Was it wrong to have come to California in the first place? Was it wrong to have been photographed showing all my legs and arms and shoulders? Doing that had been a lesson in artistic self-appreciation. Except for my elbows!! Bill had thought my elbows larger and stronger than he would like, and he taught me how to turn my arm ever so slightly to conceal that. He taught me how to hold my two central fingers together so as to make a tapering finish to the slenderizing line that he wanted. And wasn't it he who had found me my very first work in pictures, which in turn had led to more and more, and indirectly even to *The Wedding March* because of Edna Schley? Couldn't they see that?

All they could see was the little scandal of the posing and the motorcycle, elegant though it was. My mother, I learned, would have the responsibility of talking Mortensen into signing a little lie that every time he had visited us in Salt Lake City, my brother Vivien had been present—thus making her less responsible for sending me to California. Barney Hutchinson's responsibility would be to talk to the editor of the magazine to ensure no further articles. They and the great Paramount Corporation would save the day for me. None of this would relieve John of the compulsion to believe, because of his own sensual nature, that there had to be photographs to suit the images by which he tortured himself. That would go on and on.

William Mortensen signed the fiction that my mother wanted. I found it many years after and tore it up, wanting to erase the misery that it must have been for him, the shame it was that she should have asked him for it.

I feel strong now, sorting all of this out. On that day, looking at the three of them and knowing their concerns, I let myself fit into their picture of the problem. I allowed myself to believe they might be right. How miserable I was!

Gone was all the joy it had been to have Mortensen's enthusiasm surrounding me, the excitement of seeing his head come out from under the protecting curtain on the back of his eight-by-ten camera. Catch it, he seemed to be saying to himself, Catch this lovely moment—a little wild, a little crazy, the way every genuine artist should be. And I was helping, helping!

John and I went to stay at the Beverly Wilshire in a suite that included a dining room. It had a large and lonely feeling, especially when John, in a mood of restlessness, suddenly decided one evening just before retiring to leave and "go to the beach." I begged him not to go and afterward was ashamed that I had begged.

In a calmer mood, we practiced putting golf balls on the carpeted hallways, using a tumbler placed on its side as the cup. We heard David Selznick's voice talking to Jean Arthur through a wide open door in the hallway. We went to a party given for David Selznick and Irene Mayer in the hotel ballroom. Irene and her sister, Edie, had beautiful figures and, like the ladies at the Adolph Zukor country home, wore chalk-white dresses to show off their tans. Irene removed her shoes and did a Charleston, watching her own feet flying faster and faster. Considering the recently heard voices in the hallway, the solo dance that night seemed very, very solo.

While I was away in Maryland, John had left his little place on Cheremoya and rented a house that had been built by the Vidors, King and Florence. Happily, it was now for sale; happily, I had enough for a down payment. (John had given all his reserves to Avis in exchange for no more alimony.) We went to this wonderful house on Selma Avenue, just west of Fairfax. Its English farmhouse architecture, wide lawn, rose garden, and tennis court had a healing effect. John's trunk of memorabilia was taken out of storage. Prints and engravings of Oxford were hung on the walls in the library. We began to collect autographed photos of friends. We invited people to dinner to enjoy the cooking of "Mattie," whom Florence Vidor had left behind now that she was going to marry Jascha Heifetz. We played tennis. John was an athlete; I was not, and was better at Ping-Pong than tennis. Under his urging and tutelage, I became as good as anybody around who was not, let's say, *really good,* as I would find national and international tennis stars to be. Louise Brooks's brother was good. He came over to visit with her ex-husband, Eddie Sutherland. He used a pen-holder grip—very fast.

We had wonderful things to eat: Olympia oysters and caviar that we got at the Gotham delicatessen for fourteen dollars a pound. We had a "selfish" Christmas—just us. Champagne and caviar and a big tree lighted and decorated. All the furnishings that we had been able to buy from Florence were lovely in the house. I bought books on furniture, china, and silver, wanting the education. I would have been satisfied just to stay home.

John didn't stop "going to the beach" to see Bessie right away. I had not the slightest sense of physical jealousy but I wondered what they *talked* about. It must be what they talked about, I thought, that made them really close. And so, woven in with the games and the parties and the tennis and the beautiful house were the questions: Did he love Bessie? Did he love me? Or did he just love the fact that Bessie loved him?

Usually on Sunday mornings, I would drive John to the Riviera Country Club, where he would meet Jesse Lasky for golf; then I would arrive at their beach house about five o'clock in the afternoon, in time to take John fresh linen following his ocean swim. On days that he elected to drive himself to the club, a Lasky Rolls-Royce would call for me. As a hostess, Bessie seemed to make no effort at all, moving about at the large parties as though through a grove of trees. Her air of serenity found a response in me—but we never talked; the subject might have been John. More than once, she appeared grateful that I would be driving John home, it being perfectly clear that he was "unclear."

Before dinner, the younger Lasky children, Betty and Billy, would say a polite good night to the guests. The older son, Jesse Jr., wrote poetry, John said. He had published a small volume, *Listening to Silence*. He and John kept a distance from each other, as though mutually uncomfortable at close range. John wanted me to know that everything in this household was not one-sided romantically, and he pointed out a pretty young girl who, he said, was Jesse Sr.'s girlfriend.

At the Sunday parties, I met Richard Barthelmess and his wife Jessica, and beat Jascha Heifetz at Ping-Pong. Josef von Sternberg was sometimes there. John ridiculed him for using the word *epitomization*, a nonword, John said. This was probably the epitome of rudeness, von Sternberg's expression seemed to say.

Not long after we went to Selma Avenue, Mortensen phoned that he would be sending a bill for the portraits he had made of me at the Western Costume Company. The process he had used was expensive; the bill would be a thousand dollars. "Extortion!" John said, his original anger renewed, his original suspicions enhanced to such a degree that he began to make a search along Hollywood Boulevard. He engaged the help of a bookseller to locate prints made by Mortensen, and he came home with a photo of a young girl, nude, modestly in profile, and asked, "Is this you?" It was not; he had only to look closely at the face. But he would go on looking and after a while when he tired of that, he would go on believing, anyway, that there must be photos to be found.

Why, I would go on wondering, did he have such a need? In a moment of remorse, he quoted Oscar Wilde's words to me: "Each man kills the things he loves. . . ."

I would go on trying to understand about Bessie. I would go on trying to understand why he would say that if I should ever find him in bed with another woman, I should think nothing of it— because he was "oversexed." Why he wanted me to pattern my voice after Tallulah Bankhead's. Why he wanted me to try to develop my breasts to compare to Lili Damita's, which were very large. Why he wanted me to get my skin to have the texture and tone of Dolores Del Rio's. There were times I thought he loved me as I was.

Making love, he thought, was essential to him—and a danger. Drinking was essential to him—and a danger. "Make you laugh and play." This, with the first sip of a first martini, was his way of toasting the anticipated pleasure. He thought of himself as part of the Lost Generation. He admired the "membership"; Scott and Zelda Fitzgerald had visited him in his house in the Hollywood Hills. Standing on a balcony, the three had competed to see who could urinate farther. Yes, Zelda too. He liked remembering. In Ernest Hemingway's *The Sun Also Rises*, there was a matador who made the mistake of engaging in love the night before going to the bull ring. The following afternoon, he was slain by the bull.

> Shower down thy love, oh burning bright
> For tonight or yet another night
> Will come the Gardener dressed in white
> And gathered flowers are dead, Yasmin.

These lines are not Hemingway's and I never learned whose— but John had to quote them only once to make them memorable.

In the spring of 1929, he went to Paris, found a girl at the Ritz Bar, went to live with her at the Hotel Claridge, went on to Portugal (the Hemingway characters had gone from Paris to Spain), and by the time he returned home (with perfumes and a Spanish shawl for me), he was ready to begin the writing of *Single Lady*.

He wrote early in the morning. It was fine to see him at his desk, menus and bottle labels collected from his trip posted on the wall behind him. He didn't drink during the writing of that novel. A cable arrived from Paris, saying, "A sticky cablegram came from Fay." Well! Letters followed. After he had read them, and left them on his desk, I read them when he went to play golf. She had missed him so much and had drunk so much that she had to be taken to the American Hospital at Neuilly. She had spent a night in a tree in her leopard-skin coat. She signed her name "Nikki."

Again, I was not jealous in the sexual sense but wildly curious about her as a person. I asked. She had been born in Hawaii, he said, had inherited forty thousand dollars, and had gone immediately to Paris, to the Ritz bar. He said she was chic. He had a large photo of her, taken by him, inscribed to her: "To Nikki, I can walk faster in red shoes." He was quoting her. I could understand his appreciating that line and perhaps a lot about her, but when she wrote that a wirehaired terrier that she kept was "like our child," it seemed a strangeness. He bought two wirehaired terriers and named them Michael and Mary. She had kept turtles. He bought turtles for me. He cabled her for the source of "From ghosties and ghoulies and long-leggedy beasties and things that go bump in the night, dear Lord protect us." She cabled back that it was from an Old Cornish litany.

He had brought back from Paris and given to me heart-shaped stones that he (they?) had found at the tomb of Heloïse and Abelard. For a long time, I thought they were for me only; that when given, they meant "no harm will come to our true love." I kept them carefully, believing he really wanted it to be that way for us—but Nikki became a kind of ghostie or ghoulie to me.

The character in his novel was some of her, some of me—all mixed up. I was very mixed-up about what marriage was supposed to be. It was very easy to accept his instructions about what my behavior should be. "Never let a man enter your dressing room. I know. I've been in dressing rooms." I never felt a flutter of personal interest or excitement about working with Richard Arlen or Clive Brook or Gary Cooper. He didn't have to set rules for me.

When he finished *Single Lady*, the flyleaf said: "For Fay." He dated the book's ending: Lisbon, Portugal, June 15, 1929—the date of our first anniversary.

When he returned home sometime after that and I met him at the train, he reproached me for wearing the same dress in which I had said goodbye to him. I should have worn something new, he said. The preoccupation with clothes was part of a "manners maketh man" point of view.

The next Christmas was a disastrous one because of a camel's hair overcoat I had bought for him. He put it on and went into the guest bath to look in the mirror. He called out, "The sleeves are too long!" He took it off and went out and didn't come back. I sat by the Christmas tree for a while and then decided that I, too, must drink. I put the scotch he had been drinking in a tumbler and drank until my head began to spin, until I felt I could write an apology for all that I had done wrong. In *Single Lady* when Nikki was asked as she left for the powder room where she was going, she answered, "To take a Chinese singing lesson." I quoted that in my note of apology. I said that I would try to do better; that I would take a Chinese singing lesson every single day. When he read the note the next morning, he was delighted.

In the last scenes of *Single Lady*, he had Nikki say, "Haven't I been pretty good? Haven't I done better?" He liked the pleading for approval. Did he think that by writing that note, I had done better? Or did he think by drinking, I had done better? And when he wrote those words, did he write them as coming from me—or from the Nikki of Paris?

He had done something better himself that Christmas Eve. He had not "gone to the beach." He had gone to the Lewis Milestone's. He found a large gathering and music and Christmas carols and had had a good time. And something to drink.

CHAPTER II

MERIAN COOPER: PRE-SOUND, PRE-KING KONG

◆

PROBABLY BECAUSE OF JOHN, I was cast in *The Four Feathers* automatically. It would have been typical of Merian Cooper to respond to mutual friendships. They had the same legal representative in New York and common friends in publishing. It would have been enough. But once we worked together, I had an enduring regard for him and he for me. He was not a studio person. He and his partner, Ernest Schoedsack, had made *Grass*, a spectacular documentary about migratory herdsmen in Persia, and *Chang*, made entirely in Siam with tigers and gibbons and native Siamese and an elephant stampede. It was stunning. They had no script; they made up the story as chance and opportunity provided.

Now they were involved in filming a novel about the military of Victorian England. Exteriors had already been completed by Cooper and Schoedsack in Africa and the California desert (the desert playing the part of Africa for additional scenes). The script required interior scenes and a touch of romance to be provided by Richard Arlen and me. The film, otherwise silent, was premiered with a musical score and sound effects. The exterior scenes were thought to be very impressive, the interiors considered rather list-less. I wonder now whether the uncertainties I was feeling at home contributed.

Lothar Mendes, who had taken over *The Street of Sin* after the departure of Mauritz Stiller, directed. Schoedsack did some of the interiors. He was a lanky fellow, about six feet six inches, who had a wry sense of humor. He gave us a laugh unconsciously one day. Richard Arlen and I were doing a walking scene, the camera traveling backward in front of us on tracks. Schoedsack, keeping pace alongside the moving camera, saw something not to his lik-ing and called, *"Cut! Cut!"* No one stopped; the scene continued and when the camera came to the end of the track, Schoedsack said, *"Hot dog!* That was a good scene." Because the film was silent, his words had not interfered. But the switch from *cut* to *hot dog* let us know he was as yet not really comfortable inside the studio.

Merian Cooper was a fascinating combination of high imagina-tion, an implicitly rebellious nature, a political conservative, an intellect, an adventurer, and a visionary. He had a strongly chiv-alrous nature. While we were filming *The Four Feathers*, he sent orchids to my dressing room every few days. No one had done that before.

Cooper, I would learn later, had wanted to do *The Four Feath-ers* with complete sound. Because of that and other disagreements with Paramount's handling of the film, he left Hollywood for a brief time to put his energies into civil aviation. But he didn't turn his thoughts away from films completely. It was in New York that the idea for *King Kong* began to germinate.

When you weren't working in films at Paramount, you were working for the publicity department—which was pretty much the way it had been at Hal Roach. One week you were photographed carving a turkey, next you were a Red Cross nurse looking over no-man's land (for Armistice Day). You were Elaine the Lily, maid of Astelot, floating quite dead down the Thames. You did lots of hairstyles. Long hair such as mine could be done many different ways. I liked my hair and absolutely hated to have it cut off to play the role of a gangster's moll in *Thunderbolt*. Actually, I didn't feel tough enough to play that part and I'm sure it showed.

Thunderbolt was Josef von Sternberg's first sound film. I think he was frustrated by the restrictions that sound imposed. His eyes were the eyes of a painter. He saw scenes as compositions, and the awkwardness of having the camera housed inside protective blimps and the concerns for microphones and the shadows they made were distressing. He would sometimes send his vivacious wife Riza into the scene to make suggestions while he remained in the shadows.

There was a roster of stars at Paramount and there was a roster of management. The roster of management made decisions for and about the roster of stars. It was difficult for them to make choices once the added factor of sound was involved. In a film called *Paramount on Parade,* they lumped every star, major and minor, into one musical under the guidance of eleven directors. The cast numbered almost fifty. The decision may have advanced sound and proved that Paramount could make a lot of it, but it did little for any individual.

In *Pointed Heels*, I was a chorus girl. I learned a few steps, used the same false eyelashes I had worn as the gangster's moll in *Thunderbolt,* felt thoroughly miscast, happy only to be working with William Powell. He had grace, style, wit, and technique. He was not absolutely handsome, so that he was believable as a leading man or as a villain or whatever role. He was Olympian in the sense that he seemed to have achieved an elegant arrogance. When I see photos of him in splendid profile, I think of how he told me he achieved a taut chin line. "I start a swallow but do not finish it." I worked with him again in *Behind the Makeup,* which was directed by Robert Milton of the New York theater with the strong assistance of Dorothy Arzner, who knew motion pictures very well, having been an editor. More and more arrivals from the theater began to dominate production at Paramount.

John Cromwell directed Gary Cooper and me in *The Texan*. He spent about two weeks rehearsing, creating a very comfortable and sure approach. For the early sound films, there was always a dialogue director, a separate entity from that of *the* director. The dialogue man was supposed to help the actors learn their lines so there would be no delay when actual filming began. That was Jack Wagner's job on *The Texan*. He had a sense of humor and a wonderful understanding of Spanish accents. I loved learning from him and was glad to see him again many years later when he arrived at a dinner party in New York with John Steinbeck—who for some years had found his company stimulating.

George Abbott came from New York to direct *The Sea God* with Richard Arlen and me. It was George Abbott's love of dancing that caused trouble between John and me. *The Sea God* company was on location at the end of Catalina known as the Isthmus. Avalon is at the other end of the island. After work one evening, George wanted the whole company to go to the ballroom at Avalon. As many as could, got into a big water taxi. Flying fish came along, too, leaping out of the water and sometimes right into the boat, one of them landing in my lap with a great thudding plop. A dandy experience! George Abbott has always loved dancing about as much as anything in life. It has kept him slim and young and able to direct a successful musical, *On Your Toes*, at the dancing age of ninety.

I told John about the fun of that evening when we returned from location. Dancing with a director was just as bad, he said, as letting a man go into your dressing room. He said it over and over again in a variety of ways. George Abbott has, ever since, had an undeserved wickedness about him that is far from the reality I remember. Wicked George Abbott? As absurd as the flying fish! This episode served to point out the double standard of John's philosophy.

CHAPTER 12

"MY PEOPLE IS BROKE"

◆

66 I THINK MY PEOPLE IS broke," I heard Mattie the cook telling someone on the telephone. Someone at Paramount could have been saying approximately the same thing to the bankers in New York: "I think our studio is broke." There had been the stock market crash in October 1929. The following year, Paramount began loaning their contract players to other studios.

It was probably because of John that I was loaned to Warner Brothers for *The Finger Points*. It was his script. Richard Barthelmess was the star and Clark Gable had a very small part. There was talk on the set about the interesting quality of the tall young Gable playing a gangster.

With the exception of Nikki, I do not think John wrote any women's roles that had dimension. But then, almost no Hollywood writers did. The leading ladies never seemed to have background of any kind. No parents or reference to parents. Mitzi in *The Wedding March* certainly had parents. Von Stroheim couldn't write any role, he said, unless he knew what the character's parents were like. In *King Kong*, Ann Darrow at least had an uncle "somewhere." One Hollywood writer used a recurring description that summarized in total all that need be known about the leading lady: "She has an April loveliness." It's because of that not-muchness about the character that I remember nothing about *me* in *The Finger Points*. Richard Barthelmess, yes. Even he, not as an actor, but as a person. Contained, controlled, insecure even though he had been a great star in silents. He was an original; it is not possible to say, "someone *like* Richard Barthelmess." The youthful quality remained with him always, at least until he fool-ishly had plastic surgery to remove bags under his eyes, leaving him with one grotesquely pulled lower lid.

I was loaned to Fox for a Western with Victor McLaglen, *Not Exactly Gentlemen*, and I was loaned to Columbia for *Dirigible* and went to talk to Harry Cohn about the film that was to be directed by Frank Capra. I saw, at once, that there was a tiger in him; the tiger that is the driving force behind accomplishment. His mouth curved downward on one side, as if his face had been made from halves of the two theatrical masks; his eyes were a strong and eager blue, possessively alive as he talked about the genius of his director, Frank Capra.

I knew something of Capra by reputation—that he had directed Barbara Stanwyck in *Ladies of Leisure*—and I had seen for myself that she was wonderful. Also, I knew that Jack Holt would be in the film and I could nudge the memory of my oldest sister, who had seen him on the screen as one of her favorite heroes. Sweet memories, sitting beside her at the movies.

If Cohn and Paramount were pleased to arrange for me to be at Columbia, Capra probably was not. I had no contact with him in preparation for the film and when I did go on the set, he was angry because I was some moments late. A closeted resentment cleared only slowly as my hairdresser and I explained that we needed extra time to clean my dress of brilliantine that had been sprayed not just on my hair but accidentally on the gown, as well. The burden of a heavy budget was probably a weight upon him. Also, the film had its own kind of weightiness even if the title could be defined as a craft "lighter than air." The story was all strong, male-chauvinist, adventure stuff and had none of the delicate comedy sense that Robert Riskin was to help him find and establish as a trademark.

Much has been said about Harry Cohn's brutishness, but there were sensitive areas in his personality not often to surface and, therefore, all the more memorable when seen. It must have been this sensitivity that he worked diligently to conceal that was, in fact, a sixth sense and keyed his ability to recognize talent and to draw into his orbit such men as Frank Capra, Robert Riskin, and Jo Swerling.

Columbia was a physically awkward plant. A two-story building on Gower Street housed the office of himself, Harry Cohn, other executives, a few writers, dressing rooms, and the makeup and hairdressing departments. Beyond that building, a narrow path led to cutting rooms, projection rooms, and stages, and in a far corner up some creaky stairs, the wardrobe department. All the structures were squeezed into position, each one hugging the next. It had a "make-do" character. The very look of poverty made you feel generous toward it as toward a hungry child. Among the personnel and even the actors, there was not the complaining I had heard at the more affluent Paramount. Columbia, it seemed, had a long way to go and everybody had to help. This attitude did not spring from Harry Cohn, for he and his ways were held suspect. I think the attitude must have come from Columbia being considered an underdog. The underdog had a good heartbeat.

You had to go past the doorman, Captain Duncan, to get into the Columbia studios. He sat inside a booth at the back of the small entrance lobby, flanked by two doors, one for ingress, one for egress. He was a big, bespectacled, cheerful man, so nonirritating to writers Robert Riskin and Jo Swerling—who found the reverse true in Harry Cohn—that they conceived a plan to pyramid a small sum of money into a fortune sufficient to buy the studio and make Captain Duncan the benign master over all Columbia's moviemaking. The idea was no less enjoyable for being impractical and seemed to them a tangible and perfect goal . . . at least for a few inspired weeks.

The last picture I made for Paramount was again a loanout, as leading lady to Ronald Colman. The best thing about that film was the beginning of a friendship with this fine English actor. *The Unholy Garden* had been written by Ben Hecht and Charles Mac-Arthur, two gifted writers, but their gifts were less apparent in this work than usual. The story was set in a desert oasis inhabited by an assortment of nefarious refugees from justice. Colman, in the role of a thief, was reborn through his love for "the girl."

Credibility was not an essential. "The girl" (me) had blond hair, beautifully coiffed, and I wore chiffon trimmed with Alençon lace. Everyone looked better than was reasonable given the desert background. Sam Goldwyn, the producer, did not go on the set. That *was* believable because Colman and Goldwyn were not speaking.

Ronald Colman lived on Mound Street near the top of Vine, which used to rise sharply away from Hollywood Boulevard before the freeway cut it down. He gave candlelit dinner parties on his terrace that overlooked the city. Dick and Jessica Barthelmess, William Powell, Bessie Love and her husband William Hawks, and John and I shared some pleasant evenings there. Ronnie told about a time when he had been driving home too cautiously one evening, having had numerous drinks. He was pulled over by policemen.

I had been pulled over for driving too fast when I was making *The Unholy Garden*. We were to work at night. I had gone home for dinner, had champagne with John, was sailing along on the return to the studio, singing. "I was so happy," I told the two policemen who pulled alongside me. "I was happy and singing— and now you've spoiled all that." This is about credibility—of scripts or situations. Incredibly, each policeman gave me his personal card "in case they could ever be of help." I thanked them and sang along to the studio and told Ronnie. He was pleased, especially about the champagne. "You should do that more often," he said. That, too, seemed incredible. But I think it was less about champagne per se than it was about seeing more sparkle in me than usual. He was an actor of perfect discipline and I'm certain would never have drunk while working. Before and after dinner, he loved his conversational scotch-and-sodas.

CHAPTER 13

DANCING IS BETTER THAN CRYING

◆

IT WAS DAVID SELZNICK WHO told me my contract with Paramount was over. Although he had been executive producer on *The Four Feathers* and *The Texan*, this was my only meeting with him in his office at the studio. We sat facing each other as he talked apologetically about the financial trouble of Paramount and the fact that Mary Brian and Jean Arthur were also being let go. So it wasn't just me but conditions and circumstance. His big smiling face was trying to be as kindly as possible.

Was it John's idea—or was it William Powell's—that the "good news" should be celebrated that very evening? Bill Powell came to Selma Avenue for dinner and afterward when it was dark, the three of us went out to the front lawn and danced a dance of jubilation that I was *free*! They may have really meant it for me. I didn't really mean it, but dancing was better than crying.

John had been "freed" from Paramount somewhat earlier. We were going less often to the Sunday parties at the Laskys' beach house. Bessie had a new love, the sculptor Boris Lovet-Lorski. "Not as good as you," John said she had told him, making his place in her affection secure. She told him, too, that after the stock market crash, she felt the most serious result for Jesse was that he would have to carry his own golf clubs to the car. She found it easy to make Jesse the object of her joke.

Mattie, our cook, was right. Her people were feeling broke. John's family in Seattle had to be told that his monthly check to them would be reduced. My mother had to be told the same. I made the mistake of telling her over the telephone. She made the mistake of saying, "I will sue you." She didn't sue and seemed to be able to manage on the reduced funds.

Both John and I were pained by the sharpness of her reaction. For a while after that, I couldn't find her in my feelings, couldn't find a place within me where I could be comfortable about her— wondering would she sue? She must have had some anger ready and waiting to be so quick with that response. There had not always been a neat fit between the way our lives were going or the way that hers remained unchanged. She was great with my brothers, raising them with an affectionately disciplinarian style. That is to say, affectionately intolerant. She brought that intolerance along when she came to visit us. John offered her champagne, which she bravely accepted, but as soon as the bouquet of it came close to her nose, she exclaimed, "Oh, I am drunk!" and set her glass down without sipping it. It seemed just quaint and funny at the time but was a compass for the different directions of their values.

I think she sincerely wanted to let us alone, not to be a hovering mother, but had mixed feelings about it, too.

For my part, I never ran to her when John's problems overwhelmed me. I knew I couldn't tell her and shouldn't because to her my marriage to John represented an *ultimate glory*. But mostly, I couldn't talk about such things with her because I didn't really *know* her. I knew her attitudes, her praises, her reproaches, her politics, what often seemed to be her "fictions," her relationship to Supreme Court Justice John Marshall, to those particular Joneses from whom John Paul Jones chose his name. I knew her appreciation of good manners. Her, I never really knew.

The center of that not-knowing, I gradually came to understand, was her inability to express her love. Pride seemed to be in the forefront of her feelings; I do not remember ever getting a hug. There was never any light or foolish laughter. Humor, yes, a sense of satire, but never any fullness of fun. Pocketfuls of pride, a teaching background that gave her the ability to grade her children's deportment—but I wondered had she ever been in love?

There was never a thought that she should marry again after she parted from my father. Never a thought except in *my* head! I longed to have her show an interest in Patrick Powers . . . he, in her. There was never a flicker of a crosscurrent glow between them. There was no other someone, ever. That would have relieved me, and I think the other children, of bearing the burden of the big responsibility she felt in having to raise us alone. Alone? But she had made that choice. She had never been caught saying that she loved my father but a long time before, when I was maybe seven or eight, I had caught her saying that she *didn't*. "It's like Dead Sea fruit," she was telling a woman friend, not knowing I was in the house to hear. "Every time I conceived, I thought of another man." I knew I had heard something very important but it would take a long and gradual growing-up to understand. Now I use that understanding to notice those women who live warmly into later years. Only those who have given and received love and can carry the remembered glow of it as they go along are so happy.

In the spring of 1930, a letter arrived from a nurse who had been attending to my father, telling me that he was hospitalized and dying of cancer. It was the only written communication I had had in all the years of my parents' separation. And even then, it was not from him nor did the nurse say he had asked for me. She just thought I'd want to know.

But his relatives in Idaho *did* keep some things he had written, if not to me, to whatever Great Ear he believed in and hoped would listen. He must have been writing this about my mother:

LOVE

I've looked so long for you, Dear
I've hoped to see your face
Among the people passing
I've looked from place to place

And I recall a day, Dear
When we stood side by side
Declared we'd live together
Until the time we died

And things were as we hoped, Dear.
The world to us was new.
For I knew then you loved me
The same as I loved you.

We loved and lived together, Dear
Through years that hurried by
I always hoped and praid [sic], Dear
I'd be the first to die.

And now I'm left alone, Dear
I think about the past
We loved and lived together
As long as life did last.

My mother would not have been able to give good grades to this for quality or spelling. I don't know how she would have *felt* about it. But there was some *feeling* there.

CHAPTER 14

~~~~~~~~~

JOHN'S "SINGLE LADY" BECOMES MY "NIKKI" WITH CARY GRANT

◆

JOHN'S FUTURE, IF NOT FORTUNES, began to look better when he sold *The Dawn Patrol* to First National. *Single Lady*, too, enhanced his future hopes when it was published in the fall of 1930. He sold the screen rights to First National and wrote the screenplay under the title of *The Last Flight*.

These events were so rewarding and forward-looking that his reaction to a news item in May of 1931 was startling. Someone he didn't even know committed suicide. That someone, Ralph Barton, had written for magazines and done cartoons for *Life*. He had left a note—about having had a full and successful life—about it being enough. He was thirty-nine. John said he could understand; that he, himself, felt he had achieved the three things he most wanted: to be famous, to be rich, and to be married to a beautiful woman. For him, it was enough. He was then thirty-three.

"Shower down thy love, oh burning bright / For tonight or yet another night / Will come the Gardener dressed in white. . . ."

I realized, then, that there is a knowledge or understanding, an

◆ 114 ◆

appreciation of life, widely separate from what can be learned from any university—even Oxford.

When production began on *The Last Flight* at First National with Richard Barthelmess in the starring role, I would have been available to play Nikki opposite him since my contract with Paramount was over. But they made a test of me (photographic only) and decided I didn't have the chic they wanted. Helen Chandler got the role. A test was made of John, too, to play one of the supporting roles (Shep Lambert), but he didn't look right either. Dick Barthelmess, with affection and honest humor, said John looked like a nance. I thought that was because John had never stood in front of a movie camera before and showed some nervousness. Anyway, the production went forward without us, under the direction of William Dieterle. We visited the set often. The spirit of the piece (to salute the end of World War I with an avowed commitment to drinking) appealed to Dick and Jessica.

By the time the film was released in New York, a musical, *Nikki*, from the same material was at the Longacre Theater and I was in it. John had gone to New York to help with preparation of the musical, which was produced with money from the father of a young lady who hoped to be making her debut. During his absence, I went on a health diet, inspired by reading Gaylord Hauser. Vegetarianism was a pleasure and I was getting as thin as any movie star, including Constance Bennett, whose hipbones were plainly visible. I heard from John there was a possibility they might want me to do *Nikki;* rehearsals of the musical went poorly. Then the possibility became the fact and I took the train to New York.

You could get on the Santa Fe Chief at the Union Station in downtown Los Angeles or at Pasadena. In either case, a friend or friends would see you off. There would be flowers and fruit and magazines and hugs and hopes for a beautiful time. You never went up the steps without someone going along to be sure that your luggage had been placed in your compartment. If that "someone" forgot to leave before the train started moving out of L.A., there was no great concern; Pasadena was only fifteen minutes away and the extra time was worth the forgetting.

Sit back, watch the orange groves, see the train yards at San Bernardino, Azusa (everything from A to Z in the U.S.A.), Cucamongo, Redlands. Ontario. CAL ifornia CAL ifornia . . . *CLICK ety clack* . . . *CLICK ety clack*, the green groves receding faster and faster, smudge pots between the rows of trees showing like large punctuation marks. Then to the desert and no more green . . . only telephone poles and the anticipation of a telegram waiting at Needles or Williams or maybe both. Your own telegram should be ready. At the end of the corridor, there would be Western Union blanks. Hold on to the bars at the base of the windows and swing from side to side with the sway of the car and find, at the corridor's end, tucked in a recess with timetables, the yellow pads that would mean *communication*. Getting the telegrams was a sensuous joy; after each stop, expecting the porter to press the buzzer of the compartment door and hand in the rectangular, yellow envelope. Imagining the Western Union operators dotting and dashing the message, all the staccato sounds, every word significant because of brevity. At night, the grinding to a noisy halt in some strange place—what place . . . where . . . where can we be? How far have we come? Raising the window shade just enough to see into the outer darkness. Men with swinging lanterns making paths of light along the ground. Talk outside. Nothing beyond. The flashing streaks of the lanterns. Nothing beyond. Not a station, not a place to send a telegram. Let the shade down, lie back and wait for the tug, the lurch ahead, the sound of the wheels turning and soon again *clack*ety *clack*.

Maybe the next stop would be KANsas City . . . KANsas City. That would be a place where the passengers could get down to walk along the platform for a while. Wondering who would be among them. I had once seen Ronald Colman in very dark glasses that seemed to say, I don't want to be noticed. Or, rather, Notice that I don't want to be noticed. You couldn't help but notice. And I had seen Joan Crawford, a little blond girl holding on to her hand—Christina. Arthur Unger, the editor of *Variety*, once got off the train in Kansas City for the specific purpose of buying yards and yards of handkerchief linen so that Sabu, the Elephant Boy, could show me how to wrap a turban. If I learned the lesson, I never found a need for it, but had enough fine linen to make dozens of lovely handkerchiefs. The lesson of the turban was not nearly so important as learning that Mr. Arthur Unger, who appeared to be rough and gruff, could create a charming and indulgent interlude.

If thin was chic, I was absolutely chic when I arrived for a reading with the *Nikki* company. There were several men in the cast—one who was tall and dark. We sat on sofas in the director's office for the reading. I did a scene at the tomb of Heloïse and Abelard with the tall, dark, and very handsome one. I was probably better in that reading than at any time later; I was tired from the travel, my nerves keenly on edge. And it all came out sensitively to excite the director, who murmured, "Like Judith. She's like Judith Anderson." The tall one was playing the lead role of Cary Lockwood and it was easier to call him Cary than to call him by his real name, Archie. Archibald Leach.

There are some people who seem to have an incandescent light behind their eyes that turns on to the switch of their interest. The eyes have to be dark. Picasso's eyes seemed always to be on. His bodily electric bill would have been enormous. Cary's eyes flashed as a moment excited him. *OH* . . . how interesting. I love what you have to say. I like you. Say what you just said again; I love hearing it. That is fascinating. All these things he said without speaking. And after a while, I thought it wasn't because of what I said, it was just because of *me*. That's what the look of his eyes made me feel. So the tall dark one was like a source of light: caring.

Everyone else in the cast was working to do his best, hoping to advance a career, hoping to get good reviews. Cary (later to be known as Cary Grant) was a person simply enjoying what he was doing, as if not working at all, a person in the right milieu, a person who belonged. Because of him, the rehearsals were a joy. He was easily sure of himself, happy to be in the theater, generous. When we had scenes together, he would move downstage and turn toward me, as if wanting me to have all the focus of the audience.

At lunch near the theater with John, his criticism of how I was playing Nikki was strong. Any criticism had always taken the form of diatribe, never simple. I often thought this was a carry-over of what he had learned from Rupert Hughes. The most un-correct thing I was doing was sitting with my feet too close to my chair. Nikki was supposed to be nearsighted, not able to walk without her lorgnette, and I felt her body would be cautious and she would not be likely to stretch her legs out as if she were a fashion model when seated. I yielded, but not without letting John know that I thought he had overstated. That was probably chal-lenge number one.

I was enjoying my first experience in the theater. I had beau-tiful clothes, a song to sing (even if not well). The theater seemed a natural place to be. I do not remember any stage fright or even any great concern when the musical got poor reviews. One actor told me I had gotten a rave. Rave turned out to be "Fay Wray was the saving grace of the evening." But that was only one reviewer. We were not destined to last long, so it was awfully nice that Clare Boothe Brokaw gave us a party opening night before the reviews were out. She had known John when he wrote for *Vanity Fair*. At the party, Cary sat on the floor beside my chair. I felt good about that.

If this was the worst of the Great Depression, it seemed not to be affecting me. At the Pierre Hotel, John and I had a large suite overlooking the park for thirty dollars a day. We went to Jack and Charlie's (now 21), where they opened an aperture in the door to see who we were and always let us in. Other speakeasies treated us the same.

We visited George Putnam, the publisher, at his home in Rye, New York, and met his new wife, Amelia Earhart. She chased George in and out of various rooms, trying to spray him with a can of Flit. I never saw whether she actually hit him. I think it was mostly the pleasure of threatening. I saw large bowls of Beech-Nut gum everywhere, giving the house a commercial tone, she having endorsed the gum. Bernt Balchen was there. He had been on an expedition to the South Pole with Admiral Richard Byrd. Balchen was the first pilot to fly over Antarctica.

We went, in perfect safety, to Harlem after the theater, and what was John's idea of extra fun, to Grant's Tomb, where we could sit and look over the dark waters of the Hudson.

"When a Broadway Baby says good night/It's early in the morning . . ." Cleaning women were often on their knees in the lobby as we went to the elevator.

One afternoon we went up the Hudson to the home of Lenore Ulric (she had been a friend of Avis's). Fay Bainter lived next door and came over to see us. Fay Bainter had a magic about her. A lightning bug of a lady.

And every night there was *Nikki*. Even if the box office wasn't great, there was the pleasure of it. Hoping for better houses, we moved from the Longacre to the George M. Cohan. The box office didn't improve.

Edward Steichen invited us to his house in Redding, Connecticut, where he and his wife (the sister of Carl Sandburg) gave us luncheon. The lunch was all golden: scrambled eggs, corn muffins, and little yellow tomatoes. He raised delphinium, and their tall blue stalks just outside the windows made the day all blue and gold. Afterward we walked toward the river, where he took photographs of us. He was the shape of a praying mantis then, slim, eyes so alert that they seemed to want to run ahead of his body to catch what his camera would follow more slowly. Yet he worked fast, throwing large white bath towels on the ground to bounce the sun toward us.

After only six weeks *Nikki* was to close. The last scene was between Cary and me, a spotlight on our two heads, just before the final curtain. As the light went out, he kissed me on the forehead. "God bless you, Nikki."

I wanted to have a party for the company before we returned to California: "Please!" John said, *"No."*

Whereas the experience was all joy for me and the reviews of no great importance, John was realistically disappointed. He needed to recover from that and from the speakeasy experience, too, and went to Bill Brown's health farm at Garrison, New York to dry out. I waited at the Pierre in the big empty suite. There was no air conditioning then. Windows were kept open, letting any chance breezes blow the long white curtains into the room, their silk sheerness dancing about in sensuous patterns. I could hear the seals barking in the park below. It was a warm and comfortable loneliness because I was enjoying recent memories of being in the play.

After about a week, John asked me to hire a limousine and go to get him. I noted some scratches on the door of the car when it arrived, but it didn't occur to me to reject it and ask the hotel to order a scratchless one. It was, otherwise, a splendid, maroon Rolls-Royce. Perhaps it was the irritability of recovering after too brief a time at Bill Brown's that made John overconcerned, I thought, with those miserable scratches. We rode back to New York under the cloud of his disappointment.

Before returning to California, we went to a gala at the Waldorf. Cary was there, looking handsome in white tie and tails. John and I departed earlier than most and as we went up the great stairway at the end of the banquet room, I turned back, hoping to see Cary once more. He was standing beside his chair; he was looking at me. No one else at the table was standing—just Cary. A few more steps to the top of the stairs and I turned again. He was still standing. And so we looked at each other for a few seconds, saying from that considerable distance that we didn't want this to be "good-bye."

He telephoned the next day to tell us that he and Phil Charig, who had written the music for *Nikki*, would be driving to California and should be there about a week following our own arrival. The light source that was Cary would be following me! Cary's coming to CALifornia . . . Cary's coming to CALifornia. These were new lyrics to the *clickety-clack* of the train. And a song that Hoagy Carmichael had written attached itself to Cary. The "light source" and "Stardust" became one and the same.

On the train, John and I talked about the Academy Awards, which were to be given soon after our return. I thought his nomination for the most original story for *The Dawn Patrol* had no competition. We went to the awards evening (at that time the event was in November). The hotel room had perhaps a dozen tables with a speaker's dais. David Selznick, at a table near us, fell asleep. He often did that, publicly. When, finally, we heard that it was because of some metabolic problem and not because of drinking too much, it was gratifying to know that the discovery had been made and he could be treated. He was too big a fellow, physically, to fall asleep like that. He was so noticeable! John was, indeed, called to the dais to receive his Oscar. His speech of acceptance made references to "which came first, the chicken or the egg." He might have said the chicken *hawk* or the chicken *hawk's* egg. Howard Hawks had been involved with the story, as well as the direction of that film.

About one year earlier, on a Sunday morning, Howard had come to the house with a story idea that he wanted John to sell because John was most successful with scripts about aviation. Within a week's time, First National had bought the story as co-authored by John Monk Saunders and Howard Hawks. That's what Howard wanted. But he wanted no authorship credit for himself on the screen or in advertising; he instructed the studio of that choice in writing.

John, as I remember, went to the studio to prepare the script. That's the way Douglas Fairbanks, Jr., remembers it, too, remembers John working on the script, being on the set to rewrite or rearrange dialogue. Doug Jr. had a strong role and made a great hit in the film.

So, just a few years ago, I was astonished to hear Howard say in a television interview that every part of the story, every word of the script had been his.

"If it was entirely your story and script, why did John receive an Oscar for it?"

"We talked about it. I told him to go ahead and take it."

Howard and I were at a film festival in Montreal, walking away from the events of the evening.

(Really! Go ahead and take it!)

Howard walked slowly; he had just recovered from having two broken ankles . . . *two!*

Partly because of his ankles, but mostly because of the fixed position of his mind, I didn't press further. I wouldn't have been able to reverse anything. The mystery of that Sunday morning when Howard first went to John with the idea, the *why* of it, would remain!

I doubt that "Go ahead and take it" has been said very often to any Oscar nominee!

Paper No. 1:

Hollywood, Calif.
Nov. 15, 1929

Received from Howard Hawks the sum of one dollar ($1.00) and other valuable considerations, for which I agree to give said Howard Hawks the option of purchasing my aviation story *Flight Commander* for the sum of ten thousand dollars ($10,000.00) cash.

The rights to this story include picture, talking and stage rights. This option is given for the period of one week beginning this date and will terminate at twelve o'clock noon Friday, November twenty-second, 1929.

(signed) John Monk Saunders

Accepted
Howard Hawks

In presence of Eloise Brandon*
        (witness)

Paper No. 2:

Hollywood, Calif.
Nov. 15, 1929

In consideration of the option hereby attached given me by John

*John's secretary

Monk Saunders, I hereby assign any and all right, title, and
interest that I may have in the aviation story, *Flight Commander*.

(signed) Howard Hawks

In the presence of *Eloise Brandon*
         (witness)

Paper No. 3:

A standard "Assignment of Rights" to First National by co-authors
John Monk Saunders and Howard Hawks of their story *Flight
Commander* for the consideration of ten thousand dollars
($10,000.00). A rider attached as follows:
   The purchaser by its acceptance hereof agrees to give the
undersigned, John Monk Saunders, credit as author of the story on
the screen and in all paid advertising and publicity issued by it or
under its control in connection with the photoplay upon which the
above story is based. It being further understood and agreed that
the undersigned, Howard Hawks, as co-author of said story,
hereby relieves the purchaser of any and all claims relative to
screen and/or advertising credit in connection with said story.

The agreement was signed and dated November 22, 1929.

CHAPTER 15
THE TALLEST, DARKEST LEADING MAN

◆

W ITHIN A FEW DAYS AFTER we returned to California, Merian Cooper asked me to go to his new offices at RKO. He showed me large drawings for a film he was planning: sketches of jungle scenes that were exotically beautiful and then, an astonishing one: the figure of a giant ape climbing up the side of the newly completed Empire State Building.

"You're going to have the tallest, darkest leading man in Hollywood," he said. And even while my thoughts were flying toward the hope that Cooper might be waiting for Cary's arrival just as I was, Cooper went on to point at the giant ape and say, again, "The tallest, darkest leading man in Hollywood." Now my heart was pounding, not about the excitement it would have been to work with Cary but with apprehension. Such a huge animal! Cooper saw my dismay.

"He won't be real. He'll be a small figure that will be created to look this big." His capacity to tease had played out long enough. We walked out to the back lot while he told me something of the story.

The idea had begun in his mind when a friend, Douglas Burden, brought back two giant dragon lizards from the Dutch East Indies and gave them to the Bronx Zoo. Not being able to endure civilization, they died. Cooper had thought about a movie taking two gorillas to those islands and pitting them against the dragon lizards but was unable to interest Paramount or RKO in this project, the idea being considered too expensive in a time of depression. When he learned that Willis O'Brien was doing animation with miniature figures at RKO, he began to entertain the idea of doing a homegrown studio-made movie and the thought of one great gorilla became bigger and bigger. This one would be discovered in a jungle and brought back to civilization—to his downfall. A girl (of course a blond girl) would be part of the discovering expedition. For a while he had thought of Jean Harlow but recently had decided they could put a blond wig on me.

As I listened, I was being captured by Cooper's enthusiasm more than by the idea itself. He had the exuberance of a young boy whose dreams of adventure are forever in the forefront of his mind. I never thought of him as being in any way sophisticated, and that was part of his charm. He created a mood of happy mystery, as though he had ideas too many to tell. He often wore a half-grin that seemed to cover unrevealable secrets. He would sometimes run the palm of his hand over his entire head in a circular motion, as if to protect and contain the notions that were brewing inside. For a prop, he carried a pipe; a prop, I think, because he never seemed to smoke it but would twist the stem from the bowl with a "cracking" sound, then thread it back. His hands seemed not strong enough to do that. They were small and scarred—perhaps from the time in World War I when his plane went down in flames. If I had asked, he would probably have said, "Hell, yes!" This, and "Hell, no!" were often the beginning of his responses. But I never heard him use language rougher than that. He admired his own accomplishments openly and heartily but admired those of his colleagues, too. Praise came easily from him. Too easily, sometimes! He told me about an actress, Katharine Hepburn, who was to be at RKO. "She's good," he said, "not as good as you, but she's good."

We came to a setting on the back lot where Willis O'Brien had established the small figure of the ape in his appropriate habitat. He appeared to be about eighteen inches tall, the entire jungle scene no more than five feet square; I think the whole was covered with glass, as if needing protection from the elements. The little fellow was not frightening at all.

As we walked away from this first introduction to the nameless creature, Cooper slowed his pace, then stopped. "I think I'll call him Kong." A pause . . . and then, "King Kong." There was a ring to that, as though a reverberating tone had been struck on a Chinese gong and King and Kong together sounded enormous— and enormously right. And seemed to go on reverberating.

Cary arrived and came to visit one afternoon, to tell us he and Phil Charig would be staying, at least temporarily, in a court bungalow on Melrose, in Hollywood. Their host, as I remember, was Orry Kelly. But what I remember most was the pleasurable excitement it was to see Cary and the gladness I felt that he was here—would continue to be near.

Another arrival in Hollywood was Edgar Wallace. Because David Selznick, as head of production at RKO, had brought him from England to write for the studio, he thought it likely that Wallace could make a contribution to Cooper's story about the gorilla.

Wallace's diary of the time notes on January 31, 1932:

> Cooper telephoned yesterday morning or rather his sec'y did, to say we were to meet at his place at 8:30. . . . Fay Kay or Kay Fay, a lovely girl, the wife of a Rhodes scholar, the man who wrote *Wings* and *Dawn Patrol* and himself a very charming man, was there."

Cooper's "place" was the Chateau Elysee on Franklin Avenue. There was a gentle, overweight kindliness about Wallace, dark eyes warm with feeling, his roundness suggesting that he probably liked the comforts of home as well as good food; that he felt displaced just now and could navigate his way only by listening. I do not recall that he said anything except with his large dark eyes, which seemed only to wonder about what might lie just ahead.

This sense of "displacement" was recently confirmed to me by Bradley Jones, the son of Dr. Ellis Jones, who attended Wallace. He said that Wallace carried, in his luggage, a square of carpeting that represented England and that he would stand on it to keep a sense of the terra firma of his native land. He fell ill with pneumonia and died only ten days after our meeting. Bradley Jones says he died in their home. And I wonder, now, if his large-eyed silence might have been because he was already beginning to be ill.

The script he had started had little to do with *King Kong*; Cooper has said, "Nothing at all." Soon, James Creelman and Schoedsack's wife, Ruth Rose, began to prepare a script. But I would be doing scenes for *Kong* much before any script would be completed.

Cooper wanted to start making test scenes in the jungle. The word *test* pertained especially to the rear-projection process. It was intended for the "money people" in New York to see. Afterward, it became part of the film. It would take twenty-two hours to make—the longest I ever had to work for a consecutive period of time. A battle scene between Kong and a tyrannosaurus had been prepared by Willis O'Brien for rear projection onto a huge screen. I was placed in a tree alongside the screen. Photographing the two elements together gave the illusion that I was actually seeing the monstrous fight. Cooper directed these scenes. From his vantage point behind the camera, he had perspective and detailed clarity. From my position, all I could see was large blurry shadowy movements on the screen. It was like having the worst seat in the house, too close to define what the shadows were. But I kept moving, kept reacting as though I really could see the fearsome creatures, and would scream when Cooper said, "Scream! Scream for your life, Fay!"

We finished work early in the morning. I, numb with fatigue, having had little time for rest in between scenes nor much of any place to rest; two directors' chairs placed in the corner of the very crowded stage served as a cot—but not a very good one. Anyway, it was a good stretch of work and Cooper was happy and hungry. Dorothy Jordan (who would become Mrs. Merian Cooper) said she was having breakfast at the Brown Derby when Cooper came in and chortled to everyone who wanted to hear. "I've just finished making Fay Wray work for twenty-two hours!" As an actress, she thought rather poorly of that. She says she also had thought poorly of working "with one of your big animals" when Cooper had asked her earlier if she would be interested.

The pattern of work had been established: Animation and special effects would be prepared, then there would be a few days of shooting with me. But never again would there be such a sustained span of hours. Cooper also chortled over the fact that he paid me and the human actors only when we worked. He enjoyed that fact so much, you really had to enjoy it with him. There was no Screen Actors Guild then to tell you it wasn't really a laughing matter. The film took about ten months once they got into this on-again-off-again rhythm and I would be able to do other films while Kong and the prehistoric animals were performing together. I began to believe it was the rumored scariness of Kong that stimulated producers to offer other "scary" movie roles to me: *Doctor X*, *The Mystery of the Wax Museum*, *The Most Dangerous Game*, and *The Vampire Bat*—all these in the same year as the making of *King Kong*. One, *The Most Dangerous Game* with Joel McCrea, had an intriguing story and the added value of being produced by Cooper and made in the same studio with *Kong*.

Cary, quite soon after his arrival, was given a contract by Paramount. If he was in Hollywood, it followed that he should be doing motion pictures, so it was no surprise when he telephoned with the news, a little surprising, that they didn't want him to use the name he wanted: Cary Lockwood. Cary? All right. Lockwood? Too long. They settled on Cary Grant. That wouldn't take up too much space on a marquee in case it ever got there. A little time passed and he called again to say, "I've managed to get your old dressing room." I felt very glad he had wanted to do that. "I will see sunsets on the walls," he said.

John signed a writing contract with MGM. I think the first story they wanted from him was to be about Russia and the new "freedom" for women.

So, if Cary and John and I had a "flop" with *Nikki* in New York, we were all beginning a year of activity in Hollywood.

The interweaving of work on *Kong* with the four other films I made that year, fell into place without conflict. Of the five films, there was a subtle realization that *Kong* was probably the most important, but I'm convinced that was because Cooper was the most stimulating personality. When he approached me, he would beat himself on the chest in the manner of *Kong!* There was a lovely raillery that went on between us. He directed all the scenes that were considered technical and tied to the animation that was prepared by O'Brien.

Scenes in the hand of Kong were considered "technical." The big arm, about six feet long, was attached to a lever so it could be raised or lowered. I would stand on the floor while a grip (and that's not a pun by intention) would place the flexible fingers around my waist in a grip secure enough to allow me to be raised to a level in line with an elevated camera. There was a wind machine to give motion to my clothes, and I struggled to give the illusion that Kong was a fearsome forty feet tall. The more I struggled, the more the flexible fingers of Kong gave way, and when I felt that I was about to slip all the way through, I would call out to be lowered and resecured. Actually, the fear about falling out of the hand was a match for the imagined fear it would have been to be looking up at Kong himself. These scenes were put together with the animated eighteen-inch Kong. I had seen a tiny wooden doll that was carried by the miniature Kong, and when I went to the rushes with Cooper, I thought I was seeing the doll, until she began to kick. Me! Schoedsack did the "people" scenes—on the ship, the arrival on Skull Island, the scenes before the great wall.

Both of these men, Cooper and Schoedsack, gave me absolute freedom to make my own choices, and never made me feel that I was being directed; there were often scenes that were done in one take. For instance, the scene on the ship when Denham is making a "screen test" of Ann was done just once. Heads of departments in studios often got total credit for any work done in the department whether or not they were personally involved. Walter Plunkett, as such, got credit for the costumes, although my clothes were designed by a young woman from New York. I regret that I do not remember her name because there was a rightness to everything she did. The medieval gown for the screen-test scene enhanced the fairy-tale quality of that sequence. And the simplicity of the gown she gave me for the top of the Empire State Building scene had a classic timelessness.

CHAPTER 16
I'M THE BUSIEST ACTRESS IN HOLLYWOOD

◆

W HEN I GOT MERIAN COOPER for a producer-director, I also got a lot of friends that were his friends both past and present. Many were bound together with the ties of shared experiences in World War I, particularly in the air. It is unimaginable that flyers flew in the stuck-together biplanes known as Spads and did battle and survived: Edward P. (Ted) Curtis, Harold Buckley, Denny Holden, M. C. Moseley.

Cooper was a bachelor, then, and had a rented house in Beverly Hills with a tennis court and a tall black butler named William. Cooper didn't drink and didn't urge William's Sunday afternoon mint juleps on anyone—but they were available and helped to create an atmosphere of Southern hospitality. Practical joking gave him delight. When Senator Stuart Symington was a guest, Cooper arranged for a singles match between the senator and one Tom White. The senator won perhaps four games very handily when, suddenly, the power of Tom White was turned into enough straight points to make the senator realize he was facing a master. And he was: Harvey Snodgrass, the tennis pro of the Beverly Hills Hotel.

Katharine Hepburn and her friend Laura Harding were luncheon guests. Katharine wore blue jeans, as though wanting to establish an iconoclastic attitude toward Hollywood glamour. She even wore her jeans on the tennis court! Ever since that time, there has been a steadily increasing appetite for blue denim, until the material must have become sufficient to measure the circumference of the earth many times. Cooper had friendships in the so-called eastern establishment. It was Mrs. Kermit Roosevelt who brought Katharine Hepburn to Cooper's attention after she saw her in the theater.

Douglas Burden and Shirley Burden came on the set while we were making *King Kong*; also the Goodhue Livingstones. Because of Cooper, Jock and Liz Whitney began to spend time in California—and, through Cooper, establish a friendship with David Selznick that led to Whitney's financial interest in *Gone With the Wind*. Liz was a classic beauty, wearing her hair straight back and knotted at the nape of her long and graceful neck, sometimes wearing a live squirrel on her shoulder. Fortunately, she had trained the little animal to run up the draperies wherever she visited and sit on top of the valances, waiting for her departure.

Cooper was beginning to fall in love with Dorothy Jordan and enjoyed pretending that he must be strong and resistant. He beat himself on the chest à la Kong to show he was too strong to "fall." He beat his chest for Dorothy, for Maureen O'Sullivan, and he beat his chest for me. For how many more, I don't know. The three of us, he called "Woos." There was a sense of fun and joy in this tomfoolery. Sometimes, according to his nature, I thought he looked upon Kong as a great big wonderful joke. But I think, too, in a more sentimental way, he must have enjoyed the losing struggle it was "to look upon the face of beauty. . . ."

He had written the "old Arabian proverb" that is at the beginning of the picture:

And the prophet said: "And lo, the beast looked upon the face of beauty. And it stayed its hand from killing. And from that day, it was as one dead."

Doctor X and *The Mystery of the Wax Museum* were both made at Warner Brothers, both in Technicolor, both with Lionel Atwill, both directed by Michael Curtiz. Michael Curtiz was a machine of a person—efficient, detached, impersonal to the point of appearing cynical. He stood tall, militarily erect; his calculating, functional style made his set run smoothly, without humor. He had a steely intelligence and moviemaking know-how that made you feel there was a camera lens inside his cool blue eyes.

Looking through the finder one day at a group of extras, he called out to one, "Move to your right . . . more . . . more . . . more . . . *now* you are out of the scene. *Go home!*" So wicked, it was almost funny.

On location for a beach scene, he paced back and forth in front of a crew and cast who were having the usual cold box lunch. He paced and muttered, "Why should they eat? I don't eat! Why should we be wasting this time. . . ?"

There is a scene in *The Mystery of the Wax Museum* when, in self-defense, I hit the face of Lionel Atwill. His face cracks and falls away, revealing horrible scarring underneath. This couldn't be rehearsed. Only two wax masks had been made. When the mask broke and I saw the repulsively scarred face, I absolutely froze instinctively, wanting not to touch that face again. Curtiz, with his camera-eyes watching over my shoulder, wanted to see the whole revolting visage at the first strike. "You should have kept on hitting!" So we did it again with the second mask. Now that I knew what to expect, I could do it technically.

Lionel Atwill was married to a lady who had been married to General Douglas MacArthur. She often came on the set and seemed a very gracious person, in no way increasing the already military atmosphere.

Lionel and I would march on to a third film, *The Vampire Bat*, at Universal. These films, all of the horror category, were not carbons of carbons except for Lionel and me, and we had the good fortune to add Melvyn Douglas in *The Vampire Bat*. He wondered, I'm sure, what he was doing in such a film. Probably making money, just as I was. It was John's theory that you lost double the salary offered you if you didn't accept a film: You wouldn't get what was offered and, in addition, you would lose by that much, so if you didn't get twice as much as was offered, you *would* be losing twice as much, which amounted to about the same thing, he said.

MGM had abandoned the Russian movie about freedom for their women and assigned John to *West Point of the Air*, about the Air Force training field at San Antonio. "Get a prescription for chloral hydrate from Dr. Fishbaugh and come to San Antonio as soon as your last scene is finished." I knew that meant he'd been drinking a lot.

The Texas sky was a strong blue as the plane I was in approached Randolph Field. Suddenly, all the passengers were alert, looking to the right, to the left. Two smaller planes, one on each side and flying quite close to ours, were causing curiosity and concern. They were open planes and I saw a white scarf and I saw a helmeted John Saunders. He waved; I waved. He wasn't piloting, so he could wave again and again. And then we heard from our own pilot that the two Air Force planes had gone out from Randolph Field to salute us and to escort us. I didn't tell any of the passengers that the escort was for me. But, of course, I knew, I knew!

I stayed for the weekend, meeting personnel and officers and their families on the post and was treated to a ride in the smallest plane I ever saw—no larger than a bathtub—just big enough for two to be seated in tandem. General Danforth, the commanding officer, was the pilot. I sat behind him, and his wide shoulders made me·feel very secure as he did turns and banks. I wished that the capsule of a plane was not enclosed so that I might have been able to feel the rush of air throughout the maneuvers.

The pleasant experiences at Randolph Field offset the concern it was to know that John and an Air Force officer had discovered the joys and the consequent misery of drinking corn whiskey. The chloral hydrate smoothed out some of John's tension. I believe that was the first time I was aware that John looked to Dr. Ernest Fishbaugh to ameliorate the agonies that followed his drinking.

John had found Dr. Fishbaugh through Cedric Gibbons. Cedric was art director at MGM. He was married to Dolores Del Rio, had brought her to his beautiful modern home in Santa Monica Canyon, where, she said, she found for the first time a house filled with light. Cedric himself was the architect. A wide staircase rose from the entrance to turn at a right angle before long windows and reach, on the second level, a large living room. Here was a portrait of Dolores by Diego Rivera above the fireplace. There were built-in lounges and a sense of great space. Dolores's bedroom looked out onto a swimming pool and a sunken tennis court. She said Cedric had sometimes taken Greta Garbo there to play tennis, on Garbo's condition that no one, absolutely no one would even look out the window at her. That was not an easy condition for the proud Dolores to accept and she assuaged her feelings by telling, by talking about it enough so that the Garbo-Gibbons games did not continue for long.

Cedric had built the house when he was a bachelor. He had placed his own bedroom directly under the dressing room designed for "the lady" and had placed a ladder beneath a trapdoor in the floor of that dressing room so he wouldn't have to make visitations by way of the long staircase.

Dolores, to look at, was more than beautiful. She respected her own beauty. Her mother (for whom Cedric built a home next door) called her Angel and made her daughter's underwear herself by hand. Dolores didn't drink (she had once been hospitalized by Dr. Fishbaugh for a kidney problem). But she did keep large bottles of cologne, decanter-size, in her dressing room. She showed me once that one of the colognes was brandy, "just in case." She overprotected her own beauty to such a degree that she did not want to have a child, believing it would spoil her figure. In her case narcissism seemed natural.

I thought of her as the sister I had lost, accepted her as she was, and when she appealed to me to consider the feelings of two of the Gibbons' male friends "who are madly in love with you," I said only no without reproaching her. At another time, she told, with self-comforting pleasure, about her method of revenge for remarks a writer had made to her luncheon table. The talk that day had run to why Gary Cooper had fallen in love with Lupe Velez. The writer had said the obvious—that Lupe had fire, among other things. "You," he'd said to Dolores, "would do well to have some of that." Watching her face, you wouldn't have known that it touched her even remotely, that it mattered any at all. But she made a plan and was content when she carried it out. She succeeded in getting the writer's vulnerable wife to have an affair with one of the ever-present male friends. It didn't matter to her that the writer didn't know. *She* knew.

Considering these ways and what seemed to me her question-able sophistication, it was touching to hear her tell that for her saint's day, she had gone to Mexico and walked to the cathedral "on my knees—for an entire mile!" It was also touching to have her say at a time when she was to feel concern about my soon-to-be labor pains, "I will light a candle for you."

When she fell in love with Orson Welles, she apparently didn't consider just having an affair with him, but thought she must leave Cedric, must get a divorce. "If I don't, I might do some-thing I'll be sorry for." She seemed herself a lady of purity. I went to court with her and substantiated what she said, that she was unhappy with Cedric to the point of becoming ill. "He wants only to talk about sex," she told the judge. She went home with me to where I was living and called Orson. "Well, darling, it's all over." The day following the divorce, a basket of flowers came to me from Cedric. "Thank you," he said.

Before long, in about a year's time, it would be all over be-tween Orson and Dolores. She continued to be beautiful and later turned a corner in Mexico to see and know, with her husband Lew Riley, the pleasure it was to have a concerned caring for chil-dren. She established a foundation for the children of actors, par-ticularly those children who had been orphaned.

On one of her visits from Mexico, we were in New York City, standing on the corner of Fifty-fifth Street and Fifth Avenue. We were about to go our separate ways after sharing luncheon with friends at La Côte Basque. "I am more interested in cultural things, now," she said. I didn't find that cryptic. "I love you," she said. I said that to her, too.

The pleasure of the 1932 Olympic games was heightened greatly for me when I was asked to share Mary Pickford and Douglas Fairbanks's private box. They were "Hollywood Royalty." We drove right into the stadium and stepped from their limousine into perfectly situated seats, where Babe Didrikson won the javelin throw for women only yards away from us and where, among others, Lord Burghley was competing in the hurdles. To see the tired marathon runners come in from their race, handkerchiefs tied around their soaking foreheads, was to look at fortitude at very close range.

John and his friend, David Rose, had become golfing partners with Douglas. We were sometimes invited to the Fairbanks's beach house in Santa Monica on a Sunday. Even at the beach, there was the emphasis on elegance. The table was set formally with handwritten menus before each place. Only Douglas was less than formal, when he shoved a fully dressed Maurice Chevalier into the pool. Maurice climbed out, miserable, glum, looking at his gold water-soaked wristwatch. He was known to be a thrifty fellow and seemed to be very unamused—but not belligerent.

Douglas never went as far as some other jokesters did. There was a Vincent Barnett who acted as a waiter at certain banquets, doing everything possible wrong until the irritation of the targeted guests became explosive and Barnett was revealed to be what he was—a professional heckler.

Another such fellow spent part of an evening at the home of Jeanette MacDonald, trying to anger me with his criticisms of George Gershwin, who, he said, had no talent, copied from others, and so on! His own musicality was just good enough to make you believe he believed what he was saying. Johnny Mack Brown, who was sitting nearby, invited this rascal outside. Louis B. Mayer's secretary, Ida Koverman, a knowing witness, stopped the possible fight by confessing she had brought the heckler along to help make the evening jolly.

Pickfair, the Beverly Hills home of Douglas and Mary, was tasteful, elegant to the utmost, with liveried footmen attending at dinner. On a New Year's Eve, seated beside Douglas, I heard him say, "That's cute!" when he was shown the suckling pig with apple-in-mouth, by a butler who was probably expecting "Splendid!" Later, when all the twenty or thirty guests were preoccupied, he slid out of his chair, went under the table, and crawled the length of it, taking every napkin away. For some reason, everyone, including me, thought this was hilarious.

Perhaps it was this clownishness and ebullience that made me think not too seriously of Douglas arriving at Selma Avenue one morning at the very hour when he was to have been meeting John on the first tee at Riviera. His chauffeur carried in a case of wine. Douglas stood in the entrance hall shifting from foot to foot until the chauffeur placed the Chateau d'Yquem in the pantry. Then he went off to meet John and I was left to think this timing was a little odd.

I had more understanding when I was following a foursome at the Wilshire Country Club. David Rose, one of the four that included John and Douglas, took me aside. "You could have anything you want—ruby necklaces—Douglas is crazy about you. . . ." I would have to tell this to John. What he said, when I told him, was, "It might be interesting for you. Although Bessie Lasky tells me he's not very good. Always in so much of a hurry." I was stunned.

Soon, John told me that Douglas wanted us to join him and the David Roses on a trip around the world. He would want Douglas to pay him $20,000, John said, because he might be able to develop a story for Douglas on the way. If he had said these things while drinking, it would have been possible to discount them. But he was sober.

The changes in John clearly went further than just the increase in drinking. If there were psychologists or psychiatrists at that time, neither he nor I knew of them. All I knew how to do was to attend to him during those times when he had "gone under" and needed "prairie oysters," cold compresses to his forehead, sips of beef consommé, and the attention of Dr. Fishbaugh, who would come with a syringe. Beyond the syringe, the only suggestion Dr. Fishbaugh had to make was that we should go on a vacation together. At the moment of suggestion, that seemed feeble and unrealistic.

And there was the "leaking-roof syndrome." When he was suffering, you couldn't talk about the problem, you couldn't "hit him while he was down." When he recovered, there was no need. Usually, it was about three weeks before recovery came. Apprehension about what the trade papers might have to say tormented him. Sometimes he would just want to walk at night, want me to walk with him. Once, with Michael and Mary, the wire-haired terriers, along, we walked over the Riviera Country Club golf course, the dogs running ahead and disappearing into barrancas, behind trees, then reappearing, their white coats showing in the moonlight. The night was very quiet and the dogs made no sounds. I could only hope that this midnight therapy might make a better tomorrow.

Once or twice, he returned to Bill Brown's at Garrison, New York, to stay for several weeks. For a while after each of those times, he was strong and able to sustain good working habits.

Nikki came from Paris. I never saw her, ever, but I saw numerous cigarette burns on the night tables at a beach house we had rented at Las Tunas. John didn't smoke and I didn't smoke. I asked him about the cigarette burns. Nikki, he said, had gone there with her sister. No sister, I thought. Maybe he loves her.

"Do you love her?" I asked. He didn't answer at once. That means yes, I thought. Then he said, "I don't know."

That surely means yes. If yes is the answer, he must go with her. I would want him to go with her. Then he said, "There is one thing I know for certain. If we were together, we would destroy each other."

Soon after, he showed me a letter from her, describing her marriage in Los Angeles, regretting he had not been at the ceremony, saying she had looked and waited for him until the last possible moment. "Why didn't you go?" I asked. "I was afraid you would make a scene!" Why? But why should he have even thought about asking me to go?

In 1933 and 1934, I was in picture after picture after picture, beginning a new one every fourth Friday—perhaps twenty-three films in all. I had a contract with Columbia for four films a year and did individual films at every other major studio. Having the contract for four films, Harry Cohn's enthusiasm, and the clout implied, I said to my agent as we were leaving that studio one day, "There's a young man over at Paramount I'd love to work with. Please see if you can get him into one of the films with me here."

I hadn't heard yet that Paramount had begun to realize Cary Grant's value, and I thought it might be easy to draw him away for a film with me. With *me*. I would have loved that. But the agent didn't pursue the thought and I didn't push. In general, I didn't push. I did not see myself as a shaper of events. I seemed to have a subconscious sense of destiny and the responsibility to meet that destiny with resilience.

I might have been able to help John Saunders if I had been a shaper of events, a person in charge. In a rather ridiculous way, I tried one night. I was robed and ready for bed and went onto the landing at the top of the stairwell to hear John imploring his secretary to stay for the night. He would make her comfortable "right here on this lounge." The library door was open. His tone was oversolicitous; she uncertain, he cajoling. I would take charge. I went downstairs and told her it was a shame he had kept her working so late and that I would see her home. I ran to the garage and got into my car. She went out to the driveway and into her own car, with me calling out that I would follow and see her safely home. By the time we passed La Brea on Hollywood Boulevard, she did a very clever thing. She called out that she was going to stop at the Gotham delicatessen and get a sandwich.

I was relieved of the assignment I had given myself and turned for home, wishing I had on shoes instead of having to work the clutch and the brake with my bare feet. I had mixed feelings of pride that I had prevented a "situation" and feeling foolish that I had gone so far as to pretend I was concerned only with her welfare. When I got back to the house, I had the sense that John admired what I had done.

But we didn't talk. We never did have reflective time for talking together. Life, when good, was mostly action. He bought me a shotgun and one for himself and we did a lot of skeet shooting. He chartered a boat and we went deep-sea fishing. I waited at home while he went duck shooting and I waited at the nineteenth hole at the end of his golf matches, sometimes as long as three hours.

I began to feel that even if we had had quiet times together and I had talked out my feelings and tried to make him see what I saw his talents and great good fortunes to be, he wouldn't have heard. There is a scene in *Brother Saul*, a novel by the Irish writer Donn Byrne, in which a young bride takes advantage of her husband's silent introspection to tell him the fullness of her feelings, to say what she has long needed to say. Her heart and mind and soul all open, she waits for his response. He shows he has not heard her when he repeats the words he had spoken earlier, that led him into deep preoccupation, that shut him out of the world and away from her.

After MGM, John went to RKO to do two aviation stories. There, a young woman who had been a star in silent films approached him about doing publicity for me. He said she had big, lovely soft-brown eyes and seemed so nice he thought I ought to engage her. I became Helen Ferguson's first client. Helen was in no way flamboyant or contriving in her concept of what public relations meant, and I trusted her. She was a little too much of a nanny, calling at the end of the evening to "tuck each client into bed." But she was sincere and tireless. It was her efforts, as well as the initial success of *King Kong*, that made me the busiest actress in Hollywood. And that was a mistake. There was no selectivity—only commitment to the precept that "If you don't accept a film, you'll be losing double the salary."

King Kong had opened at Radio City Music Hall in New York to good notices (except, as I recall, for *The New York Times*) and two weeks later in Hollywood at Grauman's Chinese. I was very uncomfortable watching the film that night, mostly because of my screaming—Too much, too much, I thought. Before they had started editing the film, I had gone into a sound room at RKO and screamed and moaned and whimpered for several minutes, recording a kind of "Aria of Agonies," so that the sounds could be spliced into various spots as needed. This, of course, was in addition to the screaming that came naturally during the filming. I didn't give much thought that opening night to the why of all that, not realizing that the little wooden doll had to be given life by means of the sounds I made. I was not able to appreciate the splendor of Max Steiner's music, and I didn't believe my eyes when I read in *The Hollywood Reporter:* "Fay Wray brilliant in *King Kong.*" Brilliant? Brilliant meant cerebral! And I didn't realize for many years that *King Kong* had made an enduring impact.

Sometime in the late forties, I was walking on Olympic Boulevard in a lightly trafficked area. Approaching from the opposite direction, a young man stopped about ten yards away. His jaw had dropped and he appeared transfixed. *"King Kong,"* he said, as I came nearer. "You were in *King Kong!*" We exchanged a word or two and as I moved on, the powerful feeling that the film had given him trailed after me; *his* feeling, *his* appreciation, *his* caring. Maybe, I thought, there are others who feel that way, too!

Here I am, a "three-year-old with parasol" smiling at
my future.

My first bit part in Hollywood, at the Century Comedy studio. I
improvise a clown dance and think I'm just wonderful!

At the Hal Roach studio, where I got my first contract and was apparently very happy about it.

As leading lady opposite Glenn Tryon (far right). Left is James Finlayson. This Hal Roach comedy short was directed by Leo McCarey, who would later win Oscars for *The Awful Truth* and *Going My Way*.

At Universal. A fashion photo. I shouldn't be wearing patent-
leather shoes! (Phototeque)

At Universal. Hoot Gibson was a big star of Westerns.

This was the first scene Von Stroheim and I made together. There was a lovely and natural rapport between us. I am fascinated with his intensity.

Flirtation scene. Prince Nicki (Von Stroheim) is on the horse. From left: Mitzi's father (Cesare Gravina), Schani, the big oaf I'm to marry (Matthew Betz), Mitzi's avaricious mother (Dale Fuller), Schani's father (Hughie Mack), Mitzi.

Seduction scene in apple orchard in old abandoned carriage. Thousands of apple blossoms! At Von Stroheim's insistence each one was hand-made!

Wedding day: June 15, 1928. The Paramount publicity department wrote the caption for this photo: *John Monk Saunders, screen author, and Fay Wray, Paramount star, startled the film capital by being married suddenly while the bride was on location at Easton, Maryland, during the filming of* The First Kiss, *in which she co-starred with Gary Cooper. Saunders wrote* Wings, The Legion of the Condemned, *and* Dirigible.

John in Washington, D.C., a few days after our wedding. I
thought him so very handsome!

John (left) with F. Scott Fitzgerald and a still of *Wings*. Fitzgerald was an almost too-beautiful man.

John in a sleigh. St. Moritz, 1935. Photo by Fay.

At a film festival in Montreal. In French, the caption reads, *De
gauche à droite:* Gloria Swanson, Fay Wray, Ingrid Bergman.
(Nothing very gauche about these ladies!)

With Gary Cooper in *One Sunday Afternoon*. Maybe he's asking me to go for a bicycle ride. Gary often napped between takes.

On a bicycle built for two.

It's hard to tell whether Richard Arlen is arriving or departing in this scene from *Murder in Greenwich Village*.

I am a senorita in *Captain Thunder* with Victor Varconi. (Phototeque)

Various moments
in *King Kong*

As Ann Darrow I have to imagine
that Kong is about forty feet tall.

I am being kidnapped and will be taken to Skull Island.

Inset: The natives are about to tie me to two pillars for presentation to Kong.

Bruce Cabot and Robert Armstrong have rescued me, but
the three of us are still scared.

This must have been a publicity
shot. I couldn't have looked this
well-washed after the ordeal on
Skull Island.

The worst is over. But we still have
to get down from the top of the
Empire State Building!

We think we're safe in a hotel room in New York.

We give a Ping-Pong party for stars (movie and tennis). The tennis stars won! I should have known. Sidney Wood once beat me using a carpet slipper for a paddle! From left to right: Fay, Sidney Wood (the champ), Georgia Hale, Charlie Chaplin, Lilyan Tashman (the chicest actress in Hollywood), John Monk Saunders, Richard Arlen, Frank Shields (tennis star), Jobyna Ralson (Mrs. Richard Arlen), and Bessie Love.

Robert Riskin and Frank Capra during the making of *Meet John Doe*, an independent production released through Warner Bros. This collaborative relationship helped raise Columbia to the level of a first-rank studio. *It Happened One Night* swept the Academy Awards in 1934.

At home, Selma Avenue. Now this house is gone in 1988. But the wide pants and halter top are back in style.

My wedding to Robert Riskin, August 23, 1942. From left: Owen
McGivern, William J. Donovan, Judge Ferdinand Pecora, Robert Riskin,
a very happy Fay Wray, Irving Berlin, Ellin (Mrs. Irving) Berlin, David
O. Selznick, and Dorothy (Mrs. William S.) Paley. Bill Paley took the
picture with Dorothy's Brownie camera.

A "Western" party at Pickfair. Seated, from left: Betty (Mrs. David)
Rose, David Rose, John Monk Saunders, Johnny Mack Brown, Fay
Wray, Bea (Mrs. Donald Ogden) Stewart, Gary Cooper, Donald Ogden
Stewart, Countess di Frasso, Mary Pickford, Douglas Fairbanks, Guinn
Williams. Seated on floor: Elsa Maxwell.

CHAPTER 17
SOME ROLES I WANTED BUT DIDN'T GET

◆

I HAD BEEN WELL AWARE that *King Kong* was, to say the least, very successful. But I did not realize then (no one did!) that it was on its way to becoming a classic.

By the time 1969 rolled around, I was certain of its unique place in the history of filmmaking. *The New York Times* asked me to write a piece about it. I wrote it, and mailed it, and the *Times* people were pleased.

By coincidence, I arrived in New York on a Saturday the day before my article was to be printed, and heard the announcement about it over the radio as I rode in from the airport. Bellboys at the Hotel Pierre had heard the broadcast also. As soon as they got the luggage into my room, they rushed to the windows, opened them wide, leaned out, and cried "Help! Help!" A sort of reverse interpretation. We all had a good laugh and the next day they brought me extra copies of the *Times*, with my article, which the editor had titled "The Scream That Shook the World."

Many facts have been told about the making of *King Kong*. The fact that he was created by Willis O'Brien and was only eighteen inches high has been well publicized. His interior was metal with articulated joints so that O'Brien and his technicians could animate him by means of stop-motion photography. It took an artist like O'Brien to make Kong move with anatomical precision—and make him so believable.

There are other facts, not so well known. The film cost about $680,000. And while speaking of money, it seems only right to reveal that I received $10,000. That was for ten actual working weeks, which stretched out over a period of ten months. A further fact is that residual payments were not even considered—because there were no established unions to protect us. The Screen Actors Guild had not come into being.

One day, sometime in the sixties, when I was visiting Ernest Schoedsack and his wife, Ruth Rose, they were letting their lively imaginations run wild with thoughts of how much money each and all of us might have made if we had been paid residuals.

I couldn't let them feel so bad. I had to say something to elevate their (our) feelings. I said, "But if we'd gotten all that money, we wouldn't be the nice people we are. We'd be rich!"

Schoedsack must have liked that and talked about it when he was interviewed for a book, *The Making of King Kong* by Orville Goldner and George Turner. What I said was quoted. It was placed in a box right in the center of a page!

RKO did not have to wait for residuals. Their finances improved immediately and dramatically. It had been rumored, and I believe it to be true, that RKO had been about to go into bankruptcy. I believe it because I had already seen the effect of the stock market crash on the Paramount studio. The movie industry was not in very good shape.

King Kong saved RKO from bankruptcy! When I write that now, it makes King Kong seem less like a movie character than an individual who came to the rescue of a studio where he had had the pleasure of working.

And so it always seems about Kong: that he is a very real and individual entity. He has a personality, a character that has been compelling to many different people for many different reasons and viewpoints. He has been thought to have religious significance; to have sociological importance; to be a kind of King Lear.

I don't know what the rules are—or even if there are any—about when a film gets to be considered a classic. But *King Kong* had certainly reached that status in 1975 when it was honored by The American Film Institute as one of the fifty most favorite films ever made. There was a reception at the White House before clips from all the chosen films were shown at the Kennedy Center. When I came before President and Mrs. Carter in the receiving line, the President kissed me on the forehead. At the theater, I was not required to do anything except stand up and take a bow. There was a beautiful amount of applause. On that night I gave credit to Kong for being one of the better public relations men (individuals) of all time.

Most of the pictures I made at Columbia were B movies—with Jack Holt, with Ralph Bellamy, with Victor Jory, with Richard Arlen. B movies are budgeted for less money than the really big ones and made in a limited amount of time. After doing a film at Fox with Spencer Tracy, and knowing that he was going to Columbia to do *A Man's Castle*, I tried to shape events by talking to the writer Jo Swerling, and asking him please to help me get the lead in that film.

It had been the greatest pleasure working with Spencer. Nothing of the story of *Shanghai Madness* stays in my mind; his honesty as an actor, does. No nonsense, no pretension. I wanted so to complement his realities that I wore no makeup. Without having a light summer tan and without the artistry of the cameraman, Lee Garmes, I might not have been able to do that. At the close of the picture, Spencer wanted my photograph, and I signed it with the same words Cary had chosen when he signed a photograph of himself for me: ". . . with my utmost admiration." And we both hoped that I would be in *A Man's Castle*.

The very next night, John and I went to a nightclub. Spencer was there, standing at the bar. I stood about two feet from him and said hello. He looked at me but didn't know me or, apparently, even *see* me. It would be a few years before Katharine

Hepburn would take charge and rescue him from his vulnerability—and keep him from drinking.

I didn't get the part in *A Man's Castle;* Loretta Young did. A real romance developed between Spencer and Loretta. So Spencer had already turned away from his wife, Louise, before he met Hepburn. Louise had my admiration for the acceptance speech she made when Spencer won his first Oscar—sixteen words: "Thank you for Spencer, thank you for Susie, thank you for Johnny, thank you for me."

Another role I wanted and didn't get was Maria in *Lost Horizon.* Maria was a terrific role because she is the first woman who falls in love with an outsider and wants to leave. When she does leave, she turns into the ancient woman she really is . . . only in Shangri-la is there eternal youth. I would have liked to see myself, through special effects and makeup, turned into an ugly old hag. I wanted that challenge. I wanted it so much that I approached the writer who was preparing the script from the James Hilton novel just as he was about to enter a court at the Beverly Hills Tennis Club. His mind was surely on his tennis game. My mind was on Maria. I told him, after introducing myself, how much I wanted that part. He stood, patient and kindly, holding the gate open with one hand, tennis racket in the other, just as pleasant as could be, not showing that he mentally had a foot inside the court. He said yes, he'd be glad to talk to Frank Capra about me. And then I let him go. There you are. We let each other go. He went through the gate and I went back to a chair under an umbrella and thought about his quality: charmingly objective, a lighthearted dignity, an intelligent easiness. I thought he might really see the rightness of me playing Maria, and he'd surely tell Frank. I don't know whether he did and I never asked him because by the time I got to know Robert Riskin really well, it no longer mattered. The actress who used only Margo as her professional name played the part of Maria. She was lovely.

With Gary Cooper again at Paramount, I was delighted to have a bad-girl role in *One Sunday Afternoon.* Gary had changed somewhat, talking more, thought to be influenced by Countess Dorothy diFrasso, who came on the set quite often.

When Dolores Del Rio told me that Gary had gone to their house to ask Cedric Gibbons for the hand of his niece, Veronica Balfe, it was surprising on two counts: He appeared to be rejecting the high-society life that Dorothy's wealth and ways had drawn him into, and he was being more proper and formal than one would have expected. Veronica (Rocky) had gone to California only a few months earlier. At first, she had stayed with Dolores and Cedric and then found an apartment of her own. She was stunning, sleek, eyes the same gray of Gary's eyes. She had a "bit" role in *King Kong*. She leans out a hotel window in New York, sees Kong, and screams. She asked my help. "Imagine that you have to get help from someone who's at least five blocks away. You've got to make them *hear*! Imagine!"

They lived, after their marriage, in a house in Beverly Hills that Jascha Heifetz and Florence Vidor had gone to after letting John and me buy the Selma Avenue house. Then they built a modern home on Saltair Avenue in Brentwood. Gary seemed happily married.

If George Raft had been the mean, Mafia-related man he was reported to be, he might have saved me from being slapped too many times in *The Bowery*, a film with him and Wallace Beery and *little* Jackie Cooper. Cooper was so beguiling, his lower lip pouting out, that I wanted to hug him whenever he came near. George Raft, when he was supposed to hit me, couldn't bring himself to strike *hard*. Raoul Walsh, the director, wouldn't give up until it was right, which was after about twenty takes and twenty slaps. I was very much aware of the fact that George Raft didn't want to strike me, but after twenty takes, I wished he had felt belligerent right in the beginning. He said to me later, in the most gentle way, "You're the kind of girl a man would want to have for a wife."

Darryl Zanuck produced *The Bowery* and had thoughts of several more films for me. He announced them to the newspapers first, before asking me into his office to talk about them. One with Clark Gable; one with George Arliss. I was excited about them. I was not excited about Darryl. When he suddenly tried to embrace me, I pushed him away and left his office and went to tell Helen about his overtures. His decision to cancel those particular roles for me was not surprising. But we weren't enemies and I did another film, *The Affairs of Cellini*, for him. He wouldn't be so foolish as to make the same kind of approach until many years later.

Below the Sea, at Columbia, with Ralph Bellamy, a pleasant little adventure film, never became famous except for an incident that was to entertain the industry. Somewhere at sea between the mainland and Catalina, the director, Al Rogell, thought a romantic moment between Ralph and me could benefit pictorially if seagulls were seen in the background. Accordingly, the property man strewed crumbs along the rail behind us. The camera started, a cloud of gulls came down, cleaned the rail, and were off. The second take, swoosh—the same. Now Rogell's patience was gone and he shouted, "Send the seagulls through one at a time!" He really did.

An exception to most of the B films at Columbia was the quality of *Ann Carver's Profession* with Gene Raymond. The marriage-in-jeopardy that is created by the wife having a full-time career—a script written and adapted from his story by Robert Riskin—had more insight and humanity than most. Harry Cohn made much of the fact that I was playing the *title* role. He invited me to his office to tell me the importance of that. And to tell me he saw himself, now that his studio was rising to a "prima classe" level, as playing an international role. It was his intention to visit Mussolini before going on to England to supervise a Columbia production. His wife Rose, "she's my ambassador," would join him. He would like me to go, too. He was euphoric, not waiting for a response from me. He was spinning a story about himself—a tough kid who had achieved a dream. He never mentioned the trip to me again. But he was happy that day.

A bizarre circumstance during the filming of *Viva Villa* in Mexico caused that film to be recast and the recasting to include me.

In Mexico, one of the actors, Lee Tracy, had stood naked on the balcony of his hotel and urinated onto the crowd below. A scandal! The MGM picture produced by David Selznick had to be taken back to Hollywood, with David salvaging what was possible but certainly finding a sober actor for the Tracy role. I never learned why he wanted to change the leading lady or how many more of the cast that was headed by Wallace Beery as Pancho Villa. When he telephoned to say he wanted to make a test of me, I seriously objected, not liking tests. He said, "You will have to be awfully bad not to get the part." David was a straightforward person. You could believe him.

When I think of *Viva Villa*, I think first of the velvet richness of the black-and-white photography. One of the great cinematographers, James Wong Howe, made it a beautiful-looking film. In spite of the troubled history of its production, the film was nominated for an Academy Award, which testified to David's tenacity and his relentless interest in quality. I think of him as being the sum of each picture he made, so total was his caring and involvement. He plunged his whole personality into whatever he was doing. Because he was awkward physically and imprecise, you had the impression he might stumble over his own eager feet. But there was a strong intelligence that sifted by trial and by error and by copious preparation. He was credited with being the producer of *King Kong*, but he was not (except as executive producer of RKO) and he, himself, said his only contribution was to see to it that Merian Cooper got the money. He never did go on the set. At that time, he had enough to do keeping RKO afloat, and he also had the judgment and discretion to know that Cooper's *Kong* had to be just that—and something apart.

I might have done another film with David. I tested (Tests! He had to have them) for *The Prisoner of Zenda*. I think I failed that because I made an awful mistake the night before: I took one of John's sleeping pills. Of course, during the test the next day, I thought I was just fine, feeling serene and floaty. But there's one thing I *know*. Every pore of one's body has to be clear and healthy to perform well. John Cromwell had directed the test. David told me afterward that Cromwell had thought I was not sufficiently *in* the scene. I believed David even though I was, just at first, wanting to think that his decision had something to do with my not letting him embrace me when he first talked about *Zenda*. But David was not a devious person. If he was troubled by my rejection, he wouldn't have gone so far as even to do the test. Some people didn't like to work with him because of the unpredictable hours he kept and the unreasonable demands he made on their time. But all of his films had the mark of David: They were generously conceived and generously produced. He was in no sense a little man.

One evening at the Selznick house, the conversation after dinner concerned romantic relationships. Scott Fitzgerald started it, flinging out his view that no woman west of Omaha had the ability to *feel*. David took it out of geographical context into his belief that the higher the intelligence, the more rewarding the sexual experience. For instance, that must be true, he thought, for Laurence Olivier and Vivien Leigh. I made no contribution, just listened, but I like to remember within the steamingly physical preoccupation of today, that David was right.

As a practical joker, David was never in close competition with Merian Cooper, but he gave Roland Young (Uriah Heep in *David Copperfield* and later *Topper*) a hopeless chore at a party, when Roland, with champagne bubbles diffusing his sight, believed that I was Merle Oberon. Because Merle and Marlene Dietrich had recently been at odds and Marlene was present, David took advantage of Roland and asked my cooperation to let him plead with me to make friends with Marlene again. He believed he was doing David a favor, doing the whole world a favor. "Please, Merle, please . . . for David's sake . . . for the sake of everybody . . ." David stood by as "producer" of this charade. Then they both went off, they said, to make the same plea to Marlene.

Costume parties were a great fad in Hollywood. At one "turn-of-the century" party given by Freddie and Florence March, David found what seemed to be his ideal costume, going as Teddy Roosevelt in his Rough Rider's uniform, fortunately finding a balcony over the festive garden scene where he could make periodic appearances shouting, "Charge!"

If I could have had his company, looking just like that, one evening in the fall of 1932, it might have saved me a miserable confrontation over the coming election, Roosevelt versus Hoover. John was solidly a Democrat. My mother's Republicanism made me loyal to her views. We were at a restaurant in Culver City, where we had met after a working day. I had arrived at voting age but couldn't vote because I hadn't yet become an American citizen. That fault, in John's view, simply compounded the wrong it was to champion the Republicans and/or Hoover. He may have been right to get up and leave. I had never learned the art of debating in school and was probably just as stubborn as I thought my mother would have wanted me to be. We each had our own car, but I had no money and had to promise the restaurant owner, who was remarkably understanding, that I would come back and pay him the next day. When I arrived home, John's car was in the driveway but he was nowhere in the house. I got a flashlight and searched through the garden, around the tennis court, and finally found him crouched behind shrubbery, a half-empty highball glass in his hand.

Even while making an average of one picture a month, there was time for other things; for example, to sit in on the first meeting, at the home of Florence and Frederic March, when the idea of a Screen Actors Guild was proposed. Robert Montgomery was the *voice* that night; to go to Mines Airfield (where Los Angeles International Airport is today) to see aerial acrobatics performed by a German, Ernst Udet, whose handling of his biplane was so delicate that he could pick up a handkerchief from the field with a hook secured beneath the wing. The hook appeared to be no more than twelve inches long. I wondered at his skill, not knowing that he would later go to see John in our hotel room in Munich as a representative of Hitler's Luftwaffe.

There was time to cooperate with the Los Angeles police when an extortion letter arrived. A threat to kill my mother unless a packet of money was placed in a vacant lot about two blocks from our house required the performance of the request by me. Plainclothesmen watched from positions nearby. John went up on the hill above Hollywood Boulevard, carrying binoculars. I flung the packet into the lot and drove away. A car followed; a man got out and retrieved the packet. As he climbed back into his car, the police reached him in time to keep him from grabbing a Luger automatic on the seat beside him. There was drama here, more than I knew.

The young man had gone to high school with my oldest sister. They had thought themselves in love. He had come from an affluent family in Salt Lake City. This turnabout in behavior of someone my sister had cared for was painful to consider and reflected for me the complications attached to being at all well-known, the unfortunate influence it could have on an apparently normal young man. But I hadn't known him well and never would. I was glad he didn't go to jail. The mayor of Salt Lake prevailed (I was told) and he was returned to his family in that city.

The earthquake of 1933 was no less or no more shattering. Our house leaned to the south, leaned to the north, but cracked not at all. When it happened, I was just climbing out of the tub: I flung one of John's overcoats around me and ran out of the house. Then it was over. The same evening, at an Actors Guild meeting at the Writers Club, we all saw chandeliers swaying, the sign of aftershocks.

Following another disaster, John wanted an aerial view of a devastated Los Angeles when the whole area was flooded in 1934. He chartered a small plane and we saw all of the city looking like a great muddy tub with toy houses showing their roofs. We flew a ring around this sea of mud and went home with me wondering whether he had seen what he was looking for.

There was time to go to parties. Jessica and Richard Barthelmess gave a memorable one with Paul Whiteman and his band filling one side of the tennis court that had been converted into a ballroom. Hoagy Carmichael didn't go, but he was within hearing distance and he wrote about the sounds of that summer evening in his memoirs, *The Stardust Road*. "That horn! Bix

(Biederbecke) was in there that night. They all were. They were inspired. I'll never hear 'Rhapsody in Blue' like that again. I hope God was listening for there was beauty there that night."

Another great musician was there that night. Jascha Heifetz didn't play a note but he had a small triumph. In the corner of the tennis court, away from the music, he beat me at Ping-Pong— which he had long been wanting to do. And he said, laying down the paddle that had polished me off, "Now I will ask you to dance." Moving back to the music, we whirled and whirled until I saw the Italian cypresses that lined the outside of the court as one solid green wall. Slavic supremacy!

Randolph Scott was far more gentle as a dancing partner. At a formal evening, he said, "Cary is in love with you." They had become friends and were sharing a house and, I supposed, confidences. Whatever the music was that was being played became "Stardust" for me at that moment.

John's need to be at the ocean made renting beach houses mandatory. At Playa del Rey, the writer Frances Marion and the director George Hill had houses side by side that we rented alternately. One summer, James Kirkwood, Jr., who wrote the book for *A Chorus Line*, visited George, with his mother, Lila Lee, and repeatedly threw his volleyball over the wall so that he could keep going to our house to retrieve it. That is his memory, not mine.

Mine has to do with John evidently working well in cooperation with ex-aviators Harold Buckley and Denny Holden, friends made through Merian Cooper. They wrote, they sunned, they drank. They had the secretary oil their tanning backs. They ate. Our cook and butler provided good food and service. I went to work in the early morning, loving the ride in an open car and the look and smell of clear, clean blue sky.

As their work progressed, the drinking kept pace. Once in his cups, Harold Buckley needed only the telephone to keep him company and in touch with friends at far points around the world. The longer the distance, the better. When I came home one night, I knew he wouldn't be able to drive himself home, so I called his wife, whom I had never met, to ask her to come for him. She came in while he was conferring with someone in the Middle or Far or Near East. She was firm, she was threatening, she was victorious. But only after she had raised a bottle over his head in the manner that Jiggs's wife Maggie used to raise a rolling pin in the funny paper. That gesture, from a lady who looked as if she was the very essence of finishing-school conservatism, was impressive. She had courage. Later on, she would show that she had initiative and enterprise. The Buckley School is one of the more successful private schools in California.

Of Cooper's friends in the group of ex-aviators, the steadiest and the most responsible was Edward (Ted) Peck Curtis. He seemed to bear no neurotic burden from his flying experience in World War I. He was married to a woman of great good humor. Agnes went with Ted and her children to their home in Beverly Hills in the summertime and returned to Rochester, New York, in the fall, where Ted was an officer of Eastman Kodak. He was that company's representative to "Hollywood and other foreign countries" as Agnes put it.

CHAPTER 18
SOME PEOPLE BEHIND THE CAMERA

♦

T HERE WERE VERY FEW DIRECTORS who had a gift or talent
that placed them beyond being just one of the crew. Crews in
themselves were a unit of energy and resourcefulness and inge-
nuity with a most supportive attitude toward the making of a film.
They knew, I think, which takes were good. *They* knew about the
talent and character of every person attached to the film. *They*
didn't want the leading lady, if they cared for her at all, to be
crude or tough or vulgar. *They* didn't want to have to keep a
Thermos of vodka standing by for insecure actors who depended
on their secrecy. *They* established unspoken rules and created an
atmosphere of caring and responsiveness that has sometimes
made me wonder why some actors from the theater think that
when they are in films, they are without an audience.

The best directors were those who did not feel an immediate
responsibility to a boss, to the "front office," who didn't work
from a precut pattern but from their creative guts. That was the
excitement of moviemaking. The unexpected, the spontaneous

could happen. And it took a leaping intelligence to stimulate and
to know that.

Karl Freund, who had done some extraordinary camera work in
European films, had immigrated to America about the time of the
filming of *All Quiet on the Western Front*. He was often on the set
during that production. It was he who suggested to the director,
Lewis Milestone, that the ending of the film had to be quiet,
"quiet as a butterfly," which led to one of the most exquisitely
sensitive moments ever put on film.

Madame Spy was a B picture made at Universal, but it *felt*
better than that, because it was directed by Karl Freund. He had
the advantage of having worked on some of Universal's bigger
productions and the experience of having lived through the war in
Europe. His was a full and mature personality. He and his wife
were warm and life-loving.

At the end of one working day during the filming of *Madame
Spy*, instead of going directly to the beach house, I stopped at
Selma Avenue to get something, perhaps some bathing suits.
Going into the darkened driveway, I saw a limousine and a driver
standing beside it. I recognized him as someone who had often
chauffered us.

"I wouldn't go in there, if I were you," he said. My key was
ready. I unlocked the front door. I saw a woman's purse on the
hall table. I heard John's voice calling down from the second
floor, "Don't come up here!" I looked up and saw him at the rail
of the second-floor landing, naked except for a towel held across
his pelvis. I walked through the hall and into a far dark corner of
the dining room. In a few moments, through a lighted archway in
the upper half of the dining room wall, I saw the secretary who
had been working at the beach come down the stairs. I almost felt
sorry for her, being so suddenly turned out. I sat in the corner of
the dining room the rest of that night. It was early morning when I
saw him and heard his reasons and his conviction that it was vital
for us to embrace to overcome the rift that otherwise might happen. The rift was there, anyway.

It was difficult for me to know a day or so later, whether it was good or bad, that Karl Freund would be directing me in a crying scene, a scene in a muddy trench. The crying came too easily. John didn't *have* to do that! He had never been denied!

In a few months the secretary married and her husband sent John a threatening letter, claiming he had been deprived of her virginity, his marital right. Bodyguards were engaged.

By now it was autumn. As the guards sat in and around the house, eucalyptus leaves fell and swirled and made crisp sounds under their scrunching footsteps. There was an arid feeling in all directions.

At Universal making a minor movie, *Cheating Cheaters*, with Cesar Romero, I asked my stand-in, Hazel, who had been with me since *King Kong*, to bring me some sherry. I drank it and felt sorry at once and even frightened that I had imagined it would help me through a working day. No one else seemed to be aware of what I had done. But *I* knew.

John and I went to a costume party given by Countess diFrasso. Cary was there. I was glad he didn't see John when it was time to go home. John had unbuttoned the blouse of Mrs. Frank Morgan and was examining the lacy pattern of her well-filled brassiere. Neither of them seemed aware there was anyone else around.

Work itself was a panacea. There was *The Richest Girl in the World* at RKO, with Miriam Hopkins and Joel McCrea, directed by William Seiter, who was born understanding laughter. There were several pictures at Columbia, two of them with Victor Jory, whose energy and high spirits were infectious. He had been born in Alaska (it was rumored he had a dash of Indian blood). He had a belligerently exciting style. The belligerence, he said, was something he had had to learn to control, having brawled too often, too easily, when he lived in the Yukon. He and his wife had performed the play *Ramona* together for many seasons and had been a part of Gilmore Brown's company at the Pasadena Playhouse. He understood theater but not in the way it was understood by Leo Bulgakov, who was directing us. Leo analyzed everything, even the manner in which a doorknob was to be turned, investing the action with sensual implications. Harry

Cohn must have noticed in the rushes that all was moving too slowly, and we found ourselves with a new director, that same Al Rogell who had asked that the seagulls be sent through one at a time. There was a contrast in direction, to be sure—one from the Stanislavski school; one from just growing up with the movies.

There were better examples of just growing up with the movies than Al Rogell. There were John Ford, Frank Capra, Willy Wyler, King Vidor, and von Stroheim, among others, who achieved a high art without benefit of a background in the theater. They just went ahead and made movies with the life-force that was in them, the instinctive understanding of interaction between human beings.

I took Hazel with me when I went to New York to do a film, *Woman in the Dark,* with Ralph Bellamy and Melvyn Douglas. In June, New York without air conditioning was difficult to endure. We worked at a studio uptown; stuffy, hot; we returned to the Pierre, which, with all its beauty, couldn't provide a restful night, the heat making it almost unbearable to be covered by a sheet.

The producers invited me to the Baer–Carnera fight *outside!* A grateful experience to be in the night air.

Hazel was restless, or rather, Walter Daniels, the company manager of *King Kong,* who had fallen in love with her, was restless for her to return. Long distance was very expensive then, the basic call about twenty-five dollars. But Walter called Hazel. They talked. I called John. He couldn't talk, he said. Hazel was quick to realize why. "But he could put his shoes under my bed, anytime," she said.

While in New York, an extortion note arrived at the Pierre. So-and-so-much money was to be placed in the corner of a men's room at the Waldorf. I notified the studio. Joseph Schenck and Howard Hughes and a man who represented the city of New York arrived. None of them sat down, the meeting having a sense of urgency. Howard, all in summer white, altered his stance a lot, as if trying to secure a base that would accommodate his height. The man from the City was short, tough. He would assign a bodyguard, he said. Joseph Schenck, always benign, called soon afterward to ask me to the theater. Before the curtain went up, he wanted to know, "Do you love John . . . or are you *in* love with him?"

"Both." I would think about the possible difference later.

There were only two passengers on the return flight to California: Hazel and I. The solo pilot had but one leg, which made him seem a worthy veteran. The thunderstorm that had caused every other passenger to cancel didn't trouble us much after we broke through the early turbulence, and we arrived in temperate California in time to begin *The Affairs of Cellini*. That film had a fine cast: Fredric March as Cellini, Constance Bennett as a duchess, Frank Morgan as her rather foolish duke. It was based on the play *The Firebrand* by Edwin Justus Mayer.

The Darryl Zanuck production was beautiful and lavish. I loved the sixteenth-century Florentine settings and the opportunity to play a dumb model to Freddie March's Cellini. The usual fault was made: Pretty, pretty, pretty. My Angela should have looked like a stray.

There was more than the average amount of waiting between scenes. Gregory La Cava, who directed, had a penchant for rewriting, for wanting to develop scenes peripheral to the script, to improvise, which he did at less than lightning speed. Constance Bennett had her own demands, which included being the first to leave the set each day. Louis Calhern, who played a nobleman, objected. When the film was presented at the Chinese theater and all of us went, his speech to the audience ran: It had been a pleasure to work with (naming each in the cast), ending with "That is *all*." He was satisfied, having pointedly left out Constance Bennett's name. But I'm not sure the audience got the point. I heard no gasps.

A party at the home of Ernst Lubitsch was a fateful night for John. He hit Herbert Marshall, who was known to have a wooden leg. He wrote about this to a friend, John Wheeler of the North American Newspaper Alliance, in response to a request for the inside story. His counter request to Wheeler was that it be kept in confidence. Remarkable for that time (or any time), Wheeler honored John's wishes. But now, finding a copy, because it tells so much of John's "rationale" and because the evening probably affected all events in his life thereafter, it follows here:

October 26, 1934

Dear John:

Thanks for your kind letter and interest in the imbroglio.

I have been ducking fights at Hollywood parties for ten years but one finally caught up with me. As a ball-room battler I hope I have made my first, last and only appearance.

On account of your being such a cordial and helpful friend of mine over a period of years I am going to give you the low lowdown for your own information. You might file it away because it may assist your interpretation of future events.

The story in a nut-shell is this: I was born in lawful wedlock in Hinckley, Minnesota November 22, 1897. Herbert Marshall, a visiting English actor, called me a bastard in the presence of guests at the Lubitsch party for Max Reinhardt. I smote Mr. Marshall on the chin. Mr. Marshall hit the deck. In the uproar which ensued many interesting and imaginative versions came out.

Now here is the back-lighting: Marshall is married to Edna Best, and Gloria Swanson is married to Michael Farmer. Both Mr. Farmer and Miss Best are in England at the present moment and in the meantime Mr. Marshall and Miss Swanson have been playing house together. I don't know whether these facts are known to the public in general, but they are common knowledge here in Hollywood.

At this point you may be able to detect a faint taint of adultery surrounding the episode. One of the reasons why the fracas was unfortunate is that it served to bring the public's attention to an irregular situation just when Hollywood is putting on its bright Sunday morning face for the clergy. But, of course, all this is none of my business. It only helps to explain the events leading up to the tragedy.

Around mid-night Fay and I and Gloria and Bart left the Lubitsch party to play off a ping-pong match at Gloria's house, Lubitsch having no table. On account of Fay and I are the best, it was decided that Gloria and I should play against Bart and Fay. Gloria and I won the match, whereupon the ladies retired to powder their noses and Bart and I sat out in the garden and polished off a glass of brandy together. At this point everything seemed serene and I was not at all conscious of the heavy undercurrent of resentment which was rising in Mr. Marshall's breast.

It seems that the criticism to which he has been subjected in England for leaving his wife and running off with Miss Swanson has made him hyper-sensitive. They have both adopted a sort of two-against-the-world attitude.

My only theory for his behavior lately is that he either suspected something in the past between Miss Swanson and myself, or anticipated something in the future. If my theory is correct he was wrong on both counts.

At any rate I was quite insensible to any ill feeling when the ladies rejoined us and we returned to the Lubitsch house. We sat down together at a table in the Games Room downstairs which has a bar and a dance floor. Bart and Gloria sat together on the wall seat, whilst Fay and I sat at opposite ends of the table. Someone came along and took Fay away to dance, whereupon Myron Selznick sat down in the empty chair.

At this point Mr. Marshall suddenly began a startling disquisition upon my character and conduct, insofar as it related to Miss Swanson. Myron Selznick, who is a battlescarred veteran of countless Hollywood parties, (Selznick vs. Barrymore) and (Selznick vs. MacArthur), looked at me in some amazement. I listened with considerable interest to everything Mr. Marshall had to say. It was both illuminating and instructive. Emboldened by my non-resistance Mr. Marshall pursued his remarks further and ventured a few plain and fancy insults.

No retaliation being forthcoming (Mr. Marshall having a game leg) he branched out into a few choice curses and then in a voice which reached all ears round about he pronounced me a bastard. What happened immediately thereafter is history, not particularly heroic history, but at any rate history.

In order to reach Mr. Marshall I had to upset the table and poor Myron Selznick was buried under a barrage of glass and chinaware. He has been asked by practically everybody for his account of the fight but he stoutly maintains that he was under the table at the time and was, therefore, deprived of a proper view.

The crash brought everyone in the vicinity to their feet, including Mr. Marshall, although he maintains that he was seated and looking in another direction at the time.

I wonder if anyone believed that Mr. Marshall was looking in another direction when he called me a bastard? I also wonder how I could have clipped him on the chin if he was turned away from me and, I am still wondering how he wound up at full length on the dance floor from a sitting position against the wall. However, these are merely academic ponderings on my own part.

I was, of course, instantly sorry the moment I had hit him, but nothing could have checked that punch. I have often wondered what would happen if anyone looked me straight in the eye and called me a bastard—and now I know. The reflex is automatic.

There was, of course, a hell of a to-do right away. One of the funnier angles is that Fay was the first to fly to Bart's assistance. She cried, "Oh, Bart, what happened! Who hit you?" Bart said, "John." Fay said, "I'm so sorry!" and Bart replied, "I'm sorry too. I love John. I want to go to him."

However, any reconciliation at the moment was made impossible by Miss Swanson. She flew about in all directions in a furious display of hysterics and dramatics and generally took charge of the situation.

Since nothing could be accomplished whilst feeling was running so high, Fay and I departed. This, mind you, was only a little past mid-night. At five in the morning the telephone began ringing like mad. Mr. Marshall, who was now all steamed up, was on the other end of the wire and insisted that I make a public apology and contribute $500 to charity.

I declined both invitations. As I have heard nothing from Mr. Marshall since I imagine that the offers are still open and that I may take advantage of them at any time.

Now, this was a very special and exclusive party and the carefully selected guests who were present might well have kept the incident under cover, so to speak.

On Sunday noon, however, the reporters were climbing the eucalyptus trees on my front lawn. Under threats, duress, and with the aid of grappling hooks I was persuaded to present my angle of the brawl and by Sunday night the goddam thing was being shouted from the street corners. I never felt quite so silly. Later that night the London papers began to call on long distance.

By this time I had begun to feel that I had precipitated an international incident; that I had affronted Great Britain; and that diplomatic reprisals would certainly ensue.

By now I was pretty well worried and retired to the beach and organized a Brain Trust to lend me council and advice. We decided to talk to the London *Dispatch*, and so I bet I was torn limb from limb in England.

After all Marshall has a fine war record I understand, and he and Edna Best were, prior to their split-up, tops on the stage in London.

There are two schools of thought on the subject: one, the first, is that you must not under any circumstance strike a cripple, the second school holds that a cripple must not take advantage of his disability to insult others without fear of retaliation. As a matter of fact, however, neither school of thought had any influence upon my behavior. The instant the fatal words were spoken I reacted.

Nobody seems to know to what extent Mr. Marshall is disabled. He handles himself so well that no one who isn't aware of his disability would detect anything missing, particularly a leg.

Those friends of Mr. Marshall who rushed to his defense and attempted to place me in a bad light by calling attention to his missing member found themselves in a puzzling position. They could not broadcast the fact that Marshall is a cripple without damaging his usefulness as a leading man. The more they dwelt on his disability the more they destroyed the romantic illusion with which lady fans surround their screen heros [sic]. It seems that the gals like for their male stars to be sound in wind and limb.

None of the Los Angeles papers betrayed Mr. Marshall in this respect. I think Walter Winchell was the only newspaper man to describe Marshall as a "one-legged man." A statement which, although written in defense of Marshall, was more injurious to him as a screen idol than it was to me for having struck him.

Thus far there have been no serious repercussions. I trust that the affair has been laid away in moth balls alongside the other Hollywood episodes. It may come to life when the sparks begin to fly in the four-cornered divorce suits, if any.

I would have written you much sooner but the truth is that I received an emergency assignment from Warner Brothers to have a shooting script completed for Kay Francis by the first of

November. This has kept me fairly dizzy night and day and I have fallen behind in my personal correspondence. How is the syndicate business?

I hope to see you sometime this winter. Fay and I have been working steadily for a couple of years now without any holidays whatever and we are about to break loose anytime now.

Many thanks for your continued interest in me and my misbehavior.

I beg to remain,

Cordially yours,

JMS:L

Mr. John N. Wheeler
247 West 43rd Street
New York City, New York

The very significant thing John omitted in that letter is that, following the Ping-Pong, when we returned and sat at a table in the games room, John placed himself immediately next to Gloria and began exploring her décolletage. Not wanting to be an observer, I stood up and left the table. None of them seemed to notice. Herbert Marshall must have been forbearing, because it was several moments before I heard a crash and ran back to see the table overturned and Bart Marshall on his back on the floor. I knelt beside him. "I'm sorry he did that," Bart said, "I love John." That gentle remark belies any thought of his having been nurturing a resentment over losing at Ping-Pong! If, as John said, he called him a bestial bastard, it was surely not with vitriol but, rather, kindly, as a statement of fact. Ernst Lubitsch joined the scene and got on one side of John and I on the other and we helped him to the car, I saying all the while to Ernst, "I'm so sorry, I'm so sorry." Gloria telephoned that Bart had a gun and was on his way to our house. But as she continued to talk and to lecture on the enormous difference in the drinking style of Europeans and Americans, I sensed that Bart was probably beside her. A man who could say what he said about John would not be out with a gun. He probably didn't have one.

CHAPTER 19

~~~~~~~~

OH, TO BE
IN ENGLAND!

◆

I HAD ACCEPTED AN OFFER for two films in England with Gaumont British. Cary sent me orchids to wear on the way. I arrived at the Dorchester Hotel on the day that Princess Marina of Greece became the Duchess of Kent. The procession following the wedding came along Hyde Park beneath my window—a lovely sight in an otherwise gloomy day. By four o'clock in the afternoon, the sun had nearly disappeared.

Fog seeped through into the studio at Shepherd's Bush; and the photography had a softness that I suspected was fog-formed rather than the effect of gauze over the lens. In the freight-sized elevator going between the various levels of stages, I sometimes saw the unforgettable shape of Alfred Hitchcock.

Jack Hulbert, the star of the film, had a distinctive profile, a chin as long as a ski slope (that's unfair), but it was long and an important asset to his comic style. I saw no one who reminded me of Ronald Colman or my other English friend, Cary Grant. I did see a film, *The Eagle and the Hawk,* that was made from a story John had sold to Paramount. Cary was in it. He was wonderful! I cabled him to say so. But there was a gentleman of distinction in the film I was making in England. Ralph Richardson honored this whodunnit, *Bulldog Jack*, with his meticulous performance of a detective. And he told me about restaurants and places to go when John arrived.

The pace of production was extremely slow. I spent long hours waiting in my dressing room. My maid went out each day to get the only available lunch for me, plaice, potatoes, and brussels sprouts. I visited Westminster Abbey and came out, grateful for a rain that washed away the heavy feeling of walking over famous names. My spirits weren't lifted when I went for a walk in Hyde Park and saw a woman dragging a reluctant, howling little boy by the hand and heard her threaten him with "If you don't behave, I'll have Fay Wray get King Kong after you!"

Most evenings at the hotel I had French lessons from an English lady. I went to Covent Garden with John Paddy Carstairs, a friend of John's who had been a writer in Hollywood. And when John was due to arrive in England, he asked to go with me to meet the boat.

John's agent had arranged for him to do a story for Alexander Korda about the history of flying, beginning with Blériot's flight over the English Channel; he also negotiated for him to do a film for Howard Hughes about dirigibles, which was to take him to Germany to see Hugo Echner. The director of *Bulldog Jack*, Walter Forde, kindly arranged for me to be free to go to Southampton to meet John's boat.

John Paddy Carstairs and I looked up from the dock to see a very unsteady John at the ship's railing. He appeared to be in terrible shape, and although dressed for disembarking, was not likely to do so without our help. We went aboard and found him back in his stateroom. His girl companion was in slightly better form than he. As they sat on the edge of the unmade bed, she was urging him to sit up straight.

On the boat train to London, he needed champagne. He rebuked me for saying I had to go to the "can," shocked by my vulgarity. He slept well enough at the hotel that night to be ready for a cocktail party the following day. I accompanied him to meet friends he had made on the boat, but I saw only the backs of most of them through heavy cigarette smoke. I engaged a nurse to help him through a recovery so that I could go back to the studio.

What is known at a hotel is known by reporters. Ernest Betts of the *Sunday Express* came to call on us to tell us something I have never taken time to verify: Attempt at suicide is a crime in England. It had been fortunate that John already had a nurse in attendance when he cut his wrists, even though slightly.

When he was well enough, we went to Oxford, where he had not been since getting his degree. There were only caretakers about; all the students were away on holiday. He was able to locate his former digs; he dressed its barrenness with memories of pictures hung on the gray stone walls and a fire going. Just now it was cold and no more than a sizable cell. The green yard before it was surrounded by the wall he had often climbed in the early morning after a night out. We walked through the magnificently paneled common rooms of Magdalen College and along High Street without stopping in any of the pubs. He was a person healing.

In London, people rented launches along the Thames in order to view the Cambridge–Oxford boat race. We took John Paddy Carstairs along and a hamper of food. We could hear the coxswains call as the boats went by, but the boats were barely visible through the fog.

Clearer days opened some beautiful scenes of the English countryside. Jimmy Dyrenforth, who had written the lyrics for the musical, *Nikki*, took us to Knole Castle in Kent for a weekend visit with his friends, Lord and Lady Sackville. The crenellated construction of the castle with seven courtyards, 52 staircases, and 365 rooms was not awesome to us because our hosts lived in one wing that had been made warm and comfortable with central heating. Lady Sackville was American-born. As Ann Meredith, she had been in the theater. On Sundays, paying visitors were shown through the castle that had belonged to Queen Elizabeth I. But we were not aware of them as we sat in a drawing room looking out onto a deer park. In the evening, candlelight glowed from silver sconces on red-brocaded walls, a background that

contrasted keenly with the American jazz records that Lord Sackville enjoyed. Everybody danced.

Douglas Fairbanks arrived at the Dorchester with the David
Roses and the lady who had resolved his restlessness, Sylvia Ashley, the willowy English blonde who had come a-visiting to Hollywood as Lady Ashley and who was to marry Douglas. We all
spent a day together at Sunningdale Country Club. A clear day.

John felt ready to go to Germany to interview Hugo Echner
about the dirigible film for Howard Hughes. I would be free for a
few weeks before my next film. For the first time, I would be
seeing Paris and Munich and Berlin. The pleasures had to be
earned, it seemed, just by crossing the English Channel. Rough!
We stayed at the Claridge on the Champs Elysée. We had lunch
at the Tour d'Argent and at Maxim's. There, ladies in large hats
were eating oysters. It was wonderful how the hats stayed on as
their heads tilted back to let the juices from the oyster shells flow
into their open mouths. It was also wonderful to hear John speak
French to the waiter. "Du beurre, s'il vous plaît," sounded like
poetry. He took me to the Musée de Cluny, wanting me to see a
chastity belt that he found fascinating. This little bit of education
in the ways knights of the Middle Ages constrained their ladies to
be faithful when they were absent made me uncomfortable. What
torture it must have been to wear that metal contraption!

We went to the Folies Bergère. During intermission, John took
me next door, where a woman who looked like the one who ran
the brothel in *The Wedding March* took us into a room where
about a dozen nude girls were waiting in a line. John said I was
supposed to choose one. I pointed at a girl who looked a little bit
shy. Then John was supposed to order champagne. In another
moment, we were in a large room where the shy girl and another
girl were pretending that they were boy and girl and making love.
It seemed just awful and terribly sad. Two miserable mechanical
creatures. The big lady came to say it was curtain time again in
the theater. John should leave more money for champagne. As we
went back to the theater, she called after John, "Champagne,
champagne!"

The Père Lachaise cemetery was a part of Paris that John loved. You had to walk up a little rise to come to the tomb of Oscar Wilde, where Jacob Epstein had sculpted a man, winged, in horizontal flight, arms thrust forward, knees flexed, genitalia pendant. Although the wings were more than two-thirds the size of the body, no flight was possible, John said, because the genitalia held the figure earthbound. We walked down the rise and came to the tomb of Heloïse and Abelard. Here, too, was tragedy. John retold the story of Abelard's love for his young pupil, Heloïse, of Abelard's castration by order of her uncle. He retold the legend of the heart-shaped stones. A little path of them lay around the tomb inside a fence so low it was easy to bend over and select a few. When he found them, he gave some to me, exchanging his for mine while saying, according to the custom, "No harm shall come to our true love."

We had been in our room in Munich only a short time when Ernst Udet arrived, as though the wind had blown him in, full-bellied and red-faced. He talked about Hitler, his own plans for the Nazi Luftwaffe. He seemed a pleasant fellow but too gross in size to have had the finesse we saw him use as an aerial acrobat. He had come to arrange a meeting for John with Hugo Echner.

In 1935, there was a euphoria about Hitler. "You must see the beer hall where the Putsch took place." "There is an order that every citizen should fast one day a week. That's good for the common cause." "It's too bad you weren't here in this hotel yesterday. Hitler was here. You just missed him." There was euphoria—and there was fear. We had a guide as we drove about the city; he explained and re-explained that he wasn't Jewish. His family history had been searched. He knew he looked Jewish. But, he assured us . . .

I had to return to London for a second film, *The Clairvoyant*, for Gaumont British. John remained in Munich. Claude Rains was the star. He was intensely interesting as a mindreader whose wife (me) assisted him in performing for gullible audiences. When he predicted, to his own surprise, the winner of the Derby and realized that he had genuine clairvoyant power, he lost the security he had known as a phony performer.

My costumes were designed by Joseph Strassner. He took his fitter to the Dorchester, sending long-stemmed red roses in advance of each appointment. His attention was memorable.

From the south of France, John sent a request for money, wanting to extend his vacation there. Newspapers had reported an avalanche in the area. I wanted to believe that was why and wired the money with: "C'est l'avalanche, n'est-ce pas?" He responded, "Oui, c'est l'avalanche!" Our meanings, as it turned out, were different. When he returned, we found a flat in Grosvenor Square, and he found a doctor he could "depend upon." It was time for me to return to California to finalize my citizenship.

Simpsons on the Strand, with its paneled walls and shining silver roast-beef carts, was a comfortable and traditional atmosphere where John and I lunched one day. "Why don't you go back to California and divorce me?" The words had all the weight of "Why don't you pick up a *Times*?" I was sure he didn't mean it.

At the captain's table on the U.S.S. *Washington*, an Italian I had met at parties in Hollywood sat next to me. After a few nights when the gala evening meant formal dress and dancing and champagne, I answered yes when he asked whether he could take me to my stateroom at the end of the evening. When he wanted to return the next evening, I said no. This sophisticated person had no way to understand the enormous guilt I felt for having shared part of a night with almost a stranger. John's frequent infidelities were clearly not a passport for my own. I didn't try to explain. No was enough then and again when I got back to Selma Avenue. No over the telephone was enough.

I met Cary for lunch. I felt a little awkward, shy, uncertain. This was our first meeting just together alone. Perhaps we talked about each other's careers. Perhaps. I'm certain only that we talked about nothing personal.

The episode on the boat propelled me to the realization that I needed someone to love. If John couldn't accept the love I had to give, then a child would. John cabled that he wanted to rent our house to Tanis Guinness, who would be arriving in Hollywood. She was of the Guinness stout family, and John considered her "top drawer." I left the house about one hour before her arrival, after I lighted the lamps and put fresh flowers everywhere.

On my return to England, Mildred, our Swedish maid, went with me. We crossed this time on the *Europa*, a very large liner that left me in a more obscure position—not invited to the captain's table. John met us at Southampton. I hoped I looked fresh, perfect, infinitely attractive to him. I wanted to make up for my indiscretion.

We were invited to dine at the home of his doctor. On the piano, there was an eleven-by-fourteen photograph of John in a crystal frame, the only photograph in the room. It was inscribed to the wife of the doctor: "Avec mes sentiments les plus tendresses." As was often the case in London, this house included the doctor's office, but the living quarters appeared to belong more to John than to him.

Jack Buchanan was a matinee idol. He could sing, dance, look elegant, and was handsome (a little like the Prince of Wales). The film I made with him was *Come Out of the Pantry*. He had a light touch but was seriously methodical in his work. We went together to a formal luncheon attended by some members of Parliament, who were that day addressing their speechmaking to motion picture production. One expressed concern that the British industry was drawing too much upon Americans. Jack Buchanan quickly pointed out my presence, bringing forth an apology.

After that film, I took the opportunity to go to Sweden. It was a chance to see the lake country that I had learned about from Nils Asther when making *Madame Spy* with him. Mildred's Swedish would help. In the province of Dalarna, she and I walked in the woods, stopped for cold buttermilk at farms, picked raspberries and blueberries, ate filbunke (a kind of sweet yogurt), took the tiny boat through lakes and locks from Stockholm to Gothenburg.

On returning to London and to the flat in Grosvenor Square, I found a note that John had forgotten to tear up. In a scrawled, tormented handwriting, it said, "I need you." He had been having a bad time in spite of the attention of the doctor and his wife.

A second film with Jack Buchanan was produced by Herbert Wilcox, who arranged the very best contract I ever had. It was totally uncomplicated, not a "whereas" or "in the event" or any kind of legal phrasing. All on one page, it stipulated salary and billing only. Jack, of course, was to have billing over me. When the film, *When Knights Were Bold*, was finished and was about to be shown in Piccadilly Circus, Vincent Sheehan had come to town. He and John and I were en route to dinner at Boulestin's in the Strand. I saw workmen putting up lights on the huge marquee of the theater, my name on top of everything. I knew that was wrong but I enjoyed my dinner thoroughly. I had never had a French red wine before: Nuit Saint George. A lovely nuit for me! By the time we passed the theater on our return taxi ride, my lovely nuit was over. Jack Buchanan's name was up there where mine had been. I wondered if he, too, might have been dining in the Strand that night!

Just prior to making that film, I had been called to the Home Office and questioned for having said, when I returned to Sweden with my new American passport, that I wasn't planning to work in England. Once it was understood that I hadn't known about the second film with Jack, the gentleman interviewing me said, "We would like you to have a British passport." I replied, "But I've just become an American citizen!" However, he said, "It's quite natural, you living 'out there' and being married to an American. We would like you to have a British passport, as well."

My British passport has only one entry. It was stamped in France on December 19, 1935. I was on my way to meet Dorothy and Merian Cooper in St. Moritz. Cooper had phoned. "Come on over! We want you to spend the holidays with us," his tone, as usual, exuberant. John chose to remain at Claridges, where we had recently moved, and to join us for Christmas.

Herbert Kalmus, his wife Natalie, and their publicist, Margaret
Ettinger (the niece of Louella Parsons), were on the train. They
would be staying at the great Palace Hotel. By contrast, the little
hotel that the Coopers had chosen was beguiling. They could accommodate about thirty people only. The young manager did the
cooking, ran the dining room, and invited us to watch him ski
jump in the afternoons. Coop and Dorothy and I sat by the fire
before dinner, having sherry. Dorothy didn't say that pregnancy
was her reason for not joining Cooper and me when we raced
through trees down to the village below. The winner was the one
who could come out onto a meadow first, claiming victory, and
then get in line to be taken back up the hill holding on to ropes
behind a horse-drawn sleigh.

The Engadine Valley was more stunning from our vantage point
at the Villa Suvretta than from the Grand Palace. A full moon
made skiing at night on a road in front of the little hotel quite
easy. I could safely go alone.

John telephoned me to buy him ski clothes for his arrival.
What a disaster! He took them back to the shop and got plus fours
instead of ski pants, long hose to show the shape of his legs in
light gray tones instead of chocolate brown, and a yellow knitted
band for his head instead of a cap. He was, understandably, not
satisfied with the Coopers' choice of modest ski slopes, either. I
tried to keep up as he went to higher ones. He made it down just
fine. I took off my skis and carried them.

By midweek after Christmas, he was back in London. Dorothy
and Coop and I went to Malloja Kulm for New Year's Eve to a
mountain restaurant that is supposed to look over four countries.
At night you couldn't tell. What you could tell was that the
cheese fondue and the hot mulled wine were very good. We sent a
cable from there to Ted and Agnes Curtis.

At a Hotel Palace dinner with the Kalmuses, I felt ill and had
to be excused. Natalie took me up to their suite. I didn't tell her I
thought I might be pregnant.

An evening or so later, the Coopers and I visited Anthony Fokker, who had invented the Fokker airplane used in World War I.
He had a chalet above St. Moritz with a panoramic view of the

valley. He showed Coop and Dorothy and me his invention of electrically controlled curtains that he could open to let all the sweep of the valley lie before him, or he could close the drapes to make his living room fireplace-cozy. When he had closed them and he and the Coopers were sitting by the fire, I went to the phone and called John to tell him I thought I was pregnant.

"What the hell is that to me?"

I went out onto the balcony and looked down into the valley and asked whatever forces might be there or in the sky above to give me the power to hate him.

If I never succeeded in doing that, I did achieve a sense of detachment and independence. Friedrich Nietzsche was a help to me. Discovering his writings in a little bookshop near our villa, I learned that he had often sat on a huge rock that we saw through our dining room window, so that he and his philosophy seemed an actual presence.

Mildred's voice over the phone from Claridges was concerned and troubled. Not for John, but for herself. He had been trying to persuade her to leave her maid's room and spend her nights with him.

I told the Coopers I was departing but not why. As I sat in the train waiting for the engine to start, I saw the two of them come sliding along on their skis through the sparkling snow, searching the windows to find me and to give me a going-away gift of a delft-blue bottle of kirsch, a shimmering sign of affection.

In London, a Harley Street doctor John had recently been seeing, asked me to go to his office. He was thinking of reporting John's former doctor for the amount of medication he had been giving him. I had no idea of the seriousness involved, had never before heard any of the doctors express a similar concern, and told this clearly well-meaning man that I was pregnant and leaving for California.

"Why do you want to have a child with this man?"

"I want a child for myself."

As soon as we were in California and I found an obstetrician, I asked him the question: How much could a child be affected by the drinking habits of the father? "Not at all," the good doctor, dean of obstetrics at the Good Samaritan, told me. "The child lives in the mother and is entirely sustained and affected by her."

Then began several months of serenity, interrupted by making one film. Columbia was preparing a lighthearted little drama for me and Chester Morris, *They Met in a Taxi*.

Harry Cohn had a way of conducting several meetings at once. If a group was conferring with him, he suspended exchanges with them and let them listen to the secondary interview. There were several producers in his office when I told him that I thought I shouldn't do the film and why. Everybody in the room had something to say. It wasn't going to be a major production; the filming would take approximately six weeks and if I wasn't showing even slightly now, the film could surely be completed before my pregnancy was noticeable.

In a day or so, Harry Cohn wanted to see me again. This time there was no one else present. He looked across his desk at me, tears falling from his large blue eyes and running down the corners of his sloping mouth. "I never had a child. I want to give you something. There isn't a perfume you can name that I don't have in back of those curtains." He turned and pointed to printed drapes strung on wires at the rear of his office. "Name one."

"Moment Supreme." He wasn't likely to have that. He went behind the curtains and came out with a large bottle of Moment Supreme.

The director of the film was Al Green, a combination of rough-tough-gentle, easygoing style and a sense of humor. When newspapers printed the story of my "expecting," he bought enough copies to have the story pinned like a blue ribbon on the chest of each person in the cast and crew.

Dolores Del Rio returned from a trip to London with gifts from John, which she gave to me as we lunched together. A charm bracelet with a "15" in baguette diamonds and an exquisite head of Queen Nefertiti. "She has eyes like Queen Nefertiti has eyes," John had once said of me. Dolores had dined with John. "Why," she asked, "are you having this child?"

"Because I have no idea of leaving John for another man but I do need someone to love."

Irene Selznick sent me some of her maternity clothes, including a few that had been given her by Norma Shearer. Maternity shops were unknown in those days, so resourceful designing was a key to looking smart. Rocky Cooper, impressed that I still appeared slim at six months, said she was inspired to have a child, and Maria was born to her and Gary within the following year.

It was late July when John wrote that he would be returning. Soon a telegram came from Nassau in the Bahamas, where he had decided to stop for a vacation. Would I join him, bringing along my Leica?

Nassau was humid. Hurricane lamps in the hotel's dining room were smoky with neglect. There was a lazy, torpid atmosphere. John had the hotel pack a picnic lunch of sandwiches, and he rowed us in a dinghy under a clean blue sky across to a small island. I was wearing a two-piece bathing suit and obliged him by removing the top and letting him take pictures of my now well-enlarged breasts. He seemed satisfied, finally, with the size and shape of them.

He was less satisfied to find me awake at three in the morning the night before we departed. He had spent the evening saying good-bye to friends. His judgment that I had intentionally stayed awake to embarrass him made me believe that his saying good-bye was not to friends, plural, but to friend, singular. He was mistaken to think it mattered.

CHAPTER 20

~~~~~~~~~

SOMEONE
TO LOVE

♦

S EVENTEEN DAYS IS A LONG time to stay in a hospital after a
delivery. Although the obstetrician said it was an ordinary
garden variety birth, the nurse whispered that it was not.

A highly recommended young pediatrician came to see Susan
Cary Saunders (the name chosen by John). As he was leaving the
room after reporting to us, John said to him, "We will not be
needing you."

"Why did you say that?" I had liked the very bright, slender,
redheaded young man. "Why did you tell him that?"

"He's a Jew."

The nursery was exquisite—too lovely, according to Sylvia
Fairbanks, who came to inspect it. This childless lady said the
floor should have been covered with linoleum instead of the
woven white-cotton rug. But it would have been hard for anyone
to disapprove of the English nurse who came to care for Susan.

It was delicious to be in the house again. I had no interest in
work and was dismayed to hear the explosive anger of Harry Cohn

when I told him I didn't want to go to San Francisco for the opening of one of his films. How recently his weepfulness!

With the approach of the football season, Helen Ferguson brought an eleven-man "team" to the front lawn and took pictures of them holding me aloft as their mascot. It was a joy to see some of them—John Wayne, Pat O'Brien, and Johnny Mack Brown— turn their backs on the photographer and sprint across the lawn to get a look at Susan as she was wheeled down the driveway in her perambulator.

It was not easy, at first, to know whether Susan's arrival was exciting to John. He talked about some day "wearing her on his arm at Longchamps." For me, her arrival meant that I would have less and less concern for him.

When he talked about leaving and going to join Hitler, allowing Hollywood "to stew in its own Jews"—a remark he borrowed from a certain conservative male star; when my few jewels disappeared and he answered my concern with expressionless silence; when he sat across from me at dinner, the pupils of his eyes large and unseeing, his movements unrealistically slow; when he completed the sale of an adjacent lot and asked me to endorse the check, holding it down so that I would not know the face amount, I felt only numbness. When he sprained his ankle, it was the cook, not I, who went upstairs to wash away the pain. Throughout the progression of his problems, I was no help to him, wanting only relief.

Yet, when he left for a trial separation, there was a gnawing misery, a vacuum. Half of me was gone, even though I had wanted it that way. Perhaps if there had been a crisis, a confrontation, all the resentments expressed, the problems faced, it would have been acceptable.

The insidious march to separation reached a climax about fourteen months after Susan was born. John found a beach house north of Malibu. He put a large BEWARE OF DOG sign on the gate. Susan and I went to spend an afternoon with him. He took charming photos of her crawling through untrodden sand, leaving patterned furrows in her wake. She took a nap and so did I, lying face down in my bathing suit. I was awakened by a sharp sting in my right buttock. John was withdrawing a needle. He left the room quickly. I sat up on the edge of the bed, feeling a blurry sensation as though my body were made of absorbent cotton. He had never done such a thing before! I suspected he wanted me to share in his own experience so I could be more understanding. But if this was the feeling—just a nasty, fuzzy, uncomfortable feeling—why would he want it? Why would anyone want it? The fuzzy feeling cleared very soon, but the puzzled feelings were to grow and grow.

Sometimes I used to think of him: You can't mean what you're saying, you can't mean what you're doing. You can't mean that you want to "live dangerously and die young." You're brighter and better than that. And it was the same that "day of the needle." He couldn't have done that! I took Susan home that afternoon, deciding it would be best not to go to his beach house again.

Every evening, my youngest brother, Victor, came to keep me company, teaching me cribbage, using a well-crafted board of his own making. Waiting time: waiting for John to come to some resolution for himself about his future. It was not possible to guess what that might be and it's only guessing, even now, to think that that future was being planned in great bizarre detail. But I did not just stay home. I went, occasionally, to parties, one of which is unforgettable. "Unforgettable"—who wrote that song? Joan Whitney Payson gave a party at a mansion-of-a-house in Bel Air. George Gershwin was there, and when we were introduced, he asked me to dance. After a few moments he said, "I see something in your eyes I have never seen before."

"What is that?"

"Truth."

Nothing could be said after that. We just danced, while I looked at his slim aesthetic face, his dark, burning eyes. Unforgettable!

In the meantime, my mother had accepted word of John and my separation without any of the high anxiety I had expected. It is odd, in retrospect, that when I went to talk with her, we both remained standing. There was not that cozy confessional feeling of being seated closely together—where, perhaps, arms around one another, my unhappiness, as well as hers, could have been exorcised. It was as though she took it for granted that any or all marriages could come to this. She probably reserved her feelings for her solitude. I have never seen my mother cry, but she may have done so.

In a few months time, she became very ill. Sitting beside her bed, listening to her ramblings through a fevered delirium, I heard her talking of a time when she had been happy—before she had been married to anyone; a time she had often delighted in telling about: her pride in having gone to the university; in having been the best sidesaddle rider in the county, wearing a blue velvet habit and a plumed hat. She remembered herself as being slim and very stylish, daring enough to have her red curly hair trimmed to a perky shortness; her skin white, her breasts "full and firm and standing straight out—before nursing all my babies had broken them down"; her exhilaration in having traveled with her father to Washington, D.C., and to San Francisco to the World's Fair. And she recalled those actors and actresses and singers she had seen and heard in the Salt Lake City theater, infusing me with the excitement she had felt for them. That was the beautiful time of her life. I'm sure she loved her children, but as a compensating force for what she felt to be her largely tragic life. Her name, Vina, given to me by my father as a first, though unused, name, was one she had not wanted for any of her female children. To her, it was synonymous with tragedy and sorrow.

Now, after a few years of some relief, tragedy was sweeping her up again. Vina Marguerite Jones had been a thrilling person. Vina M. Wray, although, most of the time, my beloved mother, had torn and talonized my feelings often enough that I wanted to put her back into that earlier time. When she died, I was able to do that.

A few years before, she had gone to visit her brother in Arizona and had been given a front-page interview in a Mesa newspaper. She had this to say: "One of the greatest weaknesses in the modern home is the mother's lack of ability to sense a child's particular talent. At an early age, I saw that Fay's tendency was toward dramatic work and I at once set about to cultivate it. I do derive a great deal of joy from the fact that Fay has made good and when the occasion demands it, I do not hesitate to take a modest bow."

Oh, yes, Vina Marguerite Jones, oh, yes!

CHAPTER 21

SUMMER THEATER AND SINCLAIR LEWIS

♦

W HEN, AFTER SOME WEEKS JOHN returned to Selma Avenue, he seemed much better. He was enthusiastic about my accepting an offer to do summer theater in New England. My agent, Leland Hayward, would tell me later that John, in fact, had proposed the idea to him. If I could have known that, known anything at all of the plan he was formulating, I would not have gone to Cohasset, Massachusetts, in that summer of 1938.

Instead, I was glad to be in the theater, glad to have almost daily letters from the nurse about Susan's activities, and to have letters and photos of her from John. In Cohasset, I was in the play *George and Margaret*, a light comedy, and it helped to accelerate my feeling of freedom.

Sinclair Lewis, whom I had met earlier at a dinner party in Hollywood, was preparing to act in his own play, *It Can't Happen Here*. He was unattractive in appearance—tall, gangly, and skeletal, his narrow face pockmarked, his teeth and fingers yellow from smoking. A small amount of hair justified the nickname "Red." He had fallen in love with the theater and saw it as a fresh life experience. He was enchanted with the cast of his play—Flora Campbell and Barry Sullivan among others—and with all the young people at Cohasset.

When I left Cohasset, letters from him followed me, then he followed, arriving at Saratoga when I was preparing to do *There's Always Juliet*. I could admire Lewis, admire his brilliance and the mind he, himself, defined as "chained lightning," but I wouldn't want him to come near me or touch me. When he convinced the theater's director, Harold Winston, that he should play opposite me in the romantic comedy by John Van Druten, a wave of desperation came upon me. It was Ethel Barrymore who pulled me out from under by saying to Red, "Good God, are you serious? Do you think you can convince an audience that this woman could fall in love with you? Think of the audience—think of Fay Wray and all she went through in *that film!*"

It was Alexander Clark who reported this. He should have known. He was asked to come from New York as quickly as possible to learn the long role even more quickly so that we could open on schedule. Lewis, who told him how Ethel had dashed his hopes, stayed on in Saratoga and began to write a play that *would* be suitable for him and me. At first he called it *Romeo Is Fifty*. It was to be about a young girl falling in love with an older man. This, too, had problems for me. But he persevered. He retitled it *Angela Is Twenty-Two*, and continued writing and eliciting my help. Mostly, what I did was to suggest thoughts that would develop dramatic structure and/or visually interesting moments. Dialogue was no difficulty for him. He could make people talk!

Howard Hughes went to Saratoga, too. He stayed with Jock Whitney. Herbert Swope, who was also a houseguest, told me later he and Jock had saved me from a "fate worse than death." What they didn't know was that I had already had a romantic evening with Howard.

In July Howard Hughes had returned from a record-breaking flight around the world to be welcomed by a ticker-tape parade in New York. On the Sunday following, he went to Herbert and Maggie Swope's home on Long Island to escape reporters, to find

a refuge. He went into the solarium at cocktail time. He looked
weary, his white shirt rumpled, blue serge trousers held up by a
leather belt that was tied in a knot, the buckle missing. There
were whispers among the women. Maybe they were saying, "Here
is a hero; here is an eagle who circled the planet only a few days
ago." Maybe. Or maybe, as he thought, they were critical of his
appearance.

He asked me to step out to the terrace, and said, "Do you know
these people very well?"

"Not very well."

"They will kill you."

In their chalk-white dresses and summer tans and jewels, they
looked fashionable and sharp, but sharp-tongued, too, and I
thought maybe he was right to be uncomfortable.

The Swopes had invited me for the weekend knowing I was to
do a play at a theater nearby. Howard was at the stage door more
than once that week, driving me back to the Pierre, talking before
we said good night about his own personal disappointments, remembering times when he had seen me waiting overlong outside a
golf course and had stopped by the car to chat. He hoped, when I
had finished the present play, I would go for the weekend to his
friend Sherman Fairchild's, also on Long Island.

"No. I would have misgivings about that," I said.

A large box of gardenias—perhaps a hundred blooms—came
to the Pierre. In his strong handwriting, the card read, "No more
misgivings."

I went up to Cohasset to see *It Can't Happen Here*. Before I
went, Howard telephoned to say he knew my return train would
stop briefly at Stamford, Connecticut. He could meet me there
and take me across the Sound to Long Island. "You don't have to
worry, there'll be a chaperone."

It was about four on Sunday afternoon when I stepped off the
train and saw Howard hurrying toward me. "Am I glad to see you!
Reporters are following me. If you get back on the train and go to
the Pierre, I'll phone you."

When the phone rang at the Pierre, he asked me to take a taxi
and go to Thirty-fourth Street and the East River. "I'll be wait-

ing." He was—in a small seaplane—so small that his knees were almost under his chin. We flew not far above the water. (Did we go *under* the Fifty-ninth Street Bridge?)

We landed on a small lake and walked a short distance to the Fairchild house, where there was a group including Sherman and his aunt (the promised chaperone). At the end of the evening, she took me to my room. Before I turned off the light beside the great four-poster, a door at the far end of the room opened. Naïvely, I was surprised to see Howard. Realistically and emotionally, I knew I was not going to send him away.

At Suffern, New York, where I went next to do *The Petrified Forest*, he phoned. "Don't forget, there are ties that bind." At Suffern, too, Jimmie Fidler, a CBS Radio news-about-Hollywood commentator, phoned. There had been a wire-service story about the meeting at the train station. I admitted nothing. "You be a good girl," he said.

Before I left Suffern for Saratoga, Howard called. "I will be there, come hell or high water." But when he arrived in Saratoga, his host, Jock Whitney, called me in mock anger. "What are you trying to do to this poor fellow?" And Jock contrived that we should meet only at his house, and in the afternoon to watch a tennis match.

Helen Ferguson said John's reaction to the train station story was to call Los Angeles newspapers and tell them Howard was building a house for me on Catalina Island. They checked with Helen; John's story wasn't printed. But when I did see John next, he did not mention Howard—only Sinclair Lewis.

After Saratoga, I was invited to take *There's Always Juliet* (with Alex Clark) to Matunuck, Rhode Island. In Alex's Buick (with a maid and my wardrobe in the jump seat) we drove through the Berkshires. Red Lewis soon followed, continuing his work on *Angela*.

At Matunuck, a telegram came from my sister Willow. "John left this morning taking Susan with him, no one knows where." Then I learned that John had sold our lovely house to a producer at Paramount for cash (a roll of bills) and sold the entire contents of the house to an antiques dealer. He had mortgaged his mother's house in Seattle.

John's brother, Edward, was a physician in New York. He would know, surely, where John and Susan were. Over the telephone his wife said he had recently had a heart attack and she couldn't disturb him. If she learned anything, she would let me know. I thought she did know "something."

Sinclair Lewis followed me to New York. He walked with me in Central Park, tried to distract me with talking about the development of *Angela*. He lived at the Plaza Hotel, where he had now started feeding what he had written into a typewriter, hunting and punching at great speed while his ashtray piled higher and higher.

Ed Saunders's wife said, "John and Susan are at the Westbury Hotel. You can go there at three this afternoon." Susan came running to me. They were in a sizable suite and I was grateful that Susan was being cared for by a motherly nurse. When John went out, the nurse said she was puzzled, believing from what John had said that she would meet a dreadful person. I had my trunk brought over from the Lombardy, where I had been staying. There would be a lot to talk about if we could come to that point. We never did.

Leland Hayward's office said Columbia wanted me for a film. I felt I must do it; money was the only reason. John had taken every cent, every asset away. I had no thought of asking him for anything. I had his assurance that he would wait there, at the Westbury. Susan had a good nurse and a good pediatrician who was a friend of Dr. Edward Saunders. As soon as I arrived in California, I telephoned. They were already gone, leaving no forwarding address—even for his brother. My trunk had gone with them.

I went to my "second home," the Château Elysee. Second home? Now, *only* home. The Los Angeles district attorney was in touch with me about the question of whether the auctioneers had misrepresented the sale of furnishings and personal things by taking items of their own to the house to be sold as mine. For reviewing that, the district attorney promised to be in touch with Tom Dewey, district attorney in New York, to obtain his help in looking for John and Susan.

The picture at Columbia was a B film. Harry Cohn scolded me for not looking well: "Your face is your fortune." He stopped me in the parking lot. "I've never heard one word of gossip about you. But now you've gotten yourself talked about because of Sinclair Lewis."

I think he almost understood my explanation. If he had read my mail, he might have thought the talk was justified. Letters interspersed with poetry arrived from Lewis on a daily basis.

Oct. 10

To Angel

> I write my timid verse for you
> Because it's all that I can do.
> IF I could fly large aeroplanes,
> IF I could buy you ruby chains,
> IF I played polo, or could sing,
> Or any high heroic thing,
> To prove my passion grand and true . . .
> I still would stick to verse for you.

Oct. 11

It makes an astounding difference in the amount of eagerness with which I start work in the morning to have or not have you presently coming to see it. With you here, it's just as steady and solid work, but it's also a gift that I am carving, and all shining with you.

Oct. 12

Darling, I sort of wish you would save all my letters, keep them together. I think they might make for you all together a picture of something or other that might be interesting. Don't in efficiency, tear them up. I haven't these years and years talked to anyone so

intimately as in these, so I am prejudiced in favor—not of their
elegance but of their reality—and they, with my verses, are the
eagerest gift I shall ever give you.

Your blessed first criticisms came last evening, and have
already been attended to. I don't know which was the greater
thrill: to have had them written on the plane, or to have them so
sound and constructive. I accepted all of them, and have made all
the changes, with zest.

I'm going to go and get mystic on you. It must be significant of
your swift-moving life that we get this:

FAY WRAY
AIR MAIL

All of his letters and verses, pages and pages of them, were
signed with the initials of his character in the play—h. j. He was
giving himself a role and writing himself very personally into it. I
thought he felt perfectly elegant doing that and accepted them in
that way. They seemed to be less about me than about *his* feelings
about me. I felt that in each he was congratulating himself on his
ability to be all tangled up in a romantic image. He sent pictures
of himself signed, "Love, Red"—one interesting for having been
taken by Carl van Vechten.

I wrote to him about the play, the play only.

But my first thoughts each day were about John and Susan and
where they might be. It was fortunate that the film I was doing made
no great demands on me. I spent time at the district attorney's office.

Perhaps I do Lewis an injustice; perhaps he thought that all the
prose and poetry would be some balm during a time of real distress.
But it did seem to be more than that when the following arrived:

I like a family, but I want it to be my own family. Have I ever told
you about the girl I want to marry, some day, and with whom I
want to study at the Sorbonne and loaf in Venice? She is so
darling, so incomprehensibly gallant and lovely. I don't think I
COULD tell you about her.

h. j.

I asked him not to write in that way and got an immediate response:

Oct. 17

> I don't care a damn; I'm going to write to you, anyway. Good
> God, there can't NOT be a letter coming from you later
> today. . . . I don't think you're going to have a more loyal adorer,
> young lady.

He went on writing; there were fewer verses and he signed all the letters a little more curtly—with a simple *h*.

> At last I've found out where I can see *King Kong*, which I've
> never seen—on West 99th Street. I'm going up there tomorrow to
> see it.

Afterward:

> I've rarely had two hours of such violent and mixed emotions as
> first seeing you in *King Kong*.

There follows a lengthy analysis of the film and his reactions and the letter closes with:

> I was, for a long time, frankly and badly terrified by the film. For
> one who considers you as, beyond all people, a person to be
> respected and protected, it wasn't what is technically classed as
> Amusement to see you pulled about, beaten, thrown down cliffs;
> to hear you yelling in terror; and no amount of assurance to myself
> that it was all double photography and tricks consoled me, till I
> had quite got used to it and the girl there ceased to be Fay and
> became more a symbol, impersonal and distant.
>   I came out of that movie house a wreck. I herewith ship the
> shattered timbers on to you.

h.

It was not through the district attorneys but through a newspaper woman, May Craig, that Helen Ferguson learned, after about six anxious weeks, that John and Susan were known to be in Charlottesville, Virginia. I asked Ted Curtis whether he could recommend an attorney in New York. He told me about his friend, Colonel William J. Donovan. By remarkable coincidence, Donovan already had learned something of the travels of John and Susan. He had overheard, while at the offices of MGM, Adela Rogers St. John telling of a recent episode with John Monk Saunders. John had gone to her house in Great Neck. They had argued and she had protested strongly when, during the night, he left her house, taking Susan with him. It would be valuable, Donovan thought, to have Adela go with us to Charlottesville.

She and I went by train, getting to know each other for the first time, both of us concerned about what had been happening to John, but mostly concerned for Susan. Two bodyguards went along, assigned to Adela by the Hearst newspapers. It was those two men who learned that John was in the University Hospital under the care of a psychiatrist. Susan was in the children's wing. A young German nurse, employed by John, was violently rude to Adela and me when we went to see Susan.

I had a meeting with John in the hospital library. He did not look really ill but was waiting with a barrage of thoughts about what he imagined was my intimate relationship with Sinclair Lewis. I told him how it really was. When I left the library, I heard Walter Winchell's voice broadcasting over the patients' radios about my having located Susan—and where. It was a raw and exposed feeling to have the hospital corridors filled with this news—as if my life were being narrated.

Donovan arrived and arranged to have Susan brought to me where I was staying at the Farmington Country Club. A further coincidence developed; John's brother, Dr. Edward Saunders, had gone to Charlottesville to recuperate, not knowing John was there. He and his wife took me to meet members of the Saunders family. They were all warm and welcoming. I could understand John's wanting to be in Charlottesville, the possible sense of "homing" it meant to him. His father had a long family tree of

Virginians: Overton, Jefferson, Carr, Dabney, Minor, Cary. Was there a chance that he could rebuild his life in this ancestral university town? Would it really help to have Susan with him?

William Donovan seemed to be responding to these unexpressed thoughts when he asked me to meet him very early one morning and walk with him along a frosty country road. He had never had patience, he said, with the neurotic behaviors of adolescent men. He had arranged for me to take Susan back to California. Papers, agreeing to return her to Virginia, would have to be signed. "Once you get to California, you can, under California law, ask the courts there to let you keep her," he told me.

What I knew of Donovan, I had learned from Ted Curtis: that he had been a hero in World War I, a commanding officer of the Fighting 69th, and had run for the office of governor of New York State. In a matter of a year or so, he would become fully involved in serving his government as director of the COI (Office of Coordinator of Information), then become founding head of the Office of Strategic Services (OSS) and creator of the CIA. He would not have had time to go with me to Charlottesville.

Cornelia Beazley, a registered nurse, came to help me with Susan and agreed to go with us to California. "Bea" would remain with us for several years. Back in Hollywood, we stayed briefly at the Chateau Elysee—at least through the holidays. We decorated Susan's tree with whipped soap, piling it high on the branches as though it were snow—in lieu of expensive decorations. Perhaps it was my having known impoverished conditions when I was young that made me not afraid to have lost the house on Selma Avenue and to have to start all over again. Affluence and acquisitions had not made a happy home for John and me.

I went to an afternoon pre-Christmas party at the home of Lili Damita and Errol Flynn, who were married then. Cary was there and when I saw him, I had a belonging feeling. He asked me to dance and I told him how glad I was to see him again.

"But Nikki," he said, "I'm so *rich*." He made *rich* sound good and all that he needed. He had rich and, liking him so much, I had to be glad for him.

For Christmas, he sent Susan a whoppingly well-stuffed Santa Claus. On New Year's Eve, we went together to a party at the Jack Warners'. The belonging feeling didn't go away but had a pleasantly impersonal charm. Once or twice at parties when he left to go home, I knew he'd be back quite soon after he'd left whatever date he had and we'd talk. Once, after an evening of playing anagrams, he sent me roses with a note: "Terpyt osres for terpiter Kinik." Alice, in her Wonderland, would have liked that, too!

It would always go on like that, the closeness from the distance, kisses blown or a surprise kiss on the back of my neck. There was a slim young man inside the older handsome shape of him that remembered a slim young me who, in turn, remembered how nice it was of Hoagy Carmichael to enhance the sparkling feelings that we shared by writing "Stardust."

Sinclair Lewis and the producers of *Angela Is Twenty-two* were persuaded that I didn't want to act in the play and, although Red started out playing in it, he was soon replaced by a distinguished actor, Philip Merivale. As the play traveled in tryouts during the spring of 1939, criticism was kind to negative but never kind enough to warrant an opening in New York.

Sometime in February, John telephoned from Washington, D.C. "Are you going to divorce me?" It seemed strange to say what once had seemed impossible, yes.

Attorneys' fees and one film at the Monogram studio didn't balance well enough to let us continue living at the Chateau Elysee and Susan, Bea, and I moved to the less expensive Villa Carlotta right across the street on Franklin Avenue. Bea said she wouldn't want any salary "until you get straightened out." And she was resourceful in cooking for us nourishingly but thriftily, as only someone who had been raised in the country would understand. She even made butter from the cream at the top of the milk. As a registered nurse, she was able to get the pharmacist to make a tonic to increase my appetite: "Iron, wine, and strychnine," she said. Strychnine! I trusted her and took it.

Jane Wyatt and her husband Eddie Ward and their son Christopher, who was Susan's age, lived at the Château. Ann

Ronnell, a composer, had interesting guests, among them Aaron Copeland. The actress, Marjorie Gateson, entertained for C. S. Forester and arranged a doubles match of tennis with William Tilden as my partner. The exhilaration of teaming with him made me play brilliantly (I thought). Anna Wilson, an artist, did a charcoal portrait of Susan in exchange for my sitting for an oil. Samson Raphaelson, wanting to search out, as a study, what had been the course of John Monk Saunders's life, came to interview me.

These were all interesting diversions, but I was not getting enough films to do, and when Leland Hayward suggested I accept an offer to do a play in New York and Adela Rogers St. John said she could get us an apartment in Gramercy Square at a modest rent, we packed up and went to New York.

The Brown Danube was what its title suggests: about storm troopers whose brown shirts changed and darkened the lives of Middle Europeans. I'm pretty sure it was not a good play; I know I was not good in it. The director realized that, too, after an opening out of town. He wrote me a long letter of advice about needing more experience with summer theater, et cetera. Even after I was replaced, the play didn't last once it opened in New York.

What *did* last from that experience were friendships made with members of the company: Francis Cleveland (son of Grover Cleveland), who ran and still runs the Barnstormers, a distinguished summer theater in Tamworth, New Hampshire; and George Macready, who arranged with the management of the Lakewood Theatre in Skowhegan for me to spend the entire summer there.

He was going there with his family and assisted me in securing a cottage on the shore of Lake Wesserunsit, where Bea was glad to have Susan get acquainted with nature (there was lots of it— pine trees and country roads and the lake for splashing in). Bea went foraging for wild mushrooms and I trusted her and ate them and lived. A lobsterman came to the front door with green lobsters that she boiled to a brilliant red. We had picnics and

Susan's two kittens proliferated to a dozen! No house was far from another and the theater sat like a mother hen, overlooking a brood of houses and cottages.

When I first arrived, I was introduced to Hume Cronyn who was rehearsing *Dinner at Eight,* sitting up in a bed alongside an actress who did not sound like Lynn Fontanne, but Hume sounded just like Alfred Lunt. I was fascinated that summer to watch his resourcefulness in a variety of roles. Keenan Wynn was a member of the company, and his father, the remarkable Ed, lived right next door to us and bought toys for his youngest neighbor, Susan.

The schedule of work was gratifying: rehearsals each morning and performances each night. Summer theater repertory is ultimately demanding if it's work, work, work you want—and I did. There are better ways, I'm sure, to find development as an actor, because doing a new play each week just doesn't permit all the nuances in a role to be realized.

Sometimes the actors would sit around together at the end of the evening, having a snack and some beer or some fancy Maine apple juice at the store/lunchroom—and would talk about what we'd been doing.

In July, a playwright from New York joined a few of these gatherings. Clifford Odets was traveling through New England with his friend William Kozlenko. I had the feeling that Clifford would never take a vacation, that wherever he went, the theater was the body that clothed his spirit. He was intense—if velvet is intense—so smooth and softly thoughtful was the texture of his comments. Or, he listened, his gray eyes widening behind horn-rimmed glasses, as though to leap upon a possibly catalyzing invention of thought, his antennae all alert. He was sober; he was serious, his seriousness not his own doing but the enveloping nature of creativity.

At a party, he went across the room to say, "You are very handsome." Handsome? No one had ever said that to me. He moved easily and rhythmically, lightly. If he had walked through the Maine woods, you wouldn't have heard his footsteps, I thought, any more than you would those of a moccasined Indian.

He had been gone from Skowhegan for about three days when a telegram came. He would be back by Sunday; he hoped I would have dinner with him.

We went to a country tearoom. "These people are all dead," he said, looking at the American-gothic faces at the nearby tables. His own aliveness and mine found us exchanging, with a mutual respect for experiences of a similar nature, the trauma of being recently divorced. (I had been granted a divorce the previous December, which was interlocutory and would be final in December of 1940.) Clifford had, apparently, fought against his from Luise Rainer and had a sense of desperation that drove him as he held on to the wheel of his car, straight into a wall. It was a wall in Mexico, where he had gone to suffer. Now he was wearing a mustache that covered a scar from that crash. The suffering seemed faraway by now, the mustache immediate and requiring explanation.

There was more than cosmetics to talk about. Words meant less than the feeling of knowing. A mystery surrounded the knowing. He was not obvious. He was like a promise. I, too, was a reticent person but felt I was exchanging feelings with someone I could respect for the aspirations that had been born in him. Not very much, I thought, had been learned; a lot had been originally known by him. Accepting that, I didn't like hearing him say that he had learned how to make a successful play, that he knew the formula.

He had bought a car dealership. He had $75,000 in the bank. He had presented one of the cars to his mentor, Harold Clurman. He had been deprived, however, of observing the joy it would bring to this man he admired profoundly when Stella Adler flew down into the street ahead of Harold to exclaim and figuratively clasp the car to her breast, as though it were all hers.

Clifford had rented a cottage quite near mine. Following dinner, we went there and sat in his living room and continued talking.

I had the feeling that, as we talked, we were each enhancing our self-understanding as well as learning something of the other. I had never before had such an exchange. Almost always, I had been the listener. It was growing late and when I realized how late, I got up and went to the door. Clifford followed, and opened the door for me. As soon as he opened it, he slammed it shut and picked me up in his arms and carried me into his bedroom. Maybe every woman has dreamed of such a romantic moment. I certainly had. And that it had happened for the first time was a sign, for me, of fulfillment.

Clifford's letters began arriving soon after he returned to New York—letters mostly about *him*, his feelings, his searchings, his introspection. He sent books, all of his plays, and a large volume entitled *Man's Worldly Goods*.

A man representing himself as a newspaperman came all the way from New York to question me about that book. His credentials included a list of individuals suspected of Communism, as presented by the Walter Steele committee. Clifford was not named but the Group Theatre was.

How much did I know about Communism? Did I know, for instance, that they passed out copies of songs (the newspaperman had one to show me) that celebrated the killing of children. Oh God! It was awful to have this man in my living room. He looked like a fairly decent fellow, so it made his declarations that much worse. He never removed his hat but was otherwise not ill-mannered. He went away, knowing that I was dismayed, turning down the brim of his brown-felt hat like a reporter in a gangster movie. He left me to wonder how he knew about *Man's Worldly Goods*. I wrote about this to Clifford, making light of it.

In response to an invitation from the Lakewood Theatre management, Sinclair Lewis arrived to do *Angela Is Twenty-two* with me. He had been playing summer theater himself, his name, if not his acting talent, great enough to be a box-office draw. While performing in *Shadow and Substance*, he had found a young friend, Marcella Powers, who had become his companion and would continue to share his life.

Around the lunch table someone mentioned that Clifford Odets had recently been there. In a flash, Lewis was ready with a little verse:

Clifford Odets, with his little moustache,
Claims that soubrettes are exploited for
cash.
Then, at his most comradely, as soon as
he's said it,
Proceeds at once to exploit them on
credit.

Funny, critical, but it was the speed that made it stick in my mind.

It just wasn't possible to realize any drama in working with Lewis. It was more like moving about in an essay. Ideas were good, thoughts well-written, but there was no life, not even any certainty about where he would be on the stage at any moment. What had been rehearsed to play stage right was suddenly taking place stage left and we scrambled along for seven uncertain performances. But he was where he wanted most of all to be at that time of his life—in the theater.

A booklet prepared for the original presentation of *Angela Is Twenty-two* has a statement from Mr. Lewis:

I believe that America is at the dawn of one of the most
exciting theatrical eras in history and I am proud to try, as
writer and player, to be part of this dramatic explosion. Maybe
in some audience, some evening, will sit the young American
Molière or Shaw. If so, I am his humble missionary . . . well,
pretty humble!

Howard Lindsay and his wife, Dorothy Stickney, arrived with some little redheads to try out *Life with Father*. They chose Skowhegan because it was there that they had met and fallen in love. Oscar Serlin, the producer, and Leland Hayward among others were there to see what was to become one of the great successes in theater history. As a company member, I had a small role. I knew I was miscast and that it would have to be recast in New York. I wrote to Clifford that this was a pleasant lightweight play of no great consequence. It subsequently ran for more than three thousand performances!

Toward the end of the season, the news on the radio became the focal point of each afternoon's interest. Hitler's march across Europe was beginning to blight the planet.

CHAPTER 22
HOLLYWOOD AGAIN AND ROBERT RISKIN

♦

A FTER A WEEKEND VISIT WITH the Ted Curtises at their summer home in Small Point, Maine, Susan, Bea, and I returned to Hollywood. A B picture at RKO made it possible for us to stay at the Château and to buy a secondhand car in which Bea drove Susan and Christopher Ward to a preschool run by Isabelle Buckley in her rather small home on Doheny Drive, just south of Sunset Boulevard. The Merian Coopers now had a house in the Vanderlip Estates, overlooking the ocean, and had tennis parties, children's parties, and sometimes barbecue parties on the beach below their house, where their guests would sit around a bonfire and sing. Jock Whitney was good at doing "Night and Day" with gestures.

Jessica and Richard Barthelmess asked their "unattached" friends to be with them for Christmas. William Powell was there and others whom I don't remember except for one—Robert Riskin. I had observed him observing me while I was dancing, especially during an improvisational solo. Suddenly, he was asking whether I would go with him to see *The Grapes of Wrath*. Of course, I cried at the movie and I thought he seemed surprised at that, although I don't see how anyone could *not* cry at that movie.

If he was surprised at me, I was surprised that he had invited me, because I was nothing like the blond ladies he had known— Glenda Farrell and Carole Lombard. When we said good night, he gave me a respectful kiss on the forehead. And I had a comfortably respectful feeling for him.

A few dinner-dancing occasions continued in that same way. At the Mocambo nightclub, he told me about his ten-year relationship with the writer Edith Fitzgerald. "We were never married because . . . I was never in love with her." Oh, he does like me well enough to confide in me. He trusts me. He had made me his friend. And I was glad to be such a friend to this intelligent, even-tempered man. I knew what the evening's conversation meant to me; I had no idea of its meaning for him. It was his way, he later said, of proposing to me—Oblique; subtle.

I would learn that the question Why do women wear lipstick? had meant that he wanted to kiss me; that a box of long-stemmed red roses arriving with a card saying simply, "one dozen roses" was not his instruction to the florist but his signal to me to complete the sentence from the song: "Give me one dozen roses, put my heart in beside them, and send them to the one I love."

Ever since returning to California, letters (about two a week) had been arriving from Clifford, and music, music, music. Records for me and for Susan. My thoughts had been directed toward Clifford and I had no ear for discerning what Bob Riskin was trying to say. Bob went on a protracted visit to New York.

At an afternoon party at Douglas Fairbanks's beach house, where Sylvia (now Mrs. Fairbanks) was hostess to Cole Porter and Charlie Chaplin, an actress, Frances Robinson, who had sometimes been escorted by Bob Riskin, asked me whether I knew where he was. She was always hoping Bob might care for her, she said, because he was the very nicest man she had ever met. I told her that should I see him when he returned, he might tell me about her. After all, I thought, he had told me about Edith Fitzgerald.

John came back to Hollywood, briefly. He looked worn and

weary. He took Susan out for an afternoon. When she came home, she threw up.

Ben Piazza, an executive at RKO, hoped to help John return to work. He accompanied him to Palm Springs. But John was soon gone away again. His family tried to locate him. I tried to help.

On the tenth of March, I was rehearsing at the El Capitán Theatre in a play written by Clare Booth Luce, *Margin for Error*, when Helen Ferguson came to find me. She took me into an office, closed the door, and told me: "John has committed suicide." How many times people had said that those who talk about suicide are not the ones who do it!

There were three services, one in Seattle, one in Virginia, and one in a small chapel at Forest Lawn, at which I asked Edwin Hubble, the astronomer, who had also been a Rhodes Scholar, to speak. The burial took place in Virginia at a place called Caryswood. John's brothers and other members of his father's family were present. I sent a little box containing my heart-shaped stones to be buried with him.

When *Margin for Error* opened a few days later, there was applause on my entrance—too much, much too much, so that I was aware of the sympathy it suggested. For a few uncomfortable moments, it was not like being in a play but like making a personal appearance. Sinclair Lewis was there with his Marcella; Helen Ferguson with friends she had gathered round. There was a party afterward at the Hotel Roosevelt next door. I excused myself early.

There were many telephone calls and telegrams. A telegram from "Nikki of Paris" simply said: "Ask Yourself." We had never met. There was a long, caring, detailed letter from the landlady in Florida, where he had been living. Howard Hughes telephoned with concern that he might have been the cause of John's action. I could assure him he was not. But I told him I did not want to see him—or anyone.

Adela wired, "Forgive me. I needed the money." She referred to a full-page story she had done for the Hearst newspapers. It was painful to see the artist's drawing of the way John had died. He had been found hanging, in a closet. How awful to see the figure of a man in that way, almost filling the page. How awful that his pain and tragedy had to be displayed. What misery he must have known that brought him to the moment. But not for a cheap sensational newspaper rendition!

Adela had wired, "Forgive me." *Forgive me. She* had not done that drawing. She had written a piece that had some wonderful things to say but—forgive? All the time I had known of John's trouble, I had tried to protect him from the press. Even when I was divorcing him I had a promise from my attorney that the reasons for the divorce would be sealed and not made public! Not made public? Not only was there no sealing, but Jimmie Fidler, who had a national radio broadcast, induced Helen Ferguson to tell him what she knew—so that he could be protective, she said. Protective? He broadcast all of what she told him! Forgive Adela? She had been a friend of John's long before and owed him some protection, it seemed to me. But we were public figures, she was a journalist, and while I thought she had gone to Virginia to find him and Susan, as first his friend, then also mine, she had a story. She had need of money. Oh God. That money thing. If she hadn't felt sorry she wouldn't have said, "Forgive me." I appreciated all her staunchness, her support, her effort on behalf of Susan and me—but why not of him who once had been her intimate friend? I suppose once the paper got the story, the art department (what a misnomer!) got called in. A life, a person so assaulted!

My life with John had been tormenting in many ways, in many ways sweet and rewarding. I had learned a lot from him. He had such vulnerability! I have tears remembering a moment when he was sitting quietly in the living room one day, pensive, and I came near. He looked up at me to say, "I am weak." But it must have taken some wild, crazy strength to end his life that way. No one, no one should ever come to that! I do not have to open a book to find the following lines, John had quoted them so many times: "To dance to lutes, to dance to flutes is delicate and rare. But it is not sweet with nimble feet to dance upon the air," from "The Ballad of Reading Gaol" by Oscar Wilde.

But there were other lines from Wilde that he quoted, too, more gentle:

> Down the long and silent street,
> The dawn, with silver-sandaled feet,
> Crept like a frightened girl.
>> From "The Harlot's House"

And then, again, from "The Ballad of Reading Gaol": "Each man kills the thing he loves." He had quoted that to me, about me. But he didn't kill me. He killed *himself*!!! "The thing he loves." Never, until this moment, have I had that thought. I'm either very wrong or exactly right to find that meaning now, such a long, long time after. I often thought of him as narcissistic. I think he did love his looks, his clothes, the women who had judgment to love him for those things, too, for the externals. He loved his own image.

"Each man kills the thing he loves."

CHAPTER 23

CLIFFORD ODETS: BEHIND HIS OWN IRON CURTAIN

◆

SOMETIME THAT SUMMER, CLIFFORD ARRIVED. His friends, Sylvia Sidney and her husband, Luther Adler, arrived, too. They all stayed at the Château Elysee across from where we lived at the Villa Carlotta. I went to dinners with him, with *his* friends, knowing my own might not be comfortable in the company of a man with his advertised left-wing interests. In fact, a Los Angeles morning paper had him clustered with a few others as possible members of the Communist Party. That evening I asked him, Was it so? He looked at me directly. "No. I am not."

He cooked for me in his apartment, nothing fancy—noodles in the Jewish style were very good. He was happy doing that. Because he was broodingly serious most of the time, it was good to see his happiness about doing something so commonplace as preparing and serving noodles. I often wanted to shake him out of his seriousness into carefree feelings, but I respected the talent that made him reflective.

To me, Clifford had the look of someone in a painting by Monet. It would have been easy to visualize him boating on the

Seine or conversing with intellectuals in a French café. He had once sent me a postcard with a painting by Renoir, "On the Terrace," of a young woman in a blue dress and a red hat. There is a basket of fruit in her lap and a little girl in a flowered hat standing beside her. They seem to be waiting for someone. I thought of the young woman as me, the child as Susan, and the one we were waiting for, Clifford. He was part of the picture because he had chosen it. I thought of him as someone so creative as to be noncompetitive. I was not a competitive person. I believed in aspirations. I believed in Clifford.

When he was ready to return to New York, he went by train, carrying a loaf of banana bread I had baked, evidence of my caring. Neither of us had said love-words, not seeming to need them. Feeling was more important than language.

During Clifford's stay in California, I made a film at Columbia, *Adam Had Four Sons*, with Warner Baxter, Susan Hayward, and Ingrid Bergman. It was a period piece set around the turn of the century, the clothes of that "other time and place" that I had associated with Clifford. It had been pleasant to feel that when I wore my costume, I was wearing it not only for the film, but for him.

I played the wife of Warner Baxter, mother of his four sons who engages a new governess (Ingrid), then has the grace to become ill and die not long after so that the father and the governess can develop a romance.

Ingrid was learning English at the time and working with her coach, Ruth Roberts, almost constantly. We had only one scene together. She seemed so tall, I was glad we were both seated. Her quality was real, truthful, very simple. She seemed not to be an actress, but a reality.

In the early part of 1941, Loretta Young gave a ladies luncheon on the terrace of her large and handsome home on Sunset Boulevard. Flo Swerling was there. She and her husband, Jo, were very close friends of Robert Riskin. When Flo spoke of Bob, her eyes danced with the fondness she felt. This was my first meeting with Flo. There was a brightness and a softness and enthusiasm in her that made me believe she was a woman in love. I would learn that she was, indeed, in love with her husband, Jo. And he was in love with her. Their lives together were as close as the sound and look of their names. They were caring. They were caring of each other and, therefore, of their friends.

Bob Riskin was one of those friends. At the time of my meeting Flo, he was still away in New York. When he returned in late March, he brought me a gift: a radio in the shape of a piano. On the music rest he had written "To Fay—for my birthday, March 30, 1941." And he gave me the gift of a beginning friendship with Flo and Jo.

Orson Welles had finished *Citizen Kane* and had gone to New York to prepare for the premiere. Dolores Del Rio invited me to join her for the opening. Fate got her fingers around this circumstance. Of all the letters Clifford wrote to me, I would keep only one: the one that said he needed me in his life. Dolores's invitation, Clifford's wish that I go to New York, Bea's longing for Virginia and her repeated hope that she could take Susan to share some time with her family in Charlottesville, all these combined.

I told Bob about all of these plans and thought he would be a little bit sorry to see me go, but I had no idea how sorry. He asked me to join him for dinner at the Swerlings' the night before I was to depart. The atmosphere at the Swerlings' was rich with family feeling. The two little boys, Peter and Jo Jr., freshly scrubbed and wearing their pajamas and robes, gave us a violin concert before dinner. Later in the evening, I called Dolores to verify the time of the flight. I came back from the phone and told Bob the hour of my flight. When he took me home, we sat together for a while and he let me know then what I had never dreamed. Now, there was no unfinished sentences, no obscure, oblique, hidden meanings. I knew he meant it when he said he couldn't bear to see me go. My feelings were twisted all out of shape, realizing that it was probably not easy for him to let go of the controlled, debonair style I had come to know. I was listening to an impassioned Bob Riskin. I would not forget. I never did forget. But there could be no turning back from the commitment I had made. Timing, timing!

Orson had asked his attorney, Arnold Weissberger, to accompany Dolores and me on the plane. This gentleman, who looked older than his years because he had a wide path of gray hair and all the more distinguished because of it, would be a friend to me as long as he lived. He was a friend to many. Almost no one in the theater was without his consideration, his thoughtful attention. The fresh carnation he wore each day and his bowler hat reflected his turn-of-the-century spirit. For me and hundreds of others, there are memories of moments in London, New York, and California that are shining with his hospitality and captured by his camera. He took pictures, pictures, pictures. He published them under the title *Famous Faces*.

Dolores and I went to the Ambassador Hotel on Park Avenue, where Clifford met us. I went with him to see his new house on Beekman Place, and a Utrillo painting he had just bought. Stairs at the front entrance led first to his study, then into a large living room where musical speakers ran from floor to ceiling. Music could flow into every room.

The four of us went to dinner at an Italian restaurant somewhere downtown. For the first time, I had green pasta. How Orson loved to eat! Eventually, I think, the food he ate devoured *him*.

Afterward, Clifford said to me that Orson was an ebullient boy. It was much more than a boy, however, who made *Citizen Kane*. His was a towering talent.

At the opening, we all sat silent for a moment when the film concluded, absorbing the realization that we had seen a powerful work. It was Clifford who first reached across to take Orson's hand and tell him that.

Evenings in New York, you can walk and talk. Orson talked about having learned much from silent films, particularly those of von Stroheim. But his own style brought a new dimension to filmmaking.

I did not live with Clifford in the sense of living in his house. I stayed at a less expensive hotel than the Ambassador—and then

accepted Dr. Edward Saunders and his wife's invitation to stay
with them. They were excited about knowing Clifford—but more
as someone to lionize than to *know*. They gave him a cocktail
party. He acceded to that because Margaret Sanger was to be a
guest. William Donovan came, too. I told him about my feelings
for Clifford. "Stay with him," he said. "Bake bread for him. Then
you'll know."

I did not bake bread but I shared, broke bread with him very
often, arriving at Beekman Place in time to walk to dinner.

One late afternoon in April, we walked across town all the way
to wherever Lindy's used to be—maybe Broadway.

I had washed my hair earlier and knew it looked shining and
lovely. I felt the afternoon sun dance through it and I saw new
young leaves on the trees as we passed. I heard no traffic sounds.
I was conscious only of the easy way we walked together, my hair
free and loose to my shoulders, sometimes catching at the sleeve
of his jacket. A sensuous easy male and female walking. It wasn't
much to be doing—just walking—but, at the moment, it seemed
everything. A sense of being, an awareness of each other and the
sunlight and the greening trees.

He had written to me of his torment of the past year, of his
inability to work, to concentrate, to follow anything through:

Uneasy. Uneasy living, the unease of modern life! . . . This
"unease of living" is really the creative core from which I
function; and I cannot rail against it without, at the same time,
being aware and thankful for what it has done for me. . . . I know
how you can help me and I know how I need help. This sounds
selfish, perhaps, but there is another secret which, perhaps you
already know, that as one helps, as one makes, one is also made.

Yes, I knew.

I knew the soaring spirit of him, the way he bathed himself in
music, the way he wanted, even yearned, to climb to some truth
for himself and, he led himself to believe, for mankind. All that
was as clear as the sunshine.

What was more in the shadows of his person was the concern

that if he should be happy, should have the luck (or better still, the ill luck) to share all these with a woman, the worst possible thing might happen: His misery, the source of his talent, would be threatened. Danger of all dangers! What caring person could say to him, Be miserable, I will help you to be miserable. How to do that and still feel good about him—free? All these feelings were intervening subtly with my pleasures in the walk. Still the conscious sharing of his soaring spirit, the symphonic nature of him, the music that went along with us, made the walk a wondrous one.

When we got to Lindy's, there was hubbub, hellos, especially to Billy Rose, who was a prospective theater producer. Clifford surprised me by ordering turkey legs. Turkey legs on a platter before him didn't seem to go with the poetic, aspiring, searching *talent* I saw him to be. *Turkey legs!* But he *did* enjoy them!

Clifford had a struggle, I think, moving into areas and company he had not previously known. For years, he had been wrapped in the secure, blanketing embrace of the Group Theatre; these were his people, his family, his fireside. His own father and mother had always been at war, he said—and at war in him. Marriage was a turbulence. But he wanted to be married and to me and to have a home in Dutchess County.

Perhaps it was because his association with the Group Theatre people had been so long that, as I met them, I felt it would take time for *me* to know them. No one was resistant to me. But there was an atmosphere of things unspoken, as though an unseen party was present.

Paula Strasberg was openhearted and garrulous. She and her husband, Lee, invited us to go to their apartment for dinner. They were having stuffed neck, she said. Clifford told me she was a "leaden-footed Mercury" and that she ran from friend to friend to keep a network of lively information going.

Susan Strasberg's three-year-old feet flew about the house, her heels clicking sharply on the wooden floors; a staccato little brown-eyed beauty.

When we departed, I stopped in the entrance hall to admire a slender photograph of a New York street scene: a young iron-railed tree, the Flatiron building in the background. A horse-drawn carriage dated the picture as early in the century. Photographic poetry! Paula took it down from the wall and gave it to me. Very easily, very casually, she had given me an Alfred Stieglitz!

Manny Wolfe's restaurant was a short distance from Beekman Place. Clifford and I were dining there when a fellow—short, dark-eyed, dark-haired, rather dirty, very urgent—came to the table. He sat down and began at once to tell Clifford about what he had just seen in the South. It was as though he was expected here, as though this was a rendezvous, a place to pass information about coal miners, conditions, and so on. He was offered nothing to eat or to drink. When, in a matter of minutes, he left, Clifford gave no explanation, as if I might take it for granted that this sort of thing was part of his life.

I had already asked him the direct question (about Communism) when he was in Hollywood. He had said no. After that, I began to feel that I was living on the edge of a precipice.

Flo and Jo Swerling came to New York. I took them to Clifford's. The meeting was superficially fine but stayed at that level. Afterward, Jo, who was forever open-minded, made no judgments. But Flo couldn't endure geniuses, she said. If that was the worst thing she could think of, that wasn't so bad.

They told me that Bob Riskin had gone to London to work with Ed Murrow on some "People to People" broadcasts.

Clifford and I were sitting in his study. I had just arrived, prior to going to dinner with him. There was a nice light on the East River. The music wasn't on in the living room; the study had a feel of stillness and serenity.

"I'm not good enough for you," he said. Whatever else was said doesn't matter. What he said, what I said—I know there was nothing mean or harsh. I know I did not protest. I know my feeling was that I would go from this house and never come back. First, I went into the bedroom and sat under the Utrillo painting.

I sat there and wished that Clifford would never know happiness again. I was a silent Medea. Now that I had cast a spell of absolute misery upon him, I could leave. As I walked through the study, I said, "I'm ready to go now." I was. But I wasn't ready to let go of the quality I had expected from that relationship.

I went out and walked for a long time. I am not at all certain where I walked—perhaps to the Sherry Netherland Hotel, where longtime friends David and Betty Rose were staying and I knew had an extra room for me. I was not expecting any comfort from them; I really didn't want any. I wouldn't have heard anything they had to say. I remembered David saying when they first knew about Clifford that I should be careful not to repeat my experience with John Saunders. How absurd, I thought; Clifford was sober.

Yes. I must have walked to the Sherry Netherland, because, for a day or so, I remember having dinners with David and Betty. I was quiet, trying to understand what had happened. There had been the incident with what I had suspected might have been a Communist courier. The torment that caused in me must have been visible to Clifford. Two of his plays that had been produced since we'd gotten to know each other, *Night Music* and *Clash by Night*, were not successes. The latter opened after my arrival in New York. I went with a friend of Clifford's and afterward, at Sardi's, heard all the alarming nays. These were sorry sounds. My presence had not enhanced his writing talent, as he had imagined it might.

These thoughts blurred together in and out of understanding for a long time, and it was still a puzzle when I learned from Irene Selznick's book, *A Private View*, that Clifford told her I was the one love of his life.

After about six lonely months, when I was in the play *Golden Wings*, Clifford came to the theater to take me out for coffee. No, not coffee. We went to the Sherry Netherland. There was not a thought or suggestion from either of us about starting over. This was just a few hours of being together without any possible commitment. Nothing hidden. Nothing to wonder about. Free. I am glad for that unclouded memory.

*   *   *

Soon after I had walked out of Clifford's house, Leland Hayward's office was in touch to say he had a job for me.

In Marblehead, Massachusetts, a production of *The Yellow Jacket* was to have Harpo Marx, Alexander Woollcott, Alfred Drake, Clarence Derwent, and Rex O'Malley. After reading the script, I asked whether I could play both the young heroine and the mother of the hero, and was intrigued to learn from the author that, in the original production, both these roles had been played by one actress. The young heroine was just a charming pleasant little "Plum Blossom." But the older woman had to suffer. I needed to make use of her emotions, even if only in the cartoonlike drama written by Western writers in the format of traditional Chinese theater.

Harpo Marx, as the Property Man, would hand the performers their props as needed. When he handed me a bundle of twigs that would represent my infant child, he had such a wild and devilish look in his eyes, that I thought he might be about to do something outrageous. This *is* a wild one, I thought. Just the opposite. He was gentle. He didn't drink; he didn't smoke—which the classic Property Man in Chinese plays is supposed to do constantly. To achieve that effect, he had the cooperation of his devoted wife, Susan. She sat on a stool behind the scenery, smoking and blowing the smoke through a hole in back of the spot where Harpo was sitting with his props around him, so that the air in that area of the stage was heavy with the haze of cigarette smoke. And Susan was not a smoker, either!

Alexander Woollcott was truer to his acerbic reputation. *Life* magazine came to do photographs. We were all in costume; he in his authoritative Mandarin robes. When all was quiet and just before the camera clicked, he said very loudly, "I think Clare Luce is a puke!" I guess he felt very good about that, but only he could know why. It was surprising, then, that he showed sympathy and concern about my Susan when word came that a simple tonsilectomy had been followed by a hemorrhage and she had needed a transfusion. "What can I do?" he asked.

What could *I* do, I asked myself, except to keep in close touch and be grateful that all three Beazley women were nurses and that Susan was getting the best of care.

The Yellow Jacket was colorful and highly theatrical; comical, too, to remember Alfred Drake and Clarence Derwent galloping about on stick horses that represented powerful steeds—or, I suppose, me, after a death scene, climbing a ladder while Woollcott declaimed to the audience, "She ascends to heaven!"

Robert Anderson, the playwright, and his wife Phyllis were at Marblehead for the summer. She was teaching the apprentices. He was not yet "the playwright." He had written a play and paid me the compliment of asking me to read it. We met one morning together with his parents and Phyllis. The play had murders in it and slamming doors and poisoned people. He could not know and I did not know, that what I told him came from Clifford—or rather what I had learned about the quality of Clifford's thinking. I told him that he should write about something he *knew*, something that was close to him. It's a good memory, sitting with him and his family, and now knowing that he did become "Robert Anderson, the playwright."

Nothing is ever truly lost. In reading the letter that took me to New York, there are signs that indicate difficulties ahead. But I was ready to accept the hazards. Clifford certainly learned more about his own realities and I about mine. Such awareness is not lightly gained. There is much in the heart of me that came from him.

CHAPTER 24

THE REALITY OF ROBERT RISKIN

♦

ONE OF THE APPRENTICES AT Marblehead had an apartment in New York that she wanted to sublet. When I returned to the city, I went to live on East Sixty-fifth Street and was very soon in a play and very soon not in that same play; it closed in a week. There was strong talent involved: George Kaufman directed *Mr. Big* from a work that had been presented at Columbia University—a nice gimmick about a district attorney taking over the investigation of an onstage murder. The audience had, perforce, to be captive. Hume Cronyn was the D.A. Betty Furness and Barry Sullivan and I, among others, were actors who, after the murder, wandered on and offstage, sometimes talking to each other. Moss Hart went to Boston to help during the tryout. Help was needed. I think the captive audiences never felt good about their assigned roles.

Jack Benny told me he had gone to the opening, that his wife, Mary, never used crude language but, after the play, she said a four-letter word.

Raymond Burr said he had reviewed it for his college paper.

But when I later did some episodes of "Perry Mason" with him, we got along just fine anyway.

Gertrude Lawrence had actually performed on television, it was said. At that time there were as many as twenty or thirty sets in New York. I saw one at NBC. You had to stand over it and look down into a mirrored reflection of the broadcast.

With O'Malley of *The Yellow Jacket*, I did a two-character drama for television that lasted about twenty minutes—a very long time when you think about it being done all in one take with costume changes going on behind screens and the lighting so hot that you lost pounds during the performance. I believe no one reviewed this. In 1941 reviewers weren't catering to a potential audience of less than one hundred. All I gained from the experience was a loss of weight and the realization that I was probably one of the first actresses to be on television.

Pearl Harbor was in the very near future when I went to Washington, D.C., for the tryout of a play about England's Royal Air Force, *Golden Wings*. Ted and Agnes Curtis had taken a house in Alexandria, Virginia. At a gathering there, it was clear that our country's mobilization was beginning. William Donovan (now a general) had asked John Ford and Merian Cooper to join his Office of Strategic Services. They were present, as well as Donovan himself. I heard Merian Cooper say to someone, "There's going to be trouble in the South Pacific."

Everybody came to the opening of the play. General Donovan gave John Ford an "assignment" to help us with rehearsals. The young men in the play were exuberant—to be directed by the great John Ford—and our director, Robert Milton, was courteous and maybe even grateful.

John Ford, in naval uniform, was a powerful presence. He spent a long time with the young "aviators" devising some business about lighting their cigarettes—a detail that didn't help as much as he had hoped.

I got Bea to bring Susan up from Charlottesville. Signe Hasso, the very talented Swedish actress, was lovely to her, buying her books. When it was time to return to Virginia, a young aide of Ford's took us all to the train. The Navy was looking after us!

In New York, dress rehearsal for *Golden Wings* was on December 7—Pearl Harbor day. On December 8 soon after the opening-night curtain went up, the management announced to the audience that President Roosevelt would be making a speech. Backstage, the actors were told they had the option of listening there or going onstage to listen with the audience. I chose to go onstage and heard, with the audience, Roosevelt's resonant tones about ". . . a date which will live in infamy."

Golden Wings was not strong enough to survive the larger events going on outside the theater and closed soon after Pearl Harbor. I went to Charlottesville for the Christmas holidays.

The Swerlings had kept in touch with Bob Riskin. When he returned from London in March, he knew where to find me. He had telephoned and I anticipated his knock on the door. There he was, in a heavy blue overcoat. Faster than the speed of light, currents of understanding about why he was here, why he had gone to England, why—why—why. Strong, steady, genteel, kind. All these flashes of feeling, but I think what I said was simply, "I'm so glad to see you." I *was*—almost giddily pleased to see him. He stayed until midnight or maybe beyond. The embraces that had been so long delayed were welcome. And yet, a few nights later, when he wanted me to stay with him in his suite at the Pierre, I thought I couldn't bear the idea of transience. I told him that. The next day, not hearing from him, I telephoned the hotel. He was gone.

Oh, my God! I had hurt him again! I felt panic that I was losing this very good, very intelligent, decent human being. I think, when I had spoken to him of transience, I was wishing he would tell me that there was permanence ahead for us. But, as a letter he wrote very soon afterward said, he felt confusion. "I go over all that had gone before—and then I think of our evenings together and I'm thrown into a state of utter confusion. Which one is you? Or are they both you?"

* * *

Columbia very soon had the wit and the grace (although unknown to them) to ask me to go to California for a film. Bob wired: "Will meet you at Pasadena. Are you going to Villa Carlotta or where? . . . Did you make reservation . . . let me know . . . am really looking forward to seeing you . . . virtually breathless . . . get that train to shake a leg or wheel or something."

He arrived at the station to learn that my train was being delayed at a point several miles to the east. He got in his car and raced to that point only to find that the train had been freed from whatever problem it had encountered and was on its way again to Pasadena. He turned around and dashed westward and got to Pasadena in time to meet the train. So he was, indeed, virtually breathless, and all the urgency and the fun of hearing about the big dash he had made swept along with us as we went to leave my bags at the Villa Carlotta and then to a house he had very recently rented.

The white, two-story colonial had pink camellias at the doorway. Bob's sister-in-law, Katya, was inside, arranging greens, putting long tendrils of ivy into vases on the mantelpiece. And Richard, Bob's houseman of many years, was there. There was a room for me that I would use more than my rooms at the Villa Carlotta. A feeling of order, of home, even if a bachelor's home, lessened a certain sense of wickedness I felt it was to be living there.

Katya's presence was welcoming. Her marriage to Bob's brother, Everett, had been restless, turbulent, and one of the reasons that Bob had been cautious about marriage. He was to have a birthday the very next month; he would be forty-five and had never asked a woman to marry him. As it would turn out, I would be doing the asking.

Bob was writing a *Thin Man* script for Everett, who was a producer at MGM. He deplored doing it and was more eager to fix on a job with the government, wanting to be part of the war effort.

Although I haven't a sprig of memory about writing to General Donovan on behalf of Bob, a telegram from him during that time says, "Thanks for your note. I have asked Sherwood if he thinks

Riskin could be of service. You sound as if everything were well with you. Good luck." Robert Sherwood, the playwright, soon invited Bob to join him in the Office of War Information (OWI).

To remember the film I had to do for Columbia is to think of the acutely touching quality of the leading man, Paul Kelly. He had a dignity, standing tall and straight and distant, as though wanting to shield himself from any possible question about his recent tragic years in prison because of his passion for a married woman—or rather, because of the fight that had taken place after her husband had discovered them. The testimony for the defense, after the husband died, was that his head, in falling away from a blow, had hit the fireplace andirons. One of the reasons I had read all the accounts was because the happening seemed to have occurred at the same house where John had lived on Cheremoya. Now Paul and the woman he loved were married. Theirs was a better story than the one we were filming.

Being a B picture, it was finished in about three weeks and I returned to New York to begin a radio series, "Rosemary," that had been developed for me at NBC.

A letter from Bob told me:

You are missed around here. Something's gone out of the house. It's terrible, darling, I'm beginning to lose my enthusiasm for it. It's kept alive only by some vague and inner hope that you're coming back to it. I move around in it aimlessly. I never go down the stairs without peering into your room, expecting to hear you puttering about. Then, realizing you're not there, a dreadful depressing feeling sweeps over me. . . . I tried to fill the void you left. I called up Katya and asked her to send my bird back to me. Remember the canary I had? I don't suppose you do. Well, Katya cared for it while I was away. With you gone, there is no song in the house. I thought the canary might furnish it. Not yet, Angel, not yet! It refused to sing. It peeps, but does not sing. *You* could make it sing . . . as you make my heart sing . . . as everything you touch, sings. Write to me. Tell me all. Tell me more than all. I miss you and long for you . . .

The writers of "Rosemary," two ladies who shared an apartment at 25 Central Park West, let me sublet their place so that I would have room enough for Susan and Bea. They also told me about their psychiatrist, a warm and sensitive man who let me go to see him once a week for a period of six weeks for the price of five dollars per visit. (A radio series paid very little.) For the five dollars, he also offered me Russian tea, which I sometimes took and sometimes didn't. I was eager to polarize my own feelings, to make a *place* for my own entity in spite of a sense of displacement.

All of Bob's letters and telegrams had the same richness of expression as that first one. He had been enchanted because, upon learning that he would be at Rosalind Russell's house on his birthday, I had a cake sent there, saying, "To Bob from Fay." It was like a public announcement, which was what I meant it to be.

"On the couch," I talked about the beauty of Bob's letters.

"Maybe it's all too beautiful," the doctor said.

"No. It's real. He is real."

"Why don't you ask him to marry you?"

Women don't ask men to marry them!

In about two months Bob came to New York and, as usual, took a suite at the Pierre. We were lying crosswise on the bed just before going to dinner. I was wearing a taffeta dress on which I had pinned a golden brooch he had given me earlier. The brooch was shaped like a bow, the knot set with rubies. Very beautiful, simple in design and strong. To me, it was almost like a garment, so wearable, so right. But mostly it was right because I thought it had come from his heart. It was not just a bauble.

We began to talk about things of first importance, about the inner life that each of us lived, what each felt about religion. We were touching on the themes that motivated us and found that we were both free spirits, neither one bound to any denomination. He had been born to a Jewish family that found philosophical discussion of more value than going to temple. But, he said, to be Jewish was to belong to a club from which you never could, nor ever would, resign. I felt a rush of admiration, hearing that. Our talk was drawing us into a sense of unity and it was drawing me toward saying what I had thought would be difficult. Because of the pain I had given him, I knew it would have to come from me.

"Bob . . . I'd like to marry you."

He waited a short moment, then said, "I do have some hurts to overcome." He wanted to know how I was managing financially. Did I have any obligations? I had borrowed two thousand dollars and was paying it off, I said. I was managing.

If I had not gone those few times to visit the psychiatrist who had the wisdom to tell me to ask Bob to marry me—well, I don't know. But I did say it and it was a healing moment for both of us even if he didn't say yes. But words of any kind were not needed just then. There was a comfortable feeling of knowing where we were in life.

I can't be sure whether the following arrived before or after that conversation. It came, delivered by hand.

> Darling:
> I can't, I won't, have you stewing about money. There must be so many things you need that you've had to deny yourself . . . and the thought of that makes my heart ache.
>
> I love you,
> Bob

A check was enclosed.

He went to Washington for a few days to meet with Robert Sherwood and Donovan. After Bob returned to Hollywood, I told him that Donovan had phoned to say how much he had liked Bob and, he had said, "I like the way he expresses himself about you."

A telegram from Bob said, among other things: "Nice to hear about Donovan. Did you ask him about his friend, the Judge?"

What friend, what judge, and why and what about? I had not long to wonder. A wire from Bob's brother Everett said he was delighted with the "news" and Bob said he would be returning, or rather pushing back, to New York as fast as possible.

When he arrived, he brought his dachshund, Mr. Deeds, with

him and took a suite at the Hampshire House, nearer to where Susan and I were living. The four of us went for walks in the park, Susan going ahead with Mr. Deeds. During a certain walk, she stopped and waited for us. "It seems to me," she said, "that you two should be married. I'm going to marry you, now. Mr. Deeds will be the minister." Her knowledge of what should be said was surprisingly right for a six-year-old and she instructed Mr. Deeds to say, "I now pronounce you man and wife." Then those two ran ahead, leaving the two of us feeling as one.

But a judge had to be found. Bill Donovan not only had a recommendation to make but wanted to give us a noontime wedding at his suite in the St. Regis. He had a tiered cake and champagne and flowers. He and his assistant, Owen McGivern, Ellin and Irving Berlin, Bill and Dorothy Paley, and David Selznick (Irene was in California) listened to Judge Ferdinand Pecora say the same words that Susan had said, and then Dorothy Paley took lots of pictures. Bob gave Susan a ring of her own—with a real diamond.

Bob and I went with the Paleys to their home in Manhasset for the afternoon. Kay Chacqeneau, a very fashionable lady, was among the guests. She said to me, "With Bob, you will never know a dull day."

CHAPTER 25

~~~~~~~~~~~~~~~

THE OFFICE OF
WAR INFORMATION

◆

THEY WERE ALL PATRIOTIC, ALTRUISTIC men. Most, if not all, had left positions of considerable remuneration to work for token salaries. Among them were Ed Barrett, Jim Lenin, Louis G. Cowan, Bill Paley, Philip Dunne, Robert Sherwood, George Backer, Elmer Davis, and Robert Riskin.

It is my memory that General William Donovan had established the OSS soon after Pearl Harbor, that the Office of War Information was formed out of that with Elmer Davis, the nationally known radio commentator, as its head. Robert Sherwood joined the organization early. When he called upon Robert Riskin to establish a Motion Picture Bureau for the purpose of making propaganda films, Bob accepted eagerly.

Office space was rented on West Fifty-seventh Street; the office had a desk and the desk had pencils. He began there in the summer of 1942 to build an organization that would make a series of documentaries about America for release in multiple languages, that would let people in various countries know the character and quality of the average American, the basic closeness of that American to people everywhere.

He recruited men who had already had experience in the documentary field: Joe Krumgold, Irving Lerner, Peter Hackenschmied. And he asked Philip Dunne to be in charge of production.

The team he chose would make approximately thirty films. For *Swedes in America*, Ingrid Bergman went to a small town in Minnesota and spent time with families and narrated her understanding responsiveness to their way of life in this land. There was *Pipeline*, the story of the building of a line to carry oil from Texas to the East Coast. Frederic March was the narrator. *Cowboy* had the resonant voice of Ralph Bellamy to tell the story of those hard-riding westerners. And there was *The Autobiography of a Jeep*, about the birth, growth, and triumph of that vehicle. Told in the first person, the Jeep went from aspiring uncertainty about its capability to testing in the field to certain acceptance everywhere to pride and exultation when it had the privilege of carrying Winston Churchill and Franklin Roosevelt through the streets of Casablanca.

The usual length of an OWI film was 800 feet, but *The Tennessee Valley Authority* and *Toscanini* were extended to 1200 feet. The great conductor agreed, for the first time, to appear in a film. In a sense, he was the author of this work. It retold his personal celebration of the downfall of Mussolini. For that occasion, he had conducted the NBC Symphony Orchestra in a jubilant broadcast of Verdi's *The Force of Destiny Overture* and *The Hymn of the Nations*. It was his choice to augment this OWI film with the "Internationale" and "The Star-Spangled Banner." Never have I heard our national anthem played so fervently. His interest in the film was profound. With the rise of Fascism, he had exiled himself from his native Italy and now, at last, was able to give thanks for his country's release from dictatorship.

When I knew that I was pregnant (about six weeks after we were married), I felt like a perfect wife; Bob was so pleased.

What a delight to see my husband as happy as I was! This child would not be for myself, but for *us*. A greater gift could not be possible. Our mutual eagerness gave me a feeling of tranquility, the first I had ever known. I thought I was not showing very much when Flo and Jo Swerling arrived in New York, but as soon as I opened the door to greet them, Flo said, "You're pregnant!" Women are so wise. When we were dining at 21 about that same time, Constance Bennett sent a note to me from far across the room: "I think you're pregnant," it said. I waved an amazed but happy "yes" to her.

Tranquility was shattered one afternoon when I heard screams of pain from Susan's room. Bea had given her an enema, hoping to relieve some abdominal discomfort. I called her pediatrician but had to keep calling because he took so long to get there and her pains were intense. After five hours, he came. When he touched her abdomen, she screamed an angry scream as if she'd like to kill him for doing that. We got her to the Presbyterian Hospital, where a surgeon was waiting. "You have a very sick little girl," he said. Bob was standing right beside me. That's the point. He was with me.

Soon after I married John, he had said, "You mustn't get sick. Avis [his first wife] got appendicitis soon after I married her. You mustn't get sick." He had wanted my sympathy. What a fantastic instruction! What a fantastic difference between these two men!

Susan had worse than appendicitis. She had a *burst* appendix. It must have been a very demanding surgery; she had drains in place for weeks. But we got her home for Christmas.

"You're working very hard," Bob said as he watched me trim the tree. "Yes, I am working hard. But she deserves a beautiful tree!"

Throughout the spring, I coached her, especially in reading, so she would be ready for school in the fall.

Tranquility was restored.

On the night of July 2nd, my own abdomen was signaling gentle but certain indications that it was time for the new baby to arrive. Bob got a writing pad and notated the intervals and duration of the labor pains. My, I thought, you have never written a script like this! It was lovely to see his concentration, as though he were composing a masterpiece just by marking off the minutes! By six o'clock the next morning we were on our way to the Presbyterian Hospital. The taxi driver loved the opportunity to go through every red light, and by eight that morning Bobby was born—handsome, wonderfully well-shaped, with chestnut-red hair that smelled like his father's. Again, I felt like the perfect wife. A *boy*!

Now we needed more space than we had at the Hampshire House and found it at the Ritz Towers at the corner of Fifty-seventh and Park. From the window on the sixteenth floor, it was possible to watch Bob walk briskly up Fifty-seventh Street to begin his day's work. Hands in the pockets of his overcoat, he went along swiftly, heels coming down first. The style and pace with which he walked had intent—and goodness. He always wore a hat. Later, we would learn that both he and Robert Sherwood scored well with investigators on that account, for it was thought that Communists never wore hats.

Each person who worked for the OWI had to be cleared by Civil Service investigation. The recruitment of personnel was so urgent, so rapid, that investigations stumbled over the huge amount of processing to be done. Bob had been with the OWI about two years when the following arrived from the United States Civil Service Commission:

> You are advised that as a result of investigation you have been rated eligible, subject to satisfactory fingerprint clearance, for the position of Chief, Bureau of Overseas Motion Pictures, Office of War Information, New York.

Besides the work for the OWI, there were people from Hollywood to be seen as they went through New York en route to personal appearances overseas. For most, it was a new and formidable challenge. Spencer Tracy and Edward G. Robinson came by the apartment to get advice from Bob.

Another part of the Hollywood contingent attached to the Signal

Corps included Frank Capra and Anatole Litvak, who stopped by on a strictly social basis.

John Gunther lived at 530 Park Avenue and invited friends to "come to 530 at 5:30," where he had good delicatessen food and conversation that we shared once with Chaim Weizmann, who was looking for money to establish the future state of Israel, and again with Wendell Willkie, who had sought the presidency of the United States.

Laudy Lawrence, who represented MGM in Europe, came to town with his wife, Ping, and asked us to share a memorable evening at a French café with their friends, Pierre Lazaroff (of *Le Monde*) and Antoine de Saint-Exupery, who had written *Night Flight* and *Wind, Sand, and Stars* and was soon to publish *The Little Prince*. I had read *Wind, Sand, and Stars* and took this man's philosophy into my heart and soul. He expressed a faith in the potential courage, nobility, and love of men, including the "tiller of the earth as well as the explorer of unknown skies." Oh, he was wonderful to look at! Big, tall, great black eyes that themselves looked like radiant stars. When coffee came, he turned his chair away from the table and leaned back in it as if wanting more room for the great size of him. All the while, French, more than English, was being spoken. But that didn't matter to me. I was remembering what he had written: that human relationships were the source of joy in life. But ties of love should not mean looking at one another, rather "looking together in the same direction." And that, I thought, was Bob and me.

The Radio Section of the OWI was headed by Louis G. Cowan. "You will like him," Bob said when we received an invitation to dine with him and his wife Polly. I did like them both and their children and felt that family part of my own.

"You will like Sidney Bernstein." Sidney, as head of the Motion Picture Section of the British Ministry of Information, had a position comparable to Bob's. Their exchanges enhanced the cooperation between British and American filmmaking. It was a delight when Sidney came to New York.

Gregory Ratoff came to see me with a request from Darryl

Zanuck that I play Wilson's second wife, Edith, in the film *Woodrow Wilson*. I didn't want to do it but thought Bob might be glad to have me add to our coffer (Susan was in private school). He hesitated to tell me that he hoped I wouldn't want to work, and while it took a day or two to discover his feeling and for him to know mine, it was a great relief—even a pleasure. For the first time, family would be first.

We shared time with Bill and Dorothy Paley, with Phil and Amanda Dunne. We dined at the Colony and at 21. Always there was the constant awareness that Bob might have to go overseas. He came home one evening to ask me, "Do you know what's happening?"

"They're sending you overseas!"

"No. This hotel is on fire. The lobby is full of firemen!"

"Thank God! I thought you might be leaving!"

When he did leave, shortly before Thanksgiving, I knew a few days ahead only because I happened to touch his upper arm and discovered it was sore from immunization shots.

Letter from London, 1944:

I haven't written to you in an eternity and just wired you to that effect. Each day I would start to write—and then retreat from the idea, thinking "how silly—it's a matter of days."

Just when one matter gets itself nearly disposed of, a larger and more important issue looms up—requiring more meetings and more negotiations.

I tried cabling you after every raid so that you wouldn't worry . . . at the same time I didn't want you to get accustomed to the idea . . . so that if the cable was delayed, you would really have cause for concern.

Every time a raid starts, I think of you sitting at the radio, listening to Ed Murrow describe it vividly. . . . I see your face cloud. . . . I see your imagination fired. . . . I see you seeing me buried in a mass of rubble. I want to rush to a phone to tell you immediately I am whole and unhurt and not to worry and how much I love you for worrying.

During the week or so of persistent raids (none for almost ten days—or almost none) I learned something of the secret of why the British were so stoical . . . well, anyway, *one* of the reasons. It's an injustice to the British . . . but a theory of mine which I shall tell you about.

Actually, a great many people enjoyed the raids. Certainly the danger was there . . . the ever present imminence of your own destruction . . . but something else was there . . . *company*. It is difficult to be lonely when you are sharing a common danger with people all about you. I found, after the first few days, that I was disappointed when the alert failed to sound. I was alone in my room . . . removed from the world around me when nothing happened. But the moment the siren started, I was no longer alone . . . thousands . . . millions of other hearts stirred simultaneously . . . skipped a beat just as mine skipped. At that moment, they were in the room with me . . . and I was with them . . . in a million homes . . . in a million cellars. At times like that, no matter how impoverished you might feel . . . in worldly goods or in the spirit . . . you are lifted to a level of equality with the most blessed of human beings. Envy of another's riches . . . fear through insecurity . . . a floundering ego . . . all vanish. For one moment, you are the equal of the most courageous . . . for one moment, the brains, the genius, the gifts, the accumulated wealth, the high positions of the mightiest disappear . . . and all are one . . . of which you are an equal part.

What a blessing this must have been to the lonely. Think of how many sad, frustrated lives were revivified in the cellars . . . the subways and the shelters of Britain. People who found they weren't quite so inhibited as they thought. Words, thoughts, anecdotes poured forth. No wonder that even when the raids stopped in 1941, hundreds, thousands continued to sleep in shelters. They had inherited new families . . . new interests and were loathe to part with them. It was so difficult to go back to that lonely existence.

How smooth and unthreatening, comparatively, was life in New York! Pushing my handsome little Bobby in the pram to the park, counting ration stamps, making the occasional short trip to sell war bonds. Phil Dunne helped me with a speech I gave at a rally for the reelection of Franklin Roosevelt, where a skinny Frank Sinatra also appeared.

I helped Dorothy Paley trim her Christmas tree (Bill Paley was overseas). Her artistry and willingness to use no metallic decoration turned the tree into a beauty bedecked only with bows of red satin ribbon.

Bobby, now a manly six months old, lay on his beautiful belly, stretching a curious hand toward the ornaments on our tree: glass ornaments only, tied on with string or ribbon so that every bit of metal could go to the war that would "end all wars." I had photographs made of him, of him and Susan, of him and me, these to be saved for Bob's return . . . no use to send them overseas.

I thought of inviting Greta Garbo, who lived immediately next to us, to come in and see our tree and visit with the children. But her manner was formidable; if she saw anyone in the hall, she would run back to her apartment and slam the door. And in the elevator, she crouched in the corner while whoever was her escort covered her from view with a topcoat. The children's nurse was mightily disappointed; I consoled her by telling her that I knew Ronald Colman, whom she also admired greatly, and that when we returned to California, he might visit us.

When Bob came home in the spring, he was too ill to say more than hello; he had gotten food poisoning en route. It was several days before he could say hello heartily.

A short vacation took us to Hollywood and Irene Selznick gave us a party. Irene had a beautiful home, conceived by her, achieved by her (though, of course, with the help of a great architect and decorators), but I believe the choices were all Irene's. She was strong and decisive—about "things" as well as people. Where people were concerned, if she liked someone, she was loyal; if not, she could apparently turn them out to pasture with the greatest of ease. She had carried a banner for her father, Louis B. Mayer, and then for her husband, David O. Selznick. After their separation, she carried a banner for her friends. She had a strong respect for Bob and an over-the-years regard for me. She knew more about me than most people did: She had been a very close friend both to Clifford and to Cary and had known me when I was married to John. She was a very aware lady.

She lived in a lovely neighborhood. Chaplin's house was nearby, Pickfair was close, Willy Wyler had a home on the same street. A wide, sloping lawn at the rear of Irene's house led to a pool and a great sunken tennis court. At Sunday tennis matches, games were going constantly while guests who didn't play could relax and watch from an observation point well above the court, or could stroll a few steps into a recreation room and find a buffet table with wonderful food. The party she gave for Bob and me was in the evening. She gave it because she was glad that Bob and I were together.

I was so glad we were together that, on that particular trip, I began to knit a white cashmere pullover sweater for Bob, with the finest needles (number double zero!). I loved the cozy domestic feeling it gave me and I knew Bob would love the sweater even if the sleeves might be a tiny bit long; in other words, even if it weren't absolutely perfect, I was inclined to think that Bob would believe it was.

We went to an after-Oscar dinner at Chasen's restaurant. Loretta Young loaned me a gown, opening her closet for me to choose from dozens plus dozens.

Loretta was so beautiful she seemed to be very near unreal. My cook once said of her when she came for dinner, "Now I've seen a dream walking." But that "dream" could be very down to earth and practical and warm. We had a mutual friend in Flo Swerling, who had met Loretta when she and Spencer Tracy fell in love during the filming of *A Man's Castle*, written by Jo Swerling. Flo was enchanted with the romance—and happy to be a confidante. Loretta's Catholicism held a strong appeal for Flo, too. Flo was born to Jewish parents. She would never cease wishing that her mother had not died when she was an infant, and she would never cease remembering the motherly, loving kindness of nuns when she, as a child, had been hospitalized.

That memory would envelop her when she became hospitalized again near the end of her life. She asked me to tell Loretta that she longed to be embraced by the Church. Loretta was responsive, arranging for a priest to spend time with Flo, and when Flo died, services were held at St. Paul's in West Los Angeles. It was very touching to think that Flo wanted to be so "cradled" at last.

At the Beverly Wilshire Hotel, writers came to see Bob about possibly working for the OWI. A group from the Writers' Mobilization included names I would hear again and again. I think Bob felt he had his quorum of talent and writers, but he listened to what the group had to say. I did not sit in at the meeting but remember that several of them would become known as part of the Hollywood Ten.

There would be one more lonely Christmas in New York while Bob went overseas again to North Africa and to Italy. In Italy, he attacked a typewriter that retaliated by making his practice phrase, "Now is the time," come out, "Boz is the Tib," which had a certain charm but might have been thought "code" by the censor, so Bob wrote in his smooth, even script. He wrote a lot so that I was able to answer inquiries about him from the OWI and allay their strong concern when a report came through that he had been shot down over Algiers. If you write almost every day, you are not likely to have been shot down.

It may have been the enchanting scenery at Marrakesh (snow-covered mountains, orange groves) that pulled Bob's thoughts toward California. Most likely, it was the disenchantment with the official line taken toward Marshal Tito that decided Bob to offer his resignation early in 1945.

CHAPTER 26

A HOME
ON A HILL

♦

B Y THE MIDDLE OF MAY, word came that Katya had found a pretty house for us high on a hill. As usual, she had seen to it that everything was in order, had left us a gift of a Rouault print but was, herself, not to be seen. We had a sweeping view of Beverly Hills and the fragrance of flowers all around. Bob could set up a card table in the garden and write quite undisturbed by the children, even though they circled about him.

Bobby, always curious, tinkered with a bathroom doorknob and locked himself in. No one could venture climbing through a window too narrow for any but the slim Mr. Deeds, who wouldn't have known what to do anyway, even if we pushed him through. A very agreeable Beverly Hills Fire Department came to help us.

We gave a party. Irene Selznick and Cary Grant and Loretta Young were there and the Lewis Milestones and Flo and Jo Swerling. I heard Cary say to Bob something he really didn't have to say, "Be good to her. I was *so* in *love* with her!" in that cadence that was so particularly Cary's. The rest of what he said was less emphasized. "I wouldn't have been a good husband. I pay too much attention to the position of a sofa. That sort of thing." What else went into that dialogue, or monologue, I didn't hear; I had moved along to other guests. That was the first time I knew he had ever had thoughts of us being together. Of course, much earlier I had had similar thoughts, but they were never sustained and I knew instinctively that I would not have been good for him, knew that most actors seem to need more attention than most actresses are willing to give and had a sneaky certainty that that would be true of him . . . and of me.

There was a life-is-wonderful-tone in his voice, and what he had to say only added to the sweetness of the evening. I had never known him to be any other way. Mr. Feeling Good. Mr. Stardust. And when he went to the buffet table, it was a joy to hear him say, "French peas! Oh, *I love* French peas!"

We celebrated Bobby's second birthday on July 3. A month later, we had the news of the bombing of Hiroshima, Nagasaki, and the surrender of Japan. Not very long after that, there was word that Russia also had an atomic bomb. So horrendous was the way in which the war in the Pacific had come to an end, that my personal reaction to the latest news was, now, thank God, no one can ever use that bomb again.

Bobby's little sister, Vicki, was well on the way when I found a house large enough to welcome her and any possible future siblings—a forever house: a two-story English Tudor with wide lawns and terraced cutting gardens. We had been in the house for less than three weeks when Vicki presented her credentials to us at the Good Samaritan Hospital. Six and a half lovely pounds of girl. Susan, always having a sense of drama, wrote her a letter of warning. She wanted her sister to know that when she came home, there would be someone in the house (in the person of the nurse, Miss Haesloop) who would know and see everything she did. Beware!

Bob had great respect for Susan's imaginings and wanted her to write them out, to make them into stories. His records of Gilbert and Sullivan and numerous operas, especially *La Boheme*, cast a spell upon her. She performed Mimi, pantomiming the voice and fainting quite a lot.

Bob had known a Metropolitan Opera star, Marie Rappold, who was now living in California. He sought her out and arranged for her to give Susan lessons. Hers was a home of shabby gentility, cracked teacups, and memorabilia and playing cards always on the dining table waiting for a possible game of poker. I left Bobby there one day while Susan had her lesson and returned to find them all playing cards, a cat sitting atop the pennies, no one noticing Bobby's eyes tearing—the first I knew that he was allergic to cats.

He was not allergic to a beautiful collie named Please that Bob brought home. Please came in, walked to the fireplace, sat on the hearth, as if requesting that her picture be taken in the spot where she knew she belonged. Having Please led to naming a white German shepherd Thanx. Thanx had a certain restlessness; he would run up through the terraced garden, along a former bridle path, in back of the Bel Air Hotel, and come out at any one of a number of homes in upper Stone Canyon. He was never a go-and-fetch dog. He was come-and-fetch-me dog. We were doing that quite often.

A young owl representing the wildlife of the area got into the chimney and found his way onto the mantelpiece in the master bedroom. Bob and I awoke to see two luminous eyes blinking at us. His choice of a perch seemed right and appropriate and we wanted to keep him. With the help of our Japanese gardener, we made him a cage, which was a shameful mistake. None of us knew he wouldn't be able to endure.

George, the gardener, had just been released from one of the Japanese internment camps. I try not to think how sad that must have been. He was a good gardener and a friend to Bobby. Bobby was often his assistant.

Vicki, whose real name was Victoria, looked like a queen in the elegant bassinet that had been Susan's and just as little-queenly in the grand English pram. While waiting to be old enough to join in the older children's parties, she was admired by them in between their swinging and sliding and pony-riding.

Many of the children in the neighborhood came with their nannies to spend the afternoon because our lawn was the largest and most level.

At last it snowed in California! You don't often get a chance to build a snowman on your front lawn in California, but we *did*. I'm guessing it was the winter of 1947–48.

By that time, Bob had legally adopted Susan. He had also completed his first independent production. *Magic Town* was a story about a small town in Illinois that repeatedly polled in elections as infallibly representing the national vote. He had wanted Jimmy Stewart for it and went to have a meeting with Jimmy's agent. He came home to say he had found that agent so able and engaging that he wanted him to become his own representative. Later on, Lew Wasserman was.

Jane Wyman was the leading lady in *Magic Town*. She came to the house one evening to talk about the script and wardrobe and other etceteras. Her husband, Ronald Reagan, came to call for her. She and Bob and I were sitting at the far end of the thirty-foot living room. Ronnie took about two steps into the room and began to talk—about something he had just heard on the radio. It was as though there were an invisible soapbox underneath him and the stance he took. It was just so surprising that I remember nothing of the subject matter, only his need to expound.

During the filming of *Magic Town*, their marriage was breaking up, Jane had told Bob, who told me, who told no one. I was never any good at passing stories along.

It wasn't because of the cast or the story that *Magic Town* got poor reviews. It may have been that William Wellman, who was really a good and strong director, didn't have the light touch or the humor to match Bob's style of writing. There is a chemistry of forces that must work together to make a successful film. If any element is missing, there is a *miss*.

Bob relinquished the idea of independent production and wrote a filmscript for Twentieth Century-Fox. *Mister 880*, based on a story in *The New Yorker* that itself was based on a real court case, about a dear old gentleman who counterfeited one-dollar bills but only enough to sustain himself and his little dog and to give something to a needy soul or two in his neighborhood. Of course, it was criminal but, as played by Edmund Gwenn, so *understandable* that we, as audience, were delighted that when the old fellow was tried, his prison sentence was suspended and he was fined just one of the dollars he had made.

A split personality is probably not a classic theme for comedy—but that was the way Bob approached *Half Angel*. Loretta Young and Joseph Cotton starred in it. Loretta's character was a sober and serious nurse in the daytime and a fun-loving adventuress by night, with neither half of her personality knowing anything of the other, just being somewhat tired from all the effort it was to be living two lives and for twenty-four hours a day.

Edna Best and her husband Nat Wolfe, Ronald and Benita Colman, the Lloyd Nolans, and the Andy Devines, among others, were square-dance enthusiasts and captured us and swept us along. We whirled about and did do-si-dos to country music. Even Laurence Olivier joined us one night. It was giddy fun and we couldn't wait to get "squared-away" for the next event. The dress code wasn't very demanding; the ladies needed full skirts but a western tie was enough to make a man eligible, so that anyone who suddenly came to town could be handed a tie and thereby become an instant dancer.

There were times, after the "children's hour," when Bob and I had a quiet evening of gin rummy. How frustrating for me! He was so good at cards, he seemed to know exactly what I held in my hand. We kept score but never paid off. How could I? On paper, I owed him 50,000 points in what seemed like no time at all. It was better just to let the zeros run off the page. I did learn enough from him to beat a few other people. One of them was Willy Wyler and only one time—but it was a minor compensation.

Bob had once had a face-off with Darryl Zanuck in a poker game. Bluffing, Bob had lost $40,000 on one hand. Ethel Hill, a writer, had been a partner with Bob in owning horses. We carried a portable radio out to the garden one afternoon and listened to her horse War Knight win a $100,000 Santa Anita Derby. She had told Bob she stayed in the stable all the night before, pray-ing. He was glad she'd won and showed no regret that he no longer owned horses or played in super card games.

If Bob was content to relinquish those activities that had been diversional for him, he was also able to let go of the evidence of former romantic attachments. A watch-chain pendant of Carole Lombard's profile etched in gold simply disappeared. And a framed photo of an English actress, Elizabeth Allen, that I had seen on the desk in his bachelor apartment disappeared also.

For my part, it was easy to relinquish the idea of working. However much I wanted a career, I had always felt that the values of personal relationships and family life were of first importance.

Bob and I had no need to discuss our attitudes. We just knew.

The company of good friends and the discussion of ideas some-times went on until three o'clock in the morning. At the Lewis Milestones', besides good talk, there were often parties. Kendall Milestone was an imaginative hostess and her guests were gener-ous. Hearing Walter Huston sing "September Song" holds that time in place for me. Or Gene Kelly singing "Cockles and Mus-sels," or Danny Kaye not singing but conducting Christmas car-olers as they sat on the stairs with Danny at the bottom, seeming to have total control over every tone—and so vigorously.

At Romanoff's restaurant during coffee talk one night, an entire wheel of Roquefort cheese came to the table—a gift from John Huston to repay Bob for a piece of cheese he had shared with John when they had met overseas during the Allied invasion of Italy. As much as anything, that big wheel of cheese was a pungent reminder that the war really was over.

The sound of Bob's car coming into the driveway at the end of a working day was a signal for Vicki and Bobby to be ready for the "children's hour." The setting for this was in the master bedroom, where Bob relaxed with a beer or a "neat" scotch. If Susan didn't always join, it was probably because she was doing homework or because a card on her wall assured her of Bob's devotion: "If I had the choice of choosin', I'd choose a girl like Susan."

Bob did magic tricks, let Vicki sip the foam from his beer, watched Bobby use the bed for a trampoline, Vicki perform her idea of ballet dancing, and often treated both children to the amazing trick of apparently swallowing a lighted cigarette! But when he cracked walnuts on the ceiling, Susan was sure to hear and join. All of us liked that trick the best. If it was one nut he wanted to crack, he'd press the nut down into the corner of a cushion, aim it at the ceiling, then smack both sides of the cushion, and *voilá!* The nut flew up and fell down, well-cracked. Or he could do six at a time by nesting them in a depressed center of the cushion, almost covering them with the sides of it— then yank both sides suddenly open and snap! All of them flew up at once and there was a scramble to recover all the shells and nuts. This trick was best done in the living room, where there was more floor space. Occasionally, a nut would fall behind a painting and stay there maybe for months until a crackling sound told us it was trying to get out.

Typically, the "children's hour" took place upstairs, but if guests were coming to dinner, they might greet the guests and join in playing "musical hats" or watch Bob juggle oranges or squeal with all of us as we watched him and Frank Capra form a human wheel and go rolling in, out, around, and about the furniture.

My brother Dick, who was a film editor and had good movie-camera equipment, took movies of the children and prepared a film of them to present to Bob for Christmas. The title of this little feature was *Doing What Comes Naturally*. All Christmases at our Stone Canyon house must have been wonderful but I can remember almost nothing of them because suddenly there was one that was so painful, it had the power to erase all the others.

In *The Bowery*. Photo by Kenneth Alexander.

Adam Had Four Sons: On location at lunchtime.

Fay Wray, Ron Portas, Martha Graham, Milton Goldman, and Irene Worth. We have just come from a luncheon at The Four Seasons restaurant celebrating Martha Graham's birthday—she the genius of dance and of ageless magic.

He thought of his own intellect as "chained lightning," but Sinclair Lewis liked to be known to his friends simply as Red.

Norman Rockwell sketches me in a No Smoking area during filming of *The Texan*.

Flo and Jo Swerling—my happily married friends.

Fashion photo from Columbia's *Park Avenue Dame*. This Thirties gown is currently back in style. (Phototeque)

Fashion photo from the Columbia film *Murder in Greenwich Village*.

Susan, age six, wearing diamond ring Bob Riskin gave her on the day of our wedding. Bob's dachshund, Mr. Deeds, sits beside her.

From left: Vicki (six months), polka-dot puppy, Susan, and Bobby, getting to know one another.

Vicki, age seven, lets me share her lemonade.

Vicki and Bobby in California snow.

Vicki, age five.

Bobby, age seven.

Bob and Bobby in California sunshine.

My husband, Sandy Rothenberg, and me today, smiling at our future.
(W. Eugene Smith/Black Star)

At the 50th-anniversary celebration for *King Kong*, 1983.

CHAPTER 27
A BROKEN CLOCK

♦

ONE LATE DECEMBER MORNING, BOB left the house about nine o'clock to go to Twentieth Century-Fox, where he was writing a script for Clifton Webb in the role of Mr. Belvedere. He came home about ten-thirty. When I heard his car in the motor court, I opened the front door. He walked past me and upstairs without speaking. I followed. Then he told me. At the studio, it had been impossible to concentrate. For the past six weeks, he had been aware of an increasing weakness in his left hand and arm. Now, he was sure he must see a neurologist who had been recommended by his personal physician when they had been together a few days earlier on the golf course.

I drove him carefully . . . carefully, believing, crazily, that a sudden stop or lane change might make his condition worse. The first indignity was having to walk barefoot in an examining gown while the doctor observed his gait. Yes . . . a little off . . . uneven. A further indignity was a spinal tap. The headache that followed, they said, was to be expected. We went home, where he lay flat in a dark room to try to control the headache—a minimal consideration amid the enormous dark feelings about what might lie ahead.

Both his personal physician and the neurologist thought he should be hospitalized. As we prepared to go to the Cedars of Lebanon the next morning, Flo and Jo Swerling arrived with a limousine. There was little conversation as the four of us were driven toward the hospital. The physicians involved said we must have the attention of Dr. Tracy Putnam, head of neurosurgery, but he was not in the city. Attempts to reach him were begun. At the end of the day, I went by the Swerlings' house to wait beside their phone for word of Dr. Putnam. They were playing recently composed music by their friend, Frank Loesser, from *The Most Happy Fella*.

Early the next morning when I went into Bob's room, I found him on the floor—in a coma. Nurses came and got him into bed. He could only hold his right hand to his head, saying, "Tight, tight." Now, his whole left side was paralyzed.

In the late afternoon, Dr. Putnam arrived. After examining Bob, he picked up the phone. "Is Dr. Rothenberg in the house?" he asked, as if needing that person. The answer appeared to be a disappointing no.

After consultation with the medical men and with Bob's family, there was a concerted decision to follow Dr. Putnam's advice and let him do exploratory brain surgery. It was scheduled for December 27. Following the surgery, there was the reassurance that no tumor had been found but a "peculiar knot" of blood vessels had been removed. All were in what Dr. Putnam called "a silent room," so that there was "no reason why the left side would not return to normal." There was still further examination to be done—to find the *cause*. "It will be months before he is well again. But I am most encouraged," the doctor said.

At the end of those months, I thought, when he would be completely well, Bob would be fascinated to know all that he had been through. He could then have an objective look at his experience. I had already made notes from the first postoperative day.

My gift to him would be a detailed journal. It was meant to be read by him only. To this day, no one has seen it but me and my first reading of it comes approximately thirty-two years later.

Although he was never to read it, there may still be a value to someone to know how his character and special qualities revealed themselves all through even the most hazardous days. As originally written, the details are much too great, too many to sustain the interest of any but the one most secondarily involved—myself. With selectivity, his exceptional sensitivity and humor is still evident—a humor that was an inherent part of him and his talent.

For ten days after surgery, Bob was semicomatose, sometimes weeping, often restless. On January 7, he remained awake and clear for almost two hours.

A nurse asks: "Do you see me, Mr. Riskin?"

     Bob: "That's a leading question."

   Nurse: "What do I have on my head?"

     Bob: No response.

   Nurse: "He looks like he's thinking."

     Bob: "I'm always thinking—of a bon mot. Never answer a question directly if I can help it."

Extending right arm at right angle as if reaching for something and finding nothing.

     Bob: "Part of this bed is outside. Pea soup. They call solid food pea soup. Local joke."

I kneel by the bed.

     I: "Can you see me?"

     Bob: "I saw you for years. Long before anyone realized. Who's taking care of the transportation?"

I think this means who is driving the children to school. Soon, I realize you mean transportation to London. Whether you have gone back in time out of longing for England, or out of remembered apprehension, I cannot know.

Dr. Rothenberg, in resident training under Dr. Putnam, arrives. He has just returned from vacation.

> Bob: "It finally comes down to a redhead."
>
> Dr. R.: "That's a very important thing you've just said. You know I have red hair." (After a moment) "Do you have any pain?"
>
> Bob: (Weeping) "Only the pain of creation, only the pain of composition, only the pain of creation."

Dr. R. says he understands. Then:

> "You are getting better each day. It's been tough but you're improving and in a little time you will be normal in every respect. You will not have any frustration in talking. Do you understand me?"

All the while, you are studying him.

> Bob: "Yeah."

Dr. R. leaves.

> Bob: "That's man power. Straight." (Pointing to your head)
>
> I: "You mean he thinks straight? He's straightforward? Then you like him?"
>
> Bob: "Can't help liking some of 'em."

Out in the corridor, I tell Dr. Rothenberg I feel bad to see you weeping. He tells me, "This is emotional *lability* that is part of the disorder that these patients experience."

When the nurse asks you to turn over, you say to me, "She should be more serious."

It is about midnight. You are restless. I tell you to sleep, that I am going to sleep. (I am staying at the hospital.)

> Bob: "You won't know what time it is. The clock is broken— the hand."

You hold your left hand with your right.

I hold you and tell you the clock is not broken.

You are looking at the ceiling.

> Bob: "It's a beautiful version of the Bible—John. Come, peace."
>
> (To me): "We have suffered together. The strange case of the little dog, Camillo . . . Jesus Christ was particularly interested in little [word lost]. He was a Communist. Who was the Communist priest in the little town?"

You fall asleep.

Dr. R. asks me if I have noted whether or not you're oriented. I tell him of your talk about being presently in England. He says it would be good for you to be oriented. You would feel better.

In the morning:

> Bob: "That Boss Man. Redhead. Carrot Top. I like him."
>
> I: "Yes. He's honest. All the doctors are honest, but he tells you straighter."
>
> Bob: "When I saw him, I thought we could use him in the OWI. Right kind of man for the OWI. Thinks straight."
>
> I: "He told you there was no tumor. You remember, don't you?"
>
> Bob: "Poor John. For him it was worse and worse—about his son." (This refers to John Gunther)

During evening bath you tease the nurse, saying she once gave you a swift turn that nearly snapped your head off.

> Bob: "Snapped my head off. I've been looking for it ever since."

I laugh.

> Bob: "You think anything I say is funny. Even if it *is* funny."

You talk about a play you are writing for Harpo Marx. Talk about Churchill—a speech he should be making now:

> Bob: "Come on. Let's go. It looked as bad as this in 1941."

You talk about Mary, who wrote for the *Express*.

> Bob: "Genuine. She took you to London's Eastside. She shrieked for equality. Was like Hemingway's wife Martha . . ."

I: "Gillmore?"
Bob: "No. Gellhorn."

You ask me to look for pieces Mary wrote. To do research on it.

I: "May be in our files."
Bob: "Too simple."

Suddenly you remember Mary's name: Gunn.

Bob: "Mary Gunn. Shows you what research can do!
"What would you think would be the greatest war song? 'I was walking along minding my own business when slam-bang bang-slam alakazam, love walked up and hit me right between the eyes.' No language barriers. You can fill in whatever you want with slam-bang bang-slam alakazam."
I: "Was it a war song?"
Bob: "Wasn't meant to be. It's a kind of philosophy. You're as good as the next fellow. Don't know what to expect. Walking along, minding your own business, you can get hit with love or with a bomb."
I: "A bomb of love."
Bob: "Slam-bang bang-slam."

Sidney Bernstein arrived from England and came to the hospital today. Tonight, there was no reference to England.

The evening is wakeful. You say you would like to have a pillow my size and shape to keep beside you.

Bob: "A good idea for department stores. They could sell a million of 'em."

You tell me you've been trying to remember where it was you gave a "lift" to a G.I.

I: "Between Paris and Luxembourg?"
Bob: "Yes. Near Paris. I'm so grateful to be partly right about my memory."

I remind you that you remembered better than I the name of Hemingway's wife, Martha Gellhorn. I remind you that you know more about radio schedules than I do: Ed Murrow, Cecil Brown, Elmer Davis.

I ask you if you know of a book called *The Little Town of Don Camillo*.

> Bob: "That's what I was trying to tell you about. Communist priest."

Physiotherapy had begun and a schedule was established to continue treatment under the care of male nurses, so the doctors told me I could expect to take Bob home. The following days were filled with planning about how and where to establish a hospital room—downstairs? upstairs? I chose upstairs because, even though he would have nurses, I could sleep in a bedroom next to him and be aware of how things were going.

On one of those planning evenings, after saying goodnight to the children, I went downstairs where no one could hear me if I cried. I sat in the breakfast room in Bob's chair. This was the room we used for family meals around a large lazy-susan table. This room would never again be the same. Not this room or any other room in the house. I needn't have been concerned about anyone hearing me cry. Silent tears poured steadily, steadily down my face and fell onto my folded hands as they rested in my lap. Four weeks of the deepest concern had to be released. It may have taken an hour to do that, I'm not sure. I felt as though my own clock was broken. But I also felt that emptying out those tears would make a space for new energies to begin the long pull toward helping Bob recover.

During the first year, deep concern came from many. Darryl Zanuck wrote a long, handwritten letter urging consultation with a Swedish neurosurgeon. Irene Selznick, Lew Wasserman, Jack Benny, Harpo and Susan Marx, Eddie (Edward G.) Robinson, Lou Cowan, Norman Krasna, Ida Koverman, and Irving Berlin all came to see Bob. Very frequently, so did Jo and Flo Swerling.

John Gunther and his wife spent a weekend very near us at the Bel Air Hotel. John wanted to know about Bob, even though he found it too difficult to see him. His sensitivity was related to the loss of his son, who, coincidentally, had also been operated upon by Tracy Putnam.

Had Bob's devastating stroke occurred a year later, there might have been a medication to thin the blood that had clotted within his carotid artery—discovered to have been the cause of his stroke. As it was, persistent therapy did almost nothing to relieve the paralysis.

After that first year, with finances diminishing, I called Bob's friends at MCA about going back to work. Lew Wasserman asked George Chasin to see me. In a short time, George arranged for a film at Twentieth Century-Fox, *The Treasure of the Golden Condor* (released in 1952), at a higher salary than I had had before. Cornel Wilde was the star. Anne Bancroft brought her vivid personality to it, and my particular vis-à-vis was George Macready.

I was secretly pleased that, at least technically, I was still aware of camera angles. Watching them trying to adjust for a shot of me in a chair, I kept thinking, If you just put four-inch blocks under the legs of this chair, you'll have it. In a little while, they did just that. That wouldn't have done a darn thing in relation to performance but it reassured me that I had not forgotten the observations I had made over the years about what the camera was seeing.

Small Town Girl with Jane Powell and Farley Granger at MGM followed that, and then a television series, "The Pride of the Family," produced by MCA with Paul Hartmann and Natalie Wood. I have the very tenderest memories of Natalie—the look of her and her uncanny ability. She was just sixteen but wanted to be thought of as older, and the underlying restlessness caused by those feelings was evident. In one segment, she played a very old lady—so well! The last time I saw her was at Trader Vic's restaurant, where they give you gardenias. At the end of the evening, she gathered up all her blossoms and brought them to me.

In the second year of Bob's illness, we found a nursing home only a few miles distant, continuing with our own male nurses around the clock. They were pleasant fellows but sometimes erratic. One, who had seemed thoroughly dependable, became emotional because his wife had left a light on the *entire night* and he expected the electric bill would be catastrophic. Another over-reacted to a visit from Irving Berlin, who very kindly took Bob some of his favorite scotch. The nurse disappeared with the scotch *and* Bob's car, which had been kept at the nursing home for trips to physiotherapy. The nurse returned a few days later, admitting all, saying his behavior had been triggered by his wife losing a fifty-dollar bill.

Bob's brother Everett had a meeting with the board members of the Motion Picture Country Home and Hospital. They looked at my financial statement. They said Bob could go there to be cared for. No more precarious nursing! The attention and the conditions surrounding Bob were reason for the deepest gratitude. I salute the concept of the Motion Picture Country Home and Hospital and the memory of Jean Hersholt who began it.

Ellin Berlin went with me to see the smaller house I bought after selling our big English house on Stone Canyon Road. She said she was envious. High on Tigertail Road in Brentwood, the house was half the size of what we'd known but large enough so that each child had his or her own space, and Bobby his own darkroom.

With motherly enthusiasm, I went to Bobby's school to a science exhibit in which he participated. I found his work; I found his name and the legend of explanation. Two ladies looked over my shoulder, one saying to the other, "Wow! Wouldn't you hate to be that boy's mother!" The bacteria under glass was appalling to them. Not to me; I had seen it as it developed. But why should I tell *them* I was proud?

Proximity to Emily Wurtele in our new surroundings was very important. Her daughter, Nancy, was Susan's best friend. Emmy soon became best friend to me, to each of us: music teacher, cookie maker, counselor, prepared at all times to do any and every helpful thing she could, not only for us but for anyone on the hill. Neither I nor my children had ever seen our grand-mothers. It was easy to see Emmy as the imagined perfection of grandmotherliness. She had an abundantly loving heart. But when we paid her a compliment, her response was, "If you don't care what you say," tossing off the praise. She did have a fault: Even if she could understand that it sometimes was blessed to receive, she just couldn't seem to do that. Always, the giver—Emmy!

Bob had been a founder of the Writers Guild. Among other films, he had written the screenplays of *Platinum Blonde, It Happened One Night, Mr. Deeds Goes to Town, Lady for a Day, Lost Horizon, You Can't Take It With You,* and *Meet John Doe*. Several of these had enriched the Golden Age of the thirties.

It seemed appropriate that the Guild should present him with their Laurel Award for Achievement in the early spring of 1955. It would have been infinitely more appropriate if he had been able to accept it himself. When I carried it to him, although he knew perfectly well it was a permanent award, he had his little joke, asking, "Do I get to keep it?"

It was Linda Berlin who telephoned to say, "You mustn't be alone." I thought when someone died, it was all right—even *right* to be alone if you wanted.

When the doctor had phoned from the Motion Picture Hospital, I was able to get there and sit with Bob for about half an hour before he went. There was no talking; I imagined I was helping him to make a transition. Bob had been ill for five years.

Linda did come over the next day. She was dear, looking very like her dark-eyed father.

I didn't know that, after the services, food is supposed to be offered.

When the rabbi came, he found only me and Vicki. She had gone with me to the service. I didn't mind that the other children didn't; each had a right to do as he or she chose—to be alone if that was the choice.

The rabbi held Vicki on his lap for a while. Then he went, I suppose, to Everett's, where there would be food and drink.

It was only a few years later that my sister Willow would die. She had asked a rabbi to conduct a service for her. By then, I knew what to do and had food ready for her friends—Catholic, Jewish, and Protestant. It was an ecumenical feeling.

There is no beginning and no end. I do not have to go inside a church or temple to feel that.

When I was in Atlanta many years ago, I sat next to Martin Luther King, Sr., at dinner. He supposed, he said, that people in Hollywood didn't often go to church. John Carradine, who was near, said that he did—about once a week.

"And you?" Dr. King looked at me.

"Every day," I said. "Every time I go out and look at the sky, I see the dome of the church I belong to."

CHAPTER 28
A NEW BEGINNING

♦

T HE FILMS I MADE IN the next few years were not significant
except for the people I worked with. Lillian Gish was in *The
Cobweb*. I sat with her in her portable dressing room, listening to
her energetic interest in wanting a Department for the Arts to be
established in this country. Her skin was as smooth as when I had
first met her by the sea in Santa Monica.

Joan Crawford had written me a note when she knew I would be
working again. It said, "Welcome . . . we need you." At Columbia again, I played a part in *Queen Bee* with her and had the
opportunity to see how she continued to challenge each of life's
moments as she lived them: self-critical, compulsively clean,
washing her hands often and applying lotion from elbows to fin-
gertips, using every free moment between scenes to answer fan
mail, never relaxing.

Tammy and the Bachelor had the beguiling Debbie Reynolds
as Tammy. I was the mother of the bachelor. Ross Hunter was a
producer of taste.

Usually, when a person regales me with his accomplishments, I am inclined to be skeptical. Rod McKuen sat beside me during the filming of *Rock Pretty Baby* and told me about his difficult early childhood, his writing, his musical compositions, his poetry, such a flow of telling that I wondered how much I should believe. He was bursting with desire to talk about where he had been in life and where he would be going. He has indeed gone where he "would be."

Of all the medical people attending Bob, there was only one who had a high and positive energy on his behalf. The mutual interest we shared in Bob's welfare established a bond between Sanford Rothenberg and me that would endure. Exactly twenty years after Bob's illness began, Sandy and I were married. He has two children from his former marriage, and four grandchildren. He is devoted to them and they to him. I have three children, Susan, Bobby, and Vicki; two grandchildren, Nora and Jacob; and am locked with each in an embrace of deep good feeling.

Susan, an actress, continues her interest in drama, her dedication to the theater. Bob's thought of her: "She's the kind of gal . . . once she decides, won't let 'em go,'" was perceptive.

Bobby (now called Bob) has a guitar shop in Santa Monica, a shop of unique character and superior quality. Those qualities are also inherent in him.

Vicki just received her doctorate in psychology. When she was little, she was always looking after any of her friends who needed help. That is a key to her choice of career. She is married to David Rintels, a writer and producer. That keeps me circumstantially near to films even if I'm not working in them at all.

I have been in love with films since I was a very little girl. I am still in love with them. Anyone who looks back over the history of film has to be aware of their influence. Anyone who undertakes making a film today might think just a little bit about that.

Because Vicki went to school at the University of Southern California, and because I had given that institution my collection of memorabilia and Robert Riskin's, as well as all of his scripts, it was her idea to establish a screenwriting award in her father's name.

There was copious evidence that he was always ready and eager to help young writers or newcomers, for instance, Billy Wilder and James Cain; and lesser-knowns. A friend had once asked Bob's advice on behalf of a young writer who was having a tough time getting assignments. Bob told him, "Go to Harry Cohn and tell him that if he will give your friend a job, I will help him write his scripts."

He even helped not-at-all-knowns—like me. I wrote a sketch for the golfing ladies at Hillcrest—all about their trials and difficulties at getting a fair shot from the men golfers when the ladies were supposed to have priority on Tuesdays. It was pretty funny. But Bob needed only about ten minutes to add laughs where they would do the most good, and what was mildly funny became—well, a wow!

He was a judge of scripts submitted from fifty-two colleges and had no difficulty in awarding first place to John Thomas Dye, who I'm sure would have become one of our great American writers had he not been shot down over Austria during the Second World War when he was just twenty-two years old.

At the Swerlings' house in Malibu, I had listened to Bob give several hours of contribution to the developing *Guys and Dolls* when Jo Swerling and the producer, Ernie Martin, were having a Sunday conference.

He was never competitive, always wanting every film, every play, every writer to do well. James Cain wrote this to me: "He taught me that a story is 'not an abstraction based on some theoretical conception of form, but a living, individual thing. It has to be your story.' With which encouragement, I tried, at last, to set down 'my story,' queer though it seemed, and from then on began perhaps to be my own man."

At the University of Southern California, on the evening of March 22, 1987, the distinguished film critic of the Los Angeles *Times*, Charles Champlin, was master of ceremonies at an evening honoring Robert Riskin. The Dean of the School of Cinema spoke; *Toscanini*, the OWI documentary, was shown. Philip Dunne, who had produced the film under the aegis of Robert Riskin, spoke. Vicki presented the award. Before the showing of the Capra-Riskin film, *It Happened One Night*, I read the following excerpt from a letter Bob had written to me when he was in

London in March of 1944. He had been reflecting on how fragile most convictions are.

> . . . True deep-rooted convictions are rare. People see wisdom in many ideas . . . conflicting ideas . . . their hearts and their minds leap from one concept to another. In an era of chaos . . . when all the social forms and changes . . . when every concept of economic and spiritual existence is dusted off and paraded before the hard-ridden masses of the world . . . it is no wonder that John Q. Public is straddling the fence. It is no wonder that he is punch-drunk and unable to assert himself. Where is *that idea*? Where is that big, unchallengeable, fundamentally unshakable idea which snaps John Doe out of his binge and about which he says, 'Now that's what I mean. That's what I've waited for . . . that's what *I* stand for . . . and the rest is bilge.' Will that idea come in time to save us? I, personally, believe it will. Perhaps not in this generation . . . or even in the next . . . but come it must. Because, I still contend, despite all their larceny, people are good. Most of larcenous behavior is acquired . . . and the extent to which the individual practices it is dictated by necessity. Create a society of abundance for all and the need for larceny is reduced to a minimum. Of course it will never be perfect unless that green snow falls and changes the nature of man . . . but our jungle existence *can* be eradicated to some extent . . . and eventually to a great extent.
>
> I tried to say something of this sort in *Meet John Doe*. And it is interesting to note (as you and I have noted before) the number of books on religion which are successful in wartime. You see, people need goodness to lean on in times of wickedness and evil. They need to remind themselves that the human race . . . of which they are a part . . . is not all evil . . . that its impulses are virtuous and charitable and unselfish. They need this, for they cannot look upon *themselves* as wicked. No person, except for rare pathological cases, thinks of himself as anything but a good, honest human being.

This letter, and many others that Bob wrote while away, were a bridge over the vast expanse of physical distance between us.

And my letters to him, sometimes arriving in delayed bunches, nourished his spirit.

"You will have to write," he told me. "One day you will want to say something. I don't know in what form, but you will *have* to say it. And whether I encourage it or not won't matter." How very much it matters to be able to read his encouragement today!

In recent years, it has been good to have time to write. I have completed a play and had the pleasure of seeing an initial production by my good friend Francis Cleveland at his Barnstormers Theatre in Tamworth, New Hampshire. Francis Cleveland is a remarkable man. For more than a half-century he has run the Barnstormers and directed plays there with wisdom, wit, and taste. With his wife, Alice, he lives in Tamworth on "Cleveland Hill," very near the large home that was once occupied by his father, President Grover Cleveland. Francis and Alice rarely leave Tamworth, even resisting an invitation to go to the White House for an occasion that honored children of past Presidents. They love the land they live on, the view of the rolling wooded hills and purple-hued mountains on the far horizon.

Francis appears to be at least twenty years younger than he is (which is over eighty) and appears not to have gained even one pound since I met him in the spring of 1939.

When I asked him whether he would be interested in producing my play, *The Meadowlark*, his implied yes came over the telephone thus: "Will this mantle fall on us?"

The mantle fell in August of 1985. Francis gave my play a fine production. To hear the characters rise from the page and walk and speak and live on the stage was exhilarating for me. The play is based on that period when my family lived in Lark, Utah. Susan, my daughter, played the role of my mother. That was an interesting cycle of events!

No writing can be done without solitude. And Solitude is a lovely "location," a splendid place to be. You don't have to debate or defend or rationalize. You can just "be there" and, by being there, understand something of where you've been and where you may be going. In that sense, perhaps, I am at last "in charge."

I play a game about "where you may be going." When friends or loved ones die, I indulge in thoughts of where they may be born again. In a matter of seconds, I go to my atlas to look for confirmation. By doing that, I've discovered places, sometimes tiny, sometimes oddly named, about which I could never, never have known or heard. This game I play hurts no one and gives me a wonderful feeling of continuity, of endlessness.

Fan mail piles up. I look at it and wonder whether I can cope. I want to. In time, I will. I see a letter from France addressed this way: "Fay Wray . . . married with Dr. Rothenberg, near Century City. U.S.A."

With Dr. Rothenberg—my husband Sandy—I go once a year to Europe and twice a year to New York, where we are fortunate to have our own apartment and can feel the vibrance of the city and go to the theater again and again. We both love the theater. But I love the movies even more. They make a limitless imagination possible; they can embrace an enormous audience and can touch so many lives that a really good motion picture becomes a widely shared experience that has the possibility of bringing members of the human race closer together. Who of us has not been part of that caring audience?

About me, there are those who say, "What a shame she is known for *one* movie more than any other."

On the other hand, each time I arrive in New York and see the skyline and the exquisite beauty of the Empire State Building, my heart beats a little faster. I like that feeling. I really like it!

What would I have wanted to be different? I would like to have worked with and been an enduring part of a company that was small; that didn't have enormous budgets, overweighted with huge salaries; a company that could work because of the love of it and the harmony born of mutual appreciation of the art form; and where the writer would be respected first; in the beginning is the script. I would like to be thought of not as a star but as a co-worker; and much as I have regard for unions, not be afraid to move a vase on a table if I heard the cameraman say that was needed. I would like the public to be able to see a film for one-tenth of what they must pay today. I would like there to be at least one day a year when movies could be seen by poor people for absolutely nothing. I would like there to be less box-office competition and more thought about content in filmmaking.

And I would like to have had my friend Irene Selznick tell me fifty years sooner that Ernst Lubitsch was longing to work with me! She thought I knew. I would have liked Lubitsch to have told *me* instead of telling David. Oh, well!

No one who made movies during the thirties thought of those years as the Golden Age. Imagine anyone saying, "Here I am in the Golden Age!" It seems we don't know much about defining anything until long after the fact. I feel very good that there *was* a Golden Age and that I was a little, even a very little, part of it.

FILMOGRAPHY

THE COAST PATROL—Bud Barsky Corp., 1925. *Bud Barsky*. Cast: Kenneth McDonald, Clair De Lorez, Spottiswoode Aitken, Gino Corrado, 5 reels.

LAZY LIGHTNING—Universal, 1926. *William Wyler*. Cast: Art Acord, Bobby Gordon, Vin Moore, Arthur Morrison, George K. French, Rex DeRoselli. 5 reels.

THE MAN IN THE SADDLE—Universal, 1926. *Lynn Reynolds*, Cast: Hoot Gibson, Charles Mailes, Clark Comstock, Sally Long, Emmett King, 6 reels.

THE SADDLE TRAMP—Universal, 1926. *Victor Nordlinger*. Cast: Edmund Cobb, Buck Connors, Palmer Morrison, Albert J. Smith.

THE WILD HORSE STAMPEDE—Universal, 1926. *Albert Rogell*. Cast: Jack Hoxie, William Steele, Marin Sais, Clark Comstock, Jack Pratt. 5 reels.

LOCO LUCK—Universal, 1927. *Cliff Smith*. Cast: Art Acord, Aggie Herron, William A. Steele, Al Jennings, George F. Marion, M.E. Stinson. 5 reels.

A ONE MAN GAME—Universal, 1927. *Ernest Laemmle*. Cast: Fred Humes, Harry Todd, Clarence Geldert, Norbert Myles, Lotus Thompson, William Malan. 5 reels.

SPURS AND SADDLES—Universal, 1927. *Cliff Smith*. Cast: Art Acord, Bill Dyer, J. Gordon Russell, C.E. Anderson, Monte Montagu, Raven. 5 reels.

THE FIRST KISS—Paramount, 1928. *Rowland V. Lee*. Cast: Gary Cooper, Lane Chandler, Leslie Fenton, Paul Fix, Malcolm Williams, Monroe Owsley. 6 reels.

LEGION OF THE CONDEMNED—Paramount, 1928. *William A. Wellman*. Cast: Gary Cooper, Barry Norton, Lane Chandler, Francis McDonald, Voya George. 8 reels.

THE STREET OF SIN—Paramount, 1928. *Mauritz Stiller*. Cast: Emil Jannings, Olga Baclanova, Ernest W. Johnson, John Gough, Johnnie Morris, John Burdette. 7 reels.

THE WEDDING MARCH—Paramount, 1928. *Erich von Stroheim*. Cast: George Fawcett, Maude George, George Nichols, Zasu Pitts, Hughie Mack, Dale Fuller. 13 reels.

THE FOUR FEATHERS—Paramount, 1929. *Ernest B. Schoedsack*, Merian C. Cooper, Lothar Mendes. Cast: Richard Arlen, William Powell, Clive Brook, Noah Beery, Theodore von Eltz, Harold Hightoun. 81 minutes.

POINTED HEELS—Paramount, 1929. *A. Edward Sutherland*. Cast: William Powell, Helen Kane, Skeets Gallagher, Phillips Holmes, Adrienne Dore, Eugene Pallette. 61 minutes.

THUNDERBOLT—Paramount, 1929. *Josef von Sternberg*. Cast: George Bancroft, Richard Arlen, Tully Marshall, Eugenie Besserer, James Spottiswood. 94 minutes.

BEHIND THE MAKE-UP—Paramount, 1930. *Robert Milton*. Cast: William Powell, Hal Skelly, Kay Francis, E.H. Calvert, Paul Lukas, Jacques Vanaire. 70 minutes.

BORDER LEGION—Paramount, 1930. *Otto Brower*, Edwin H. Knopf. Cast: Richard Arlen, Jack Holt, Eugene Pallette, Stanley Fields, Ethan Allen, Sid Saylor. 68 minutes.

CAPTAIN THUNDER—Warner Brothers, 1930. *Alan Crosland*. Cast: Victor Varconi, Charles Judels, Robert Elliott, Don Alvarado, Natalie Moorhead, Bert Roach. 66 minutes.

PARAMOUNT ON PARADE—Paramount, 1930. *Dorothy Arzner*, Edmund Goulding, Victor Heerman, Edwin H. Knopf, Rowland V. Lee. Cast: Jean Arthur, Clara Bow, Gary Cooper, Maurice Chevalier, William Powell, Fredric March, Jack Oakie. 102 minutes.

THE SEA GOD—Paramount, 1930. *George Abbott*. Cast: Richard Arlen, Eugene Pallette, Robert Gleckler, Ivan Simpson, Maurice Black, Robert Perry. 75 minutes.

THE TEXAN—Paramount, 1930. *John Cromwell*. Cast: Gary Cooper, Emma Dunn, Oscar Apfel, James Marcus, Donald Reed, Veda Buckland, Edwin J. Brady. 79 minutes.

THE CONQUERING HORDE—Paramount, 1931. *Edward Sloman*. Cast: Richard Arlen, Claude Gillingwater, Ian MacLaren, Frank Rice, Arthur Stone. 76 minutes.

DIRIGIBLE—Columbia, 1931. *Frank Capra*. Cast: Jack Holt, Ralph Graves, Hobart Bosworth, Roscoe Karns, Harold Goodwin, Clarence Muse, Selmer Jackson. 100 minutes.

THE FINGER POINTS—Warner Brothers, 1931. *John Francis Dillon*. Cast: Richard Barthelmess, Regis Toomey, Robert Elliott, Clark Gable, Oscar Apfel, Robert Glecker. 88 minutes.

THE LAWYER'S SECRET—Paramount, 1931. *Louis Gaznier*, Max Marcin. Cast: Clive Brook, Buddy Rogers, Richard Arlen, Jean Arthur, Francis McDonald. 65 minutes.

THREE ROGUES—Fox, 1931. *Benjamin Stoloff*. Cast: Victor McLaglen, Lew Cody, Robert Warwick, Franklin Farnum, David Worth, Joyce Compton. 70 minutes.

THE UNHOLY GARDEN—Goldwyn-United Artists, 1931. *George Fitzmaurice*. Cast: Ronald Colman, Estelle Taylor, Tully Marshall, Warren Hymer, Mischa Auer. 75 minutes.

DOCTOR X—Warner Brothers, 1932. *Michael Curtiz*. Cast: Lionel Atwill, Preston Foster, Lee Tracy, George Rosener, Leila Bennett, Arthur Edmund Carewe. 80 minutes.

THE MOST DANGEROUS GAME—RKO, 1932. *Ernest B. Schoedsack, Irving Pichel*. Cast: Joel McCrea, Leslie Banks, Robert Armstrong, Noble Johnson, Steve Clemento. 63 minutes.

STOWAWAY—Universal, 1932. *Phil Whitman*. Cast: Betty Francisco, Leon Waycoff, Roscoe Karns, Lee Moran, James Gordon, Maurice Black, Montagu Love. 75 minutes.

ANN CARVER'S PROFESSION—Columbia, 1933. *Eddie Buzzell*. Cast: Gene Raymond, Claire Dodd, Arthur Pierson, Claude Gillingwater, Frank Albertson. 68 minutes.

THE BIG BRAIN—RKO, 1933. *George Archainbaud*. Cast: George E. Stone, Phillips Holmes, Minna Gombell, Lillian Bond, Reginald Owen, Berton Churchill. 72 minutes.

BELOW THE SEA—Columbia, 1933. *Al Rogell*. Cast: Ralph Bellamy, Fredrik Vogeding, Esther Howard, Trevor Bland, William Kelly, Paul Page. 79 minutes.

THE BOWERY—20th Century-Fox-United Artists, 1933. *Raoul Walsh*. Cast: Wallace Beery, George Raft, Jackie Cooper, Harold Huber, Fletcher Norton, John Kelly, Pert Kelton. 90 minutes.

MASTER OF MEN—Columbia, 1933. *Lambert Hillyer*. Cast: Jack Holt, Theodore von Eltz, Walter Connolly, Berton Churchill. 78 minutes.

KING KONG—RKO, 1933. *Ernest B. Schoedsack*, Merian C. Cooper. Cast: Robert Armstrong, Bruce Cabot, Frank Reicher, Sam Hardy, Noble Johnson, Steve Clemento, Victor Wong. 103 minutes.

MYSTERY OF THE WAX MUSEUM—Warner Brothers, 1933. *Michael Curtiz*. Cast: Lionel Atwill, Glenda Farrell, Frank McHugh, Allen Vincent, Gavin Gordon. 78 minutes.

ONE SUNDAY AFTERNOON—Paramount, 1933. *Stephen Roberts*. Cast: Gary Cooper, Neil Hamilton, Frances Fuller, Roscoe Karns, Jane Darwell, Sam Hardy. 70 minutes.

SHANGHAI MADNESS—Fox, 1933. *John Blystone*. Cast: Spencer Tracy, Ralph Morgan, Eugene Pallette, Herbert Mundin, Reginald Mason, Arthur Hoyt. 63 minutes.

THE WOMAN I STOLE—Columbia, 1933. *Irving Cummings*. Cast: Jack Holt, Noah Beery, Raquel Torres, Donald Cook, Edwin Maxwell, Charles Browne. 69 minutes.

THE VAMPIRE BAT—Majestic, 1933. *Frank Strayer*. Cast: Lionel Atwill, Melvyn Douglas, Maude Eburne, George E. Stone, Dwight Frye, Rita Carlisle. 63 minutes.

THE AFFAIRS OF CELLINI—20th Century-Fox/United Artists, 1934. *Gregory La Cava*. Cast: Constance Bennett, Fredric March, Frank Morgan, Vince Barnett, Louis Calhern. 90 minutes.

BLACK MOON—Columbia, 1934. *Roy William Neill*. Cast: Jack Holt, Dorothy Burgess, Cora Sue Collins, Arnold Karff, Clarence Muse, Lumsden Hare. 68 minutes.

CHEATING CHEATERS—Universal, 1934. *Richard Thorpe*. Cast: Cesar Romero, Minna Gombell, Francis L. Sullivan, Hugh O'Connell, Henry Armetta. 70 minutes.

THE COUNTESS OF MONTE CRISTO—Universal, 1934. *Karl Freund*. Cast: Paul Lukas, Reginald Owen, Patsy Kelly, Paul Page, Carmel Myers, Robert McWade. 76 minutes.

MADAME SPY—Universal, 1934. *Karl Freund*. Cast: Nils Asther, Edward Arnold, John Miljan, David Torrence, Douglas Walton, Oscar Apfel, Vince Barnett. 70 minutes.

ONCE TO EVERY WOMAN—Columbia, 1934. *Lambert Hillyer*. Cast: Ralph Bellamy, Walter Connolly, Walter Byron, J. Farrell MacDonald, Billie Seward. 70 minutes.

THE RICHEST GIRL IN THE WORLD—RKO, 1934. *William A. Seiter*. Cast: Miriam Hopkins, Joel McCrea, Henry Stephenson, Reginald Denny, Beryl Mercer. 76 minutes.

VIVA VILLA—MGM, 1934. *Jack Conway*. Cast: Wallace Beery, Leo Carillo, Donald Cook, Stuart Erwin, George E. Stone, Joseph Schildkraut. 110 minutes.

WHITE LIES—Columbia, 1934. *Leo Bulgakov*. Cast: Walter Connolly, Victor Jory, Leslie Fenton, Robert Allen, William Demarest, Oscar Apfel, Mary Foy. 63 minutes.

WOMAN IN THE DARK—RKO, 1934. *Phil Rosen*. Cast: Ralph Bellamy, Melvyn Douglas, Roscoe Ates, Ruth Gillette, Joe King, Nell O'Day. 68 minutes.

BULLDOG JACK—Gaumont-British, 1935. *Walter Forde*. Cast: Jack Hulbert, Claude Hulbert, Ralph Richardson, Paul Graetz, Gibb McLughlin, Athol Fleming. 73 minutes.

THE CLAIRVOYANT—Gaumont-British, 1935. *Maurice Elvey*. Cast: Claude Rains, Jane Baxter, Mary Clare, Ben Field, Athole Stewart, Felix Aylmer. 80 minutes.

COME OUT OF THE PANTRY—United Artists, 1935. *Jack Raymond*.

Cast: Jack Buchanan, James Carew, Ronald Squire, Olive Blakeney, Fred Emney, Kate Cutler. 71 minutes.

MILLS OF THE GODS—Columbia, 1935. *Roy William Neill*. Cast: May Robson, Victor Jory, Raymond Walburn, James Blakey, Josephine Whitell, Mayo Methot. 66 minutes.

ROAMING LADY—Columbia, 1936. *Alfred Rogell*. Cast: Ralph Bellamy, Thurston Hall, Edward Gargan, Roger Imhof, Paul Guilfoyle, Arthur Rankin. 66 minutes.

THEY MET IN A TAXI—Columbia, 1936. *Alfred E. Green*. Cast: Chester Morris, Lionel Stander, Raymond Walburn, Henry Mollison, Kenneth Harlan. 69 minutes.

WHEN KNIGHTS WERE BOLD—General Film Distributors, 1936. *Jack Raymond*. Cast: Jack Buchanan, Garry Marsh, Kate Cutler, Martita Hunt. 75 minutes.

IT HAPPENED IN HOLLYWOOD—Columbia, 1937. *Harry Lachman*. Cast: Richard Dix, Victor Killian, Franklin Pangborn, Granville Bates, Zeffie Tillbury. 70 minutes.

MURDER IN GREENWICH VILLAGE—Columbia, 1937. *Albert Rogell*. Cast: Richard Arlen, Raymond Walburn, Wyn Calhoun, Scott Colton, Thurston Hall. 67 minutes.

THE JURY'S SECRET—Universal, 1938. *Ted Sloman*. Cast: Kent Taylor, Larry Blake, Nan Grey, Samuel S. Hinds, Halliwell Hobbes, Granville Bates. 66 minutes.

NAVY SECRETS—Monogram, 1939. *Harvey Gates*. Cast: Grant Withers, Dewey Robinson, Craig Reynolds, George Sorrell, Robert Frazer. 60 minutes.

SMASHING THE SPY RING—Columbia, 1939. *Christy Cabanne*. Cast: Ralph Bellamy, Regis Toomey, Walter Kingsford, Ann Doran, Warren Hull, Lorna Gray. 62 minutes.

WILDCAT BUS—RKO, 1940. *Frank Woodruff*. Cast: Charles Lang, Paul Guilfoyle, Don Costello, Paul McGrath, Joseph Sawyer, Roland Drew, Oscar O'Shea. 63 minutes.

ADAM HAD FOUR SONS—Columbia, 1941. *Gregory Ratoff*. Cast: Ingrid Bergman, Warner Baxter, Susan Hayward, Richard Denning, Johnny Downs, June Lockhart. 81 minutes.

MELODY FOR THREE—RKO, 1941. *Erle C. Kenton*. Cast: Jean Hersholt, Walter Woolf King, Patsy Lee Parsons, Maude Eburne, Irene Ryan, Leon Tyler. 67 minutes.

NOT A LADIES MAN—Columbia, 1942. *Lew Landers*. Cast: Paul Kelly, Douglas Croft, Ruth Lee, Lawrence Dixon, Don Beddoe, Louise Allbritton. 60 minutes.

SMALL TOWN GIRL—MGM, 1953. *Leslie Kardos*. Cast: Jane Powell, Farley Granger, Ann Miller, Bobby Van, Robert Keith, Chill Wills, S.Z. Sakall. 93 minutes.

TREASURE OF THE GOLDEN CONDOR—20th Century-Fox, 1953. *Delmar Daves*. Cast: Cornel Wilde, Finlay Curie, Constance Smith, George Macready, Leo G. Carroll. 93 minutes.

THE COBWEB—MGM, 1955. *Vincente Minelli*. Cast: Lauren Bacall, Charles Boyer, Lillian Gish, Richard Widmark, Gloria Grahame, John Kerr. 124 minutes.

QUEEN BEE—Columbia, 1955. *Ronald MacDougall*. Cast: Joan Crawford, Barry Sullivan, Betsy Palmer, John Ireland, Lucy Marlow, William Leslie. 95 minutes.

HELL ON FRISCO BAY—Warner Bros., 1956. *Frank Tuttle*. Cast: Alan Ladd, Edward G. Robinson, Joanne Dru, Perry Lopez, William Demarest, Paul Stewart. 93 minutes.

CRIME OF PASSION—United Artists, 1957. *Gerd Oswald*. Cast: Barbara Stanwyck, Sterling Hayden, Raymond Burr, Royal Dano, Virginia Grey, Dennis Cross. 84 minutes.

ROCK PRETTY BABY—Universal-International, 1957. *Richard Barlett*. Cast: Sal Mineo, John Saxon, Luana Patten, Edward C. Platt, Rod McKuen, Shelley Fabares. 89 minutes.

TAMMY AND THE BACHELOR—Universal-International, 1957. *Joseph Pevney*. Cast: Leslie Nielsen, Walter Brennan, Mala Powers, Sidney Blackmer, Debbie Reynolds. 89 minutes.

DRAGSTRIP RIOT—American-International, 1958. *Basil Bradbury*. Cast: Yvonne Lime, Gary Clarke, Bob Turnbull, Connie Stevens, Gabe DeLutri, Steve Ihnat. 68 minutes.

SUMMER LOVE—Universal-International, 1958. *Charles Haas*. Cast: John Saxon, Molly Bee, Rod McKuen, Judy Meredith, Jill St. John, John Wilder, Edward C. Platt. 85 minutes.

INDEX

Abbott, George, 105
Academy Awards, 57, 86, 120–121, 146, 149
Ace of Aces, 86
Acord, Art, 55
Adam Had Four Sons, 205, 261
Adler, Luther, 204
Affairs of Cellini, The, 148, 159, 260
All Quiet on the Western Front, 156
Allen, Elizabeth, 237
American Film Institute, The, 145
Anderson, Phyllis, 213
Anderson, Robert, 213
Angela Is Twenty-Two, 183, 185, 186, 192, 196, 197
Ann Carver's Profession, 148, 259
Arlen, Richard, 102, 103, 105, 145
Arthur, Jean, 96, 110
Atwill, Lionel, 133, 134

Balchen, Bernt, 118–119
Balfe, Veronica, 147
Bancroft, Anne, 246
Barnstormers Theatre, 193, 254
Barrymore, Ethel, 183
Barrymore, John, 71
Barsky, Bud, 51
Barthelmess, Jessica, 98, 109, 152, 199
Barthelmess, Richard, 98, 106, 107, 109, 115, 152, 199
Beazley, Cornelia (Bea), 191, 192, 193, 194, 199, 206, 213, 215, 219
Beery, Wallace, 147, 149

Behind the Make-up, 104, 258
Bellamy, Ralph, 145, 148, 158, 223
Below the Sea, 148, 259
Bennett, Constance, 115, 159, 224
Benny, Jack, 214, 245
Bergman, Ingrid, 205, 223
Berlin, Ellin, 221, 247
Berlin, Irving, 221, 245, 247
Berlin, Linda, 248
Best, Edna, 160, 163, 236
Big Brain, The, 259
Black Moon, 260
Border Legion, 258
Bowery, The, 147, 259
Brown, Danube, The, 193
Buchanan, Jack, 171, 172
Buckley, Harold, 131, 153–154
Buckley, Isabelle, 199
Bulgakov, Leo, 157
Bulldog Jack, 165, 166, 260
Burr, Raymond, 214–215

Cain, James, 252
Calhern, Louis, 159
Capra, Frank, 107, 108, 146, 158, 226, 238, 252
Captain Thunder, 258
Carr, Harry, 66, 74, 75, 76
Carstairs, John Paddy, 166, 167
Carter, President and Mrs. Jimmy, 145
Celebrity Pictures, 59, 64
Century comedy studios, 41–42
Champlin, Charles, 252

Charig, Phil, 120, 126
Chase, Charlie, 53
Chasin, George, 246
Cheating Cheaters, 157, 260
Citizen Kane, 206, 207
Clairvoyant, The, 169–170
Clark, Alexander, 183, 185
Clash by Night, 211
Cleveland, Alice, 254
Cleveland, Francis, 193, 254
Coast Patrol, The, 51, 257
Cobb, Eddie, 55
Cobweb, The, 250, 262
Cohn, Harry, 107, 108, 140, 148,
    157–158, 175, 177–178, 187, 252
Cohn, Rose, 148
Colman, Benita, 236
Colman, Ronald, 109, 116, 236
Columbia, 107, 108, 140, 145, 148,
    157, 175, 186, 187, 205, 217,
    218, 250
Come Out of the Pantry, 171, 260–261
Communism, 196, 210
Cooper, Gary, 81, 83, 89, 91, 92, 104,
    136, 146–147, 176
Cooper, Jackie, 147
Cooper, Merian, 102, 103, 124–127,
    128, 129, 131, 132–133, 149,
    150, 153, 154, 172, 173, 174,
    199, 215
Cooper, Rocky, 176
Costello, Dolores, 56, 71
Countess of Monte Cristo, The, 260
Cowan, Louis, G., 222, 226, 245
Cowan, Polly, 226
Crawford, Joan, 56, 116, 250
Creelman, James, 127
crews, film, 155
Crime of Passion, 262
Cromwell, John, 104, 149
Cronyn, Hume, 194, 214
Curtis, Agnes, 199, 215
Curtis, Edward (Ted) Peck, 131, 154,
    190, 191, 199, 215
Curtiz, Michael, 133

Davis, Elmer, 222
Dawn Patrol, The, 86, 114, 121–122
Day, Marceline, 56–57
Day, Captain Richard, 76
Del Rio, Dolores, 57, 135–137, 147,
    175, 206, 207

Derwent, Clarence, 212, 213
Detleffson, Paul, 35, 41
Devil Dogs of the Air, 86
Dietrich, Marlene, 88, 150
diFrasso, Countess Dorothy, 147, 157
directors, film, 155–156
Dirigible, 107–108, 258
Doctor X, 128, 129, 133, 259
Donovan, Colonel William J., 190, 191,
    208, 215, 217–218, 220, 221, 222
Douglas, Melvyn, 158
Dragstrip Riot, 262
Drake, Alfred, 212, 213
Dunne, Amanda, 227
Dunne, Philip, 222, 223, 227, 228, 252

Eagle and the Hawk, The, 86, 165
Earhart, Amelia, 118
Earle, Charlotte, 33, 34–35
Earle, Ferdinand Pinney, 32, 33
Echner, Hugo, 166, 168, 169

Fairbanks, Douglas, 137, 138, 168, 200
Fairbanks, Douglas Jr., 121
Fairbanks, Sylvia Ashley, 168, 177,
    200
Fairchild, Sherman, 184, 185
Farmer, Michael, 160
Farrell, Glenda, 200
Ferguson, Helen, 141, 178, 185, 190,
    201, 202
Fidler, Jimmie, 185, 202
film(s). *See also specific title*
    B, 145
    horror, Wray in, 128, 133–134
    propaganda, 222–223, 252
    and rear-projection process, 127
    "rock and tree," Wray in, 50
    silent, 80, 88, 89
    sound introduced into, 80, 88, 89,
        103, 104–105
    Westerns, Wray in, 55–56, 57, 58
Finger Points, The, 106, 107, 258
First Kiss, The, 89, 91, 92, 257
First National, 114, 115, 121
Fishbaugh, Dr. Ernest, 134, 135, 139
Fitzgerald, Edith, 200
Fitzgerald, Scott, 99, 150
Fitzgerald, Zelda, 99
Flight Commander, 121–123
Flynn, Errol, 191

Fokker, Anthony, 173–174
Ford, John, 158, 215
Forty Years Among the Indians (Jones), 7
Four Feathers, The, 102–103, 110, 258
Fox studio, 50, 107, 145
Freund, Karl, 156, 157
Furness, Betty, 214

Gable, Clark, 106, 148
Garbo, Greta, 87, 88, 229
Gaumont British, 165, 169
Gaynor, Janet, 53, 54, 55, 56, 57
Geneology of Daniel Webster Jones, 7
George and Margaret, 182
Gershwin, George, 179
Gibbons, Cedric, 135, 136, 147
Gibson, Hoot, 55
Gish, Lillian, 33–34, 75, 250
Golden Wings, 211, 215, 216
Goldwyn, Sam, 109
Gordon, Robert, 30, 31, 50, 51
Grant, Cary, 53, 117–118, 119, 120, 124, 126, 128, 129, 140, 145, 153, 157, 165–166, 170, 191–192, 229, 232–233
Grapes of Wrath, The, 199–200
Green, Al, 175
Group Theatre, 196, 209
Gunther, John, 226, 245
Gwenn, Edmund, 236

Hal Roach studio, 39, 52, 53
Half Angel, 236
Hart, Moss, 214
Hawks, Howard, 121–123
Hayward, Leland, 182, 186, 193, 197, 212
Heifetz, Jascha, 97, 98, 147, 153
Hell on Frisco Bay, 262
Henriod, Fred, 22, 23
Hepburn, Katharine, 126, 132, 145–146
Hill, Ethel, 236–237
Hollywood Reporter, The, 142
Holt, Jack, 107, 145
Honeymoon, The, 79
Howe, James Wong, 149
Hoxie, Jack, 55, 58
Hughes, Avis, 85, 87, 93, 94, 97, 119

Hughes, Howard, 85, 158, 166, 168, 183–185, 201
Hughes, Rupert, 85–86
Hulbert, Jack, 165
Huston, John, 237
Hutchinson, Barney, 95, 96

It Can't Happen Here, 182, 183, 184
It Happened in Hollywood, 261
It Happened One Night, 248, 252

Jannings, Emil, 39, 87–88
Jones, Dan (uncle), 12, 13
Jones, Daniel Webster (grandfather), 6, 7
Jones, Edward (uncle), 13
Jones, Emily Colton (grandmother), 6
Jones, Helen, 19
Jones, Richard, 39, 52–53
Jones, Wesley (cousin), 19
Jordan, Dorothy, 128, 132, 172, 173, 174, 199
Jory, Victor, 145, 157
Jury's Secret, The, 261

Kalmus, Herbert, 173
Kalmus, Natalie, 173
Kaufman, George, 214
Kelly, Paul, 218
King, Martin Luther, Sr., 249
King Kong, 103, 106–107, 124–128, 129–130, 132–133, 141–145, 147, 149, 157, 158, 183, 189, 259
 as classic, 143, 145
 cost of making, 144
 residuals not given for, 144
 Wray's payment for, 144
Kohner, Paul, 54, 59, 63

La Cava, George, 159
Lady for a Day, 248
Laemmle, Carl, 57–58, 63
Laemmle, Ernst, 58, 72
Lasky, Bessie, 84, 85, 87, 94, 97, 98, 99, 110–111, 138
Lasky, Jesse, 75, 85, 87, 98, 111
Lasky, Jesse, Jr., 94, 98
Last Flight, The, 114, 115
Laurel, Stan, 53

Lawyer's Secret, The, 258–259
Lazy Lightning, 58, 257
Legion of the Condemned, The, 80, 81, 82, 83, 86, 257
Leigh, Vivien, 150
Lewis, Sinclair, 182–183, 185, 186, 187–189, 190, 192, 196–197, 201
Life with Father, 197–198
Lindsay, Howard, 197
Loco Luck, 257
Lombard, Carole, 200, 237
Los Angeles Times, 66, 252
Lost Horizon, 145, 146, 248
Lubitsch, Ernst, 159, 160, 164, 256

McCarey, Leo, 53
McCrea, Joel, 128, 157
McKuen, Rod, 251
Macready, George, 193, 246
Madame Spy, 156, 171, 260
Magic Town, 235
Making of King Kong, The, (Goldner and Turner), 144
Man in the Saddle, The, 257
Man's Castle, A, 145, 146, 230
March, Florence, 150, 151
March, Frederic, 150, 151, 159, 223
Margin for Error, 201
Marshall, Herbert, 159–164
Marx, Harpo, 212, 245
Marx, Susan, 212, 245
Master of Men, 259
Mayer, Irene, 96, 97
MCA, 246
Meadowlark, The, 254
Meet John Doe, 248
Melody for Three, 261
Mendes, Lothar, 103
MGM, 128, 134, 149, 217, 226, 246
Milestone, Kendall, 232, 237
Milestone, Lewis, 101, 156, 232, 237
Mills of the Gods, 261
Milton, Robert, 104, 215
Mister 880, 235–236
Monogram Studio, 192
Montgomery, Robert, 151
Morgan, Frank, 159
Morgan, Mrs. Frank, 157
Mortensen, William, 27–29, 30–32, 34, 35, 36, 37, 38–39, 40, 41–42, 44–46, 89–90, 94, 95, 96, 98
Most Dangerous Game, The, 128, 129, 259

Motion Picture Country Home and Hospital, 247, 248
Moulton, Herbert, 56
Mr. Big, 214
Mr. Deeds Goes to Town, 248
Murder in Greenwich Village, 261
Mystery of the Wax Museum, The, 128, 129, 133, 259

Navy Secrets, 261
NBC, 215, 218
Negri, Pola, 75–76
New York Times, The, 141, 143
Nietzsche, Friedrich, 174
Night Music, 211
Nikki, 115, 117–118, 119, 120, 129, 167
Not Exactly Gentlemen, 107
Not a Ladies Man, 261

Oberon, Merle, 150
O'Brien, Willis, 125, 126, 127, 129, 144
Odets, Clifford, 194–196, 200, 204–205, 206, 207, 208–209, 210–211, 213, 229
Offeman, Emil, 59–60, 61, 62, 67, 89
Office of Strategic Services, 191, 215
Office of War Information, 218, 222–223, 225, 226, 231, 252
Olivier, Laurence, 150, 236
O'Malley, Rex, 212, 215
Once to Every Woman, 260
One Man Game, A, 257
One Sunday Afternoon, 146, 259

Paley, Bill, 221, 222, 227, 229
Paley, Dorothy, 221, 227, 229
Paramount, 78, 79, 80, 83, 87, 88, 95, 96, 103, 104, 106, 107, 108, 110, 128, 140, 146
Paramount on Parade, 104, 258
Payson, Joan Whitney, 179
"Perry Mason," 215
Petrified Forest, The, 185
Pickford, Mary, 137, 138
Pitts, Zasu, 67, 76
Platinum Blond, 248
Pointed Heels, 104, 258
Powell, William, 104, 109, 110, 199
Powers, Marcella, 196, 201

Powers, Patrick, 64–65, 72, 78, 80, 89, 90, 112
"The Pride of the Family," 246
Prisoner of Zenda, The, 149–150
publicity pictures, 53, 103
Putnam, George, 118
Putnam, Dr. Tracy, 240, 245

Queen Bee, 250, 262

radio series, 218
Raft, George, 147
Rainer, Louise, 195
Rains, Claude, 169–170
Rappold, Marie, 234
Ratoff, Gregory, 226
Reagan, Ronald, 235
Richardson, Ralph, 166
Richest Girl in the World, The, 57, 157, 260
Riley, Lew, 136
Rintels, David (son-in-law), 251
Riskin, Bobby (son), 225, 228, 229, 232, 233, 234, 237, 238, 247, 251
Riskin, Everett (brother-in-law), 217, 220, 247
Riskin, Katya (sister-in-law), 217, 232
Riskin, Robert (husband), 108, 146, 148, 199–200, 205, 206–207, 210, 216, 217–218, 219–221, 224–225, 226, 227, 230, 232, 233, 234, 235, 236–237, 238, 251–252
  adopting Susan Saunders, 235
  death of, 248
  honored at University of Southern California, 252
  Laurel Award for Achievement given to, 248
  in Motion Picture Country Home and Hospital, 247, 248
  in nursing home, 246–247
  with Office of War Information, 222–223, 227–228, 231, 253–254
  proposed to by Wray, 217, 220
  stroke of, 239–246
  wedding of, 221
Riskin, Victoria (Vicki) (daughter), 233, 234, 237–238, 248, 251, 252
RKO, 124, 125, 126, 141, 144, 149, 157, 199, 201
Roaming Lady, 261

Robinson, Edward G., 225, 245
Robinson, Frances, 200
Rock Pretty Baby, 251, 262
Rogell, Al, 58, 59, 148, 158
Roosevelt, President Franklin D., 216, 228
Rose, Betty, 168, 211
Rose, David, 137, 138, 168, 211
"Rosemary," 218
Rothenberg, Dr. Sanford (husband), 240, 242, 243, 251, 255

Sackville, Lord and Lady, 167, 168
Saddle Tramp, The, 257
Saint-Exupery, Antoine de, 226
St. John, Adela Rogers, 190, 193, 201, 202
Saunders, Dr. Edward (brother-in-law), 186, 190, 208
Saunders, John Monk (husband), 54, 80, 81, 82–85, 89, 91, 98, 101, 102, 105, 106, 109, 110, 111, 114, 115, 118, 119, 122–123, 128–129, 134, 135, 137, 138–140, 152, 153, 157, 158, 159–164, 166–167, 168–169, 170, 172, 173, 176, 182, 185, 200–201, 224
  Academy Award won by, 121
  affairs of, 84, 85, 94, 97, 99, 100, 110–111, 139–141, 156, 166, 201
  assets taken by, 185–186
  background of, 86–87, 190–191
  and daughter, 178, 185, 186, 187, 188, 190, 201
  divorced from Wray, 192, 195, 202
  at health farm for alcohol problem, 119–120, 139
  on honeymoon, 93–97
  marital separation of, 178–179
  proposing to Wray, 84
  political beliefs of, 151
  psychiatric hospitalization of, 190
  suicide of, 201–202, 203
  suicide attempt of, 167
  wedding of, 91–92
  wife of, first. *See* Hughes, Avis
Saunders, Susan Cary (daughter), 178, 191, 192, 193, 199, 206, 212–213, 215, 219, 221, 224, 226, 233–234, 237, 238, 247, 251, 254
  adopted by Robert Riskin, 235

Saunders, Susan Cary (*cont*.)
  birth of, 177
  and father, 178, 185, 186, 187, 188,
    190, 201
Schenck, Joseph, 158–159
Schley, Edna, 38, 59, 61, 62, 64,
    88–89, 95
Schoedsack, Ernest, 102, 103, 129, 144
Scott, Randolph, 153
Screen Actors Guild, 151, 152
Sea Beast, The, 71
Sea God, The, 105, 258
Seiter, William, 57, 157
Selznick, David, 96, 110, 121, 126,
    132, 149, 150–151, 221, 229, 256
Selznick, Irene, 176, 211, 221,
    229–230, 232, 245, 256
Selznick, Myron, 161
Shanghai Madness, 145, 259
Sherwood, Robert, 217, 218, 220, 222
Sidney, Sylvia, 204
Single Lady, 54, 99–100, 101, 114
Small Town Girl, 246, 261
Smashing the Spy Ring, 261
Snodgrass, Harvey, 131–132
Spurs and Saddles, 257
Stackpool, Dr. and Mrs. Harry, 4, 5, 8
Steichen, Edward, 119
Steinbeck, John, 105
Steiner, Max, 142
Stewart, Jimmy, 235
Stickney, Dorothy, 197
Stiller, Mauritz, 87, 88, 103
Stowaway, 259
Strasberg, Lee, 209
Strasberg, Paula, 209, 210
Street of Sin, The, 39, 87–88, 103,
    257–258
Sullivan, Barry, 183, 214
Summer Love, 262
Swanson, Gloria, 160, 161, 162, 164
Swerling, Flo, 205–206, 210, 216, 224,
    230–231, 232, 240, 245
Swerling, Jo, 108, 145, 205, 206, 210,
    216, 224, 230, 232, 240, 245, 252
Swope, Herbert, 183, 184
Swope, Maggie, 183, 184
Symington, Senator Stuart, 131–132

Tammy and the Bachelor, 250, 262
television, 215
  Wray performing on, 215, 246

Texan, The, 104, 105, 110, 258
theater, Wray acting in, 115, 117–118,
    193, 201, 211, 214, 215, 216
  summer, 182–183, 104, 105,
    193–194, 196, 197–198, 212, 213
There's Always Juliet, 183, 185
They Met in a Taxi, 175, 261
Thin Man, 217
Three Rogues, 259
Thunderbolt, 104, 258
Tilden, William, 193
Too Many Kisses, 87
Toscanini, Arturo, 223
Toscanini, 223, 252
Tracy, Lee, 149
Tracy, Spencer, 145, 146, 225, 230
Treasure of the Golden Condor, The,
    246, 262
Twentieth Century-Fox, 235, 239, 246

Udet, Ernst, 151, 169
Unger, Arthur, 116–117
Unholy Garden, The, 108–109, 259
Universal, 54–55, 57, 59, 62–63, 133,
    157
University of Southern California, 251,
    252

Vampire Bat, The, 128, 129, 133, 134,
    260
Vidor, Florence, 29, 97, 147
Vidor, King, 29, 97, 158
Viva Villa, 148–149, 260
von Sternberg, Josef, 88, 98, 104
von Stroheim, Erich, 59–60, 61–62,
    63, 65, 66, 67, 68, 70, 71, 72–74,
    75, 76, 77–78, 79, 88, 106, 158,
    207
von Stroheim, Valerie, 65, 74, 77

Wagner, Jack, 105
Wallace, Edgar, 126–127
WAMPAS Baby Stars of 1926, Wray as,
    56, 57
Ward, Christopher, 192, 199
Warner Brothers, 106, 133
Wasserman, Lew, 235, 245, 246
Wedding March, The, 59, 60, 62,
    65–75, 76–79, 84, 87, 88, 107,
    258

Weissberg, Arnold, 207
Welles, Orson, 136, 206, 207
Wellman, William, 235
West Point of the Air, 86, 134
Western Costume Company, 65, 73, 89, 98
Wheeler, John, 159–160
When Knights Were Bold, 172, 261
White Lies, 260
Whitney, Jack, 132, 183, 185, 199
Wilcox, Herbert, 172
Wild Horse Stampede, The, 56, 257
Wildcat Bus, 261
Wilde, Cornel, 246
Wilder, Billy, 251
Wilson, Anna, 193
Wings, 80, 81, 84, 86
Woman in the Dark, 158, 260
Woman I Stole, The, 260
Wood, Natalie, 246
Woollcott, Alexander, 212, 213
Wray, Fay
  adolescence of, 30–63
  in Arizona, childhood in, 12–14
  in Canada, childhood in, 1–5, 8–9
  child desired by, 171, 174
  childhood of, 1–5, 8–9, 11–37, 181
  children of. *See* Riskin, Bobby;
    Riskin, Victoria (Vicki); Saunders,
    Susan Cary
  divorce of, 192, 195, 202
  in England, 165–168, 169, 170, 171,
    172, 174
  extortion letters sent to, 151–152,
    158
  family placed before work by,
    177–178, 227, 237
  films loved by, 251, 255
  grandchildren of, 251
  on guilt imposed by parents, 47, 95
  as honorary member of Indian band, 9
  and Hughes, Howard, 184–185
  journal written by, for Riskin,
    241–245
  Lewis, Sinclair in love with, 186,
    187–189
  marital separation of, from Saunders,
    178–179
  marriages of. *See* Riskin, Robert;
    Rothenberg, Dr. Sanford;
    Saunders, John Monk
  memorabilia of, given to University of
    Southern California, 251
  needing someone to love, 170–171,
    176
  in New York, 214, 216, 218–221,
    223–225, 226–227, 228–229,
    231
  Nietzsche's writings helping, 174
  and Odets, Clifford, 195–196, 200,
    204–205, 206, 207, 208–209,
    210–211
  in Paris, 168–169
  photographs of, 32, 36, 41, 44–46,
    53, 90, 94, 95, 96, 98, 103
  as Ping-Pong player, 97, 98, 153,
    160, 161
  play written by, 254
  political views of, 151
  pregnancies of, 173, 174–175, 176,
    223, 225
  psychiatrist seen by, 219, 220
  religious beliefs of, 219, 249
  Saint-Exupery's writings influencing,
    226
  at St. Moritz, 172–174
  in Salt Lake City, childhood in,
    14–17, 21–28
  in school plays, 12, 17, 20, 48, 49
  sent to Los Angeles, 28–29
  stand-in for, 157, 158, 159
  on vegetarian diet, 115
Wray, Joseph Herber (father), 2, 3, 4,
  8, 12, 14, 16, 17, 20, 112–113
  marital problems of, 19, 20, 112
Wray, Joseph Vivien (brother), 3, 11,
  15–16, 24, 26, 27, 53, 90, 91, 96
Wray, Richard (brother), 13, 22, 43,
  45, 238
Wray, Vaida Viola (sister), 11, 19, 22,
  23, 25, 44, 107, 152
Wray, Victor (brother), 16, 22, 43, 45,
  179
Wray, Vina Fay. *See* Wray, Fay
Wray, Vina Marguerite Jones (mother),
  2, 3, 4, 6–7, 8, 12, 18–19, 21,
  22, 23, 25, 26, 27, 28, 43, 44, 45,
  46, 47, 50, 51, 76–77, 82, 83, 90,
  95–96, 111–112, 113, 151–152,
  179–181
  marital problems of, 19, 20, 112
Wray, Willow Winona (sister), 3, 4, 11,
  13, 19, 23, 24, 27, 28, 46–47, 90,
  91, 185, 248–249
  husband of, 46, 47
"Wrayland," 2, 4, 10

Wright, Katherine, 24, 36, 37, 38, 39, 46
Writers' Club, 56
Writers Guild, 248
Writer's Mobilization, 231
Wurtele, Emily, 247–248
Wyler, William, 58, 158, 236
Wyman, Jane, 235
Wynn, Ed, 194
Wynn, Keenan, 194

Yellow Jacket, The, 212, 213
You Can't Take It With You, 248
Young, Loretta, 146, 205, 230, 232, 236
Young, Roland, 150

Zanuck, Darryl, 147–148, 159, 226–227, 236, 245